HERONSGATE — *Freedom, Happiness and Contentment*

HERONSGATE

Freedom, Happiness and Contentment
The First 150 Years of the Estate

BY IAN FOSTER

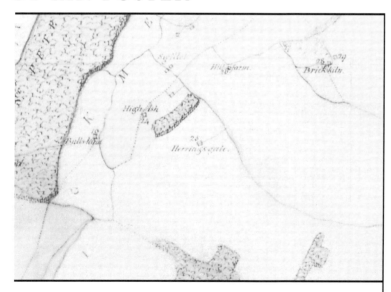

1999 MANTICORE EUROPE LIMITED

First published in Great Britain in 1999 by Manticore Europe Limited, Silver Birches, Heronsgate, Rickmansworth, Herts. WD3 5DN

British Library Cataloguing in Publication Data
A CIP record for this book is available from the British Library

ISBN 1 900887 05 3

Printed and bound in Great Britain by Bookcraft Limited, Midsomer Norton, Somerset

Cover Illustrations

Background Map: 'A map of Charleywood and the Country adjacent, containing Sixteen Square Miles' by George Thomson, 1805. Courtesy of Chorleywood Library. Drawn for the owner of Chorleywood House and presented on 9th April 1956 to the Urban District Council of Chorleywood by Miss K Barnes who resided in the former Chorleywood House.

Estate map: 'Plan of O'Connorville'. Courtesy of Francis O'Loughlin.

Photograph of Author: Courtesy of Tony Bell of the Bucks Examiner.

'Crowthorne chimney': a drawing by Dorothy Haigh. Courtesy of Linda Fernandez.

📖 Foreword

MANY WILL HAVE VISITED the spot on the quay by the River Usk from which three Chartists sentenced to transportation to Van Diemen's Land (Tasmania) for their part in the uprising at Newport in 1839 took ship. On arrival at the grim penitentiary of Port Arthur in its spectacular and remote setting, John Frost, William Jones and Zephaniah Williams were evidently treated as 'political prisoners'. They were not required to wear the distinctive, yellow convict uniform and were given junior positions as civil servants. None of the three went on to make a significant mark on the political development of the land which they had involuntarily adopted. I do not think that the same could be said, however, of the ideas which had prompted what they may have come to think of as their rash action in Newport. As new British societies fashioned themselves in lands less trammelled by the realities and traditions of political life in Great Britain, views like those encapsulated in the six points of the Chartists exercised considerable sway. They were also powerfully opposed by those who worked to frame constitutions and to limit franchise in such a way as would preserve a special place of power and influence for those who had already acquired large holdings of property. Indeed terms like 'chartist', 'radical', and 'leveller' were part of the vocabulary of political abuse in New South Wales. The extent to which Chartist ideas had gathered sway was shown when the separate colony of Victoria was established in the 1850s with its capital in Melbourne. At the first elections in 1856 the secret ballot was used for the first time, becoming known in the USA as the "Victorian ballot". In that election virtually every man in Victoria had the right to vote at a time when only one in five of their counterparts in England possessed it. From 1857 candidates did not have to own property to stand for election, as candidates for the House of Commons still did, and from 1870 members of the Victorian assembly were paid. There was no question of annual parliaments, but the second election in Victoria, held in 1859, established the rule that elections should be held every three years, rather than every five as in the Mother of Parliaments in Westminster. In New Zealand and for Federal elections in Australia the three-year rule has applied to this day. In New Zealand the franchise was widely extended amongst European males from mid-century, and in 1893 – a pioneering venture not envisaged by the Chartists – the right to vote was extended to women.

Against a background of this kind it was, perhaps, not surprising that Chartism was one of the special topics of the 19th Century British history which, as schoolboys in New Zealand in the 1950s, we were required to study. I must presume that it was still part of the syllabus taught by Ian Foster in the 1960s when we were teaching colleagues at my own old school in Auckland. What was clear was the enthusiasm which Ian brought to the teaching of history generally and to the coaching of another way of life transported to the colonies - cricket. It was not until the 1970s that my wife and I discovered Ian in his home, haven, sanctuary and castle at Heronsgate or in the 'Land of Liberty' beyond Feargus O'Connor's pale. My schoolboy introduction to the Chartist movement had omitted reference to the land settlements promoted by O'Connor, and to discover something about them via the domestic arrangements of an old friend and former colleague was especially fascinating. It has been equally fascinating for me, as I am sure it will be for Ian's readers, to take that discovery further via the pages of his book.

John E. Lewis M.A.
Head Master, Eton College, Windsor

Author's Biography

As a schoolboy at Leighton Park Ian Foster developed a keen interest in history which led to his gaining an Honours Degree in the subject at Trinity College, Dublin. He captained the Trinity Cricket Eleven and enjoyed prominence as a cricketer; a career as a schoolmaster in Preparatory and Public Schools followed naturally. His flair for motivating pupils in the classroom and on the playing field was a distinctive feature; in particular, many young New Zealanders remember with affection the enthusiasm he generated at King's College, Auckland. As a resident of Heronsgate for many years Ian has developed a deep love and knowledge of its community. Having recently retired he shares his time between gardening, golf and breeding labradors.

Roger Bass
Second Master, Haileybury College

Author's Acknowledgements

I would like to thank all those who have been patient with me and interested enough to talk about Heronsgate's history and their memories of Heronsgate. The list is too long to name all to whom I am most grateful; many Heronsgate residents and friends of Heronsgate have been very generous in supplying material and information and in imparting their own knowledge.

I would like to thank the staff at the Hertford Records Office, the Post Office archives centre in London, the Diocesan archivists at Rochester and St Albans, the archivists at the YWCA, the office manager at Esperanto House and the librarians at the Royal Society for their time and cooperation. Then, more particularly, I wish to thank Roy Underwood, who provided the information about those killed in action in the two World Wars; Bob Sharpe and his staff at Chorleywood Library who have been most courteous and helpful; the historians at Dodford who have been very enthusiastic and supportive; Amy Redhead and Simon Treanor for making available valuable material from their university work, Michael Bowler for his research and time, John Jackson for providing the Beaumont House material and Angela Grezo for making available the picture of the sampler. Also, Brian Dumbleton, Pam Hatfield, Jane Broadbent and the Rickmansworth Museum for providing photographs.

Finally, I thank Dorothy Thompson and James Epstein for their contributions of two chapters, Hugh Norwood for his interest and cooperation, Betty Gardiner (née Bird), Mrs Geraldine Bird, wife of the late Michael Bird and Peter Davidson, for supplying many of the photographs from their family albums, and many others who have lent maps and other documents; Gordon Templeton who did the majority of the work in scanning the maps and photographs and producing the final manuscript; Greg Smith and James Bond of Manticore in Canada for the design of the book; Barbara Hicks for her very great help and conscientious work as copy editor and Richard Warman and my sister for their encouragement, without which the book would not have been possible.

6

Contents

 CHAPTER ONE

Introduction

I T WAS EARLY SUMMER 1996 when Richard Warman came to me and said that, as chairman of the Heronsgate Residents Association, he was setting up a committee to consider how to celebrate the 150th anniversary of the O'Connorville Estate. Was I interested in becoming involved and what about writing a book? I thought about it. I knew some people thought of Heronsgate as a rich man's enclave complete with swimming pools, large cars and people working mainly in London. But this was not how I saw Heronsgate.

I knew there to be a sense of mystique, a pride and a love of Heronsgate present and past. Richard and I began to talk to people and soon there emerged a picture of a caring community, with the church and the hall as important focal points. Residents were interested in protecting their environment, and this had shown itself in the recent past in the concern about Heronsgate becoming a conservation area and the alarm about the construction of the M25 nearby. Residents wanted to be involved in community affairs, whether it be the lanes, the church, the hall or social and garden events. People were keen to talk of their memories: some hinted at class and social divisions, many spoke of an enthusiasm for the smallholding principle. The war years are remembered for their feelings of comradeship and everyone working together to achieve a common goal; the hard times and deprivation and sadness are largely brushed under the carpet.

As the prewar years and the decades back to 1847 come into focus the memories fade and the inaccuracies begin to appear. Which was the first post office? How many post offices were there? When did the Laurel Cottage post office open and close? Have the family and descendants of Prowting Roberts, the Chartist lawyer, the longest connection in terms of years with Heronsgate or can the Birds or Birdwoods or Fords or Clarks or Fitzsimmons or McCullochs claim this honour? Were there significant periods of post-Chartist building development? Was Ladywalk originally a monastery? People seem to like to put an earlier date than is indicated by research for the building of their homes. It has been said, for instance, that Rowandene was erected in 1860 and Sherwood's main extensions done in the 1870s. Many believe that a church existed before 1865. People speak of O'Connor, the creator of the Heronsgate Estate, in unsure terms, and for some, Chartism is regarded as an insignificant movement.

This book sets out to be partly serious history and partly anecdotal. Thus it attempts to answer some questions. Who were the Chartists? What sort of a man was O'Connor and what were his ideals? Were the original settlers freehold owners? Was the Estate sold by auction at the Swan Inn, Rickmansworth? What was being auctioned in 1857? Two eminent and highly respected historians, Dorothy Thompson and James Epstein, put forward their views on the Chartists and on O'Connor in two separate chapters.

It attempts to present a survey of the settlement first under the auspices of the Land Company (1845-1851) and later under the Official Government Receiver (1851-1860), and for the first time to present a history of Heronsgate from 1860 to the present day. It cannot be claimed to be a definitive work of history; where dead-ends have been reached or questionable assumptions made, these may provoke the reader to do his or her own research.

The book has been a happy task; it has been a pleasure talking to people about the history of Heronsgate, using the facilities of many record offices and libraries, gleaning information from maps, studying directories, electoral rolls, census statistics, ledgers and Beaumont House magazines. I would like to take this opportunity to thank Richard Warman for his expertise and encouragement, Roger Bass — a school-master friend from New Zealand days and currently Second Master at Haileybury College (Hertford) for reading the manuscript and offering suggestions for improvements, and my sister for her hours of calm and methodical labour in putting the written word on to a word processor. There are, of course, many other people who have contributed in one way or another and they are acknowledged elsewhere.

Throughout the book, reference is made to Plot numbers. The plan opposite should be used as a guide and reference for those plots. At the end of the book, Appendix Two also provides a detailed account of the development of each plot.

At right: Plan of the Estate
O'Connorville, the first Estate purchased by the Chartist Land Company, situated in the Parish of Rickmansworth, Hertfordshire; founded by Fergus O'Connor, 1846.

Holders of the Plots at O'Connorville in 1846

Two Acres

1.	John Westmorland	London
2.	John Lambourne	Reading
3.	Michael Fitzsimmons	Manchester
4.	William Mann	Northampton
5.	Philip Ford	Wotton-under-Edge
6.	George Hearson	Leeds
7.	George Mansfield	Bradford (Wilts.)
8.	Richard Eveson	Stockport
9.	Charles Brown	Halifax
10.	John Walwark	Ashton
11.	John Neale	Heywood
12.	William House (Howse)	Pershore
13.	Henry Smith	Keighley
14.	George Ramsbottom	Ashton
15.	William Mitchell	Whittington & Cat, London
16.	John Firth	Bradford
17.	Ralph Kerfoot	Rouen

Three Acres

18.	James Short	Bilston
19.	William Oddy	Bradford
20.	George Richardson	Westminster
21.	Benjamin Knott	Halifax
22.	Isaac Jowitt	Bradford

Four Acres

23.	Thomas Mayrick	Worcester
24.	Joseph Mills	Ashton
25.	David Watson	Edinburgh
26.	Martin Griffiths	Worcs.
27.	James Cole	Bradford
28.	Barbara Vaughan	Sunderland
29.	Alfred Hay Crowther	Ashton
30.	Thomas Smith	Wigan
31.	James Greenwood	Hebden Bridge
32.	Thomas Smith	Greenford (nr London)
33.	Thomas Bond	Devizes
34.	James Taylor	Manchester
35.	Joseph Openshaw	Manchester
36.	School and Land Attached	

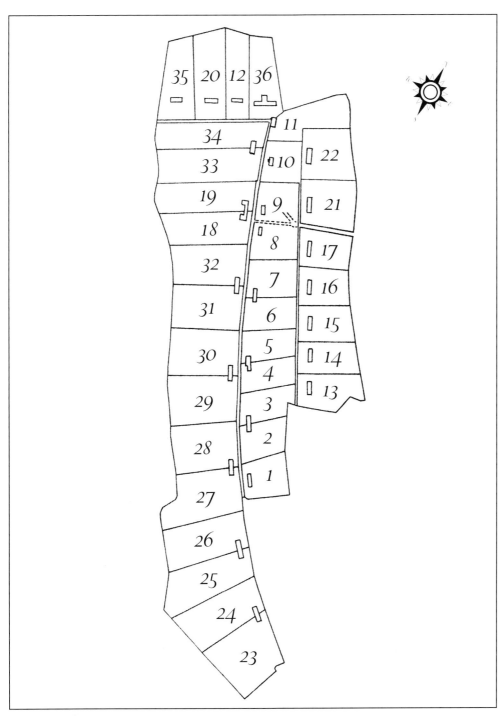

Plot numbers of O'Connorville

 CHAPTER TWO

The Chartist Movement 1836-1856
by Dorothy Thompson

IT WAS AT A CONFERENCE on Chartism at Birmingham in the autumn of 1996 that I first met Dorothy Thompson. It soon became clear after various papers had been delivered and discussed by the conference of university lecturers, students and others that one person was the accepted expert and her opinion sought to clarify areas of doubt. It was, of course, Dorothy Thompson.

Dorothy Thompson and her husband before her have, for many years, been prominent in the academic world of historical research. She earned her reputation as a lecturer in modern history at the University of Birmingham and as the author of a number of works on English Labour history. Probably her most important research was into the Chartists, the first working class movement of the 19th Century.

I felt it important as a background to this book that readers should have a basic knowledge of Chartism, for it was Feargus O'Connor, one of the Chartist leaders, who founded the Chartist Land Company and it was Heronsgate which was the first established estate. My keenness to include chapters on Chartism and O'Connor was reinforced when Iain Campbell my ex-headmaster (Canford and Oxford University) from King's College, Auckland, New Zealand visited me in May 1997 and we discussed the book.

Later he wrote saying, 'Feargus O'Connor was a good talking point on my trip round the UK and it was interesting to note how many people (so-called intelligent), had never heard of Chartism'.

Dorothy Thompson writes:

The editors of this volume have asked me for a short general essay on the Chartist movement to provide a background to the story of the establishment and history of the land colonies which are the book's main subject. Chartism is now included in the National Curriculum as a subject for study at school. A number of local Chartist leaders will be included among the figures to be remembered in the New Dictionary of National Biography, and the bibliography of writings about Chartism has expanded into its second full volume. Most of us, therefore, have some idea of what the movement represented and when it occurred. As with all areas of history, however, scholarship and research continue. New discoveries and new interpretations are continually being made, and there are lively discussions going on about the nature of the movement and its effects. In spite of current interest, it is still the case that many mistaken and outdated ideas about the movement abound, and even some quite serious historians of the nineteenth century can be found repeating clichés which have been out of date almost since they were first uttered in the early days of the modern Labour Party. For Chartism has a characteristic which it shares with a few other important moments in our history, that is that it seems to shed important light on contemporary affairs and contemporary politics. Just as it is said that in some remote parts of the North Country people still identify themselves as Cavaliers and Roundheads, so in some political circles the divisions among the Chartists about political tactics colour the language of political programmes and activity to the present day. It was Asa Briggs in one of the essays in his seminal collection 'Chartist Studies' (1958) who urged that Chartism should be seen as part of social history rather than as part of the history of socialism. We must resist the temptation to see the past in terms of modern political structures and look at Chartism as it was, a phenomenon of the first half of the nineteenth century in Britain.

Several major works had been written about the Chartist movement before the Second World War, works which still hold the respect of modern historians. Some of these saw the movement as largely a political one, but most tended to see it as the reflection of economic change in British society in the early industrial period, as, in the words of one of the early Chartists, a 'Bread and butter question, a knife and fork question'. The revival and expansion of social history as a discipline in the years after the war saw social historians break away from being minor partners in economic history departments and begin to establish their right to examine all aspects of society – political as well as economic – with a new, more flexible discipline, and to ask questions which went beyond the oversimplified categories of conventional historical discourse. The study of the land problem among the Chartists is only one of the questions which illustrates the need for a more flexible and less present-minded approach to the ideals and beliefs of the Chartists.

It is often said that Chartism failed, and a great deal of breath and printer's ink has been expended in examining the reasons for this failure. The Chartists, as it has been suggested, were premature democrats – demanding the vote before a national system of education had been established which could teach them to make political judgements. Or they were failed revolutionaries who drew back – in a typically British failure of nerve – from the final violent confrontation which would have brought them to power. Or they were romantics who opposed the inevitable march of science and technology in the name of traditional communities and a system of smallholding agriculture which could never have fed the growing cities or maintained the imperial armies. Their ideology was faulty and their leadership was fatally divided, or self-interested or cowardly. All these and many more answers have been given to what was basically the wrong question.

Chartism was the demand for access to lawmaking and to the political system of Britain on the basis of citizenship rather than of property. The six points by which it was proposed to achieve this aim were none of them gained during the years of Chartist activity, only one of them indeed, the ballot, was to be gained during the nineteenth century. But if political campaigns are to be judged as successes or failures by whether or not their aims are immediately achieved, very few would be judged successful in the short term. The often quoted Anti-Corn Law League which was contemporary with the Chartists did, indeed, see the Corn Laws finally repealed. This did not however produce the results the campaigners had claimed would follow. Cheap food wanted for refrigerated transport to bring supplies from beyond Western Europe and complete freedom of trade was never more than an aspirational myth during the century following repeal. Of most other mass movements the results can be seen in changes of attitude or perception rather than in the actual literal achievement of immediate aims. Chartism brought many new issues into the political arena. It may also be said to have put the working class vote on to the agenda, even if the first responses by authority were a modernised police force and a national system of education which sought to dilute the too prominent talk of the rights of man and universal brotherhood with the teaching of discipline, obedience and the Christian religion.

Perhaps the first interesting point about Chartism is why, at that particular moment in history, a programme demanding political reform should catch the imagination of millions of men and women in the British Isles. Parliament had been in existence for centuries and the interests which controlled it had been contested by small numbers of excluded people in earlier years. But the mass movement for its reform was a new phenomenon in the early nineteenth century. Writing later in the century George Eliot described the period of the reform agitation as one in which 'Faith in the efficacy of political change was at fever heat in ardent reformers'. Why should this have been so? Already, before Britain had been shaken by the two decades of war that followed the revolution in France, considerable changes in society and in social administration had been taking place. Until the eighteenth century authority had been maintained and the law had been administered by locally based powers – the magistrates, the Church of England parsons, the landowners and other employers and local charities. But as population expanded and industrial change led to population movement and to greater and greater concentrations of population, old forms of authority were breaking down. New methods of production for an expanding home and world market called for a more flexible attitude to work and to skills in some major industries. Attempts had been made to deal with grievances and to assert traditional rights and customs through the old local systems of authority or by traditional methods of withholding labour to enforce wage and payment levels, but these had proved increasingly ineffective. Strikes, many of them long and painfully drawn out, in nearly every trade and industry during the twenty years after the ending of the French wars had all been defeated. At the same time the old system of poor relief, based since the days of Elizabeth I on the parishes, could not cope with the new concentrations of manufacturing and of population or with the new irregularities of trade and large scale manufacture. As traditional local systems of law enforcement and the regulation of wages and working conditions broke down in the growing manufacturing districts, and as new kinds of wealth and influence grew up, the classes which had so far been largely outside the political system, based as it was on landed property and the moral and political hegemony of the established church, began to look to the reform of Parliament as the means of adjustment to the new way of life.

Between the end of the wars in 1815 and the beginning of Chartism in the mid 1830s a series of notable victories had been won by hitherto excluded classes. In 1828 the repeal of the Test and Corporation Acts had opened the way to public office for Protestant Nonconformists, and thus to many of the commercial and manufacturing classes. In 1829 an even more remarkable achievement was seen in the Catholic Emancipation Act by which a Protestant Parliament voted for the removal of the remaining barriers to nearly every public office for Roman Catholics. In 1832, most dramatic of all, a Parliament of landowners and their protégés admitted to the electorate a large sector of the shopkeeping and urban property owning population which ended only just above the level of the skilled artisan – indeed, in parts of London it did include some members of that radical stratum. Access to parts of the lawmaking process, that is the right to vote for Members of Parliament and for the right to serve as Members and as other officers of the state, had ceased to be the prerogative of the Anglican landowning classes. What is more, the achievement of these changes showed that Parliament and the lawmaking structure generally could be vulnerable to external pressure. It did not seem wildly utopian to believe that mass pressure and the display of huge numbers could force the adoption of universal adult manhood suffrage which could establish the poorest people as a legitimate constituency to whose interests Parliament would be bound to listen.

Although there were those among the crowds who rallied to demand reform in 1831 and 1832 who believed that the Act would be the first instalment of a wider extension of the franchise, most of those who were to become leaders of the Chartists saw the admission of employers and traders to a franchise which still excluded working men as likely to harm rather than help the lower orders. The Charter with its six points was a document that grew out of the disappointment felt by the working people in the provisions of the 1832 Reform Act. This immensely important act saw the British 'ancien régime' alone among those of the major European powers, relinquish its monopoly of power without armed conflict. If King William wept as he signed, the Duke of Wellington saw in the signing the onset of a revolution, 'England which was once governed by gentlemen has been handed over to shopkeepers, many of whom are Socinians or even atheists'.

The more hard-headed among the Whig and Tory politicians recognised that they had won valuable support among the powerful new trading and manufacturing classes without seriously reducing the power of large landed and financial property owners. The boys in the streets of Belper were alleged to have been heard singing,

'The Revolution has begun
So I'll go back and get my gun
And shoot the Duke of Wellington'

but the more perceptive of the political spokesmen among the working class warned that the new electorate was likely to be wooed with a programme of reforms which would do little to deal with the grievances of the poor, the corrupt and oppressive poor law, the abolition of apprenticeship regulations, the penalties put upon combinations of tradesmen, the draconian administration of Ireland, the restrictions placed upon a cheap press and the lack of restrictions placed upon the work of women and children in the rapidly growing factory districts. They were to be proved right, as the legislation of the 1830s proceeded to deal with all these questions, and in every case in the interests of the new electorate of traders and employers.

The document which became known as the People's Charter was first written out and circulated in 1836. Its effect when it became generally adopted by radical groups throughout the country in the two years which followed was to draw together a series of campaigns and actions on specific issues, some the continuation of aims which were already part of the reform movement before 1832 but which had not been achieved by the Act, others started in direct response to a series of measures carried out by the reformed Parliaments of the early and middle 1830s.

The Charter was issued in the form of an appeal to the House of Commons to receive petitioners calling for an Act of Parliament embodying the six points which would introduce universal – i.e. male adult – suffrage. The points were: universal adult male suffrage, vote by secret ballot, the abolition of property qualifications for members of Parliament, the payment of members of Parliament, equal electoral districts and annual Parliaments.

Petitioning was the traditional means by which non-electors or any groups with a special interest approached Parliament, but the idea of a national petition with identical words and backed by massive numbers was new. Bronterre O'Brien, radical journalist and the most articulate of the early Chartist spokesmen, had called for such a massive petition to register opposition to the 1834 Poor Law Amendment Act. The idea had, he said, been suggested to him by the Irish radical leader, Feargus O'Connor, and what they proposed was 'that the poor of England shall be heard by council at the Bar of the House of Commons against the tyrannical and inhuman enactment miscalled the Poor Law Amendment Act'.[4]

The 1834 Act had been one of the first of the Whig 'reforms', and under it outdoor poor relief was to be abolished in favour of relief in a 'properly regulated workhouse'. The proper regulation was to include the separation of the sexes and the reduction of the standard of food and of comfort generally to one below that of the poorest employed labourer outside the workhouse. The Act had provoked anger among radicals which began to reach unmanageable proportions in the winter of 1836-7 when attempts were made to introduce its provisions into the manufacturing districts of the north. These districts were to be the heartlands of the Chartist movement – not the rural areas and not the cities but the manufacturing villages in which textiles and metal goods were made for the markets in the towns and cities.

Three or four main streams came together in 1838-9: the universal suffrage movement which produced the Charter itself and which was based in London and Birmingham as well as in Lancashire, Yorkshire and Nottinghamshire; the anti-poor law and factory reform movements which were closely connected and which were strongest in the manufacturing districts; the demand for a radical press which had been strongest in London and Manchester, and which now began for the first time to produce legal, national and stamped journals led by 'The Northern Star' in Leeds and including 'The Manchester and Salford Advertiser' in Manchester and 'The Northern Liberator' in Newcastle. The Chartist movement was to see a flowering of journals, mostly small and local and rarely breaking even in terms of financial gain, but providing a national network of information and debate for a largely working-class readership which was totally unprecedented in Britain or the rest of the world. The radicals had always supported Catholic emancipation and had opposed the Act of Union of 1801 which had abolished the Irish Parliament and brought Ireland under the direct rule of Westminster. There were large numbers of first and second- generation Irish workers in Great Britain, many of whom were to be found among the radicals and Chartists. The draconian

Irish Coercion Act of 1833, another early Act of the reformed Parliament, brought out large demonstrations of the Irish and their supporters, and was undoubtedly another of the precipitants of the movement. It was the idea that all these grievances could be solved by legal action, just as some of them had been created by such action that gave the enormous power of enthusiasm and numbers to the campaign for the vote. In its early days a few of the ultra-radicals in the Liberal and Tory parties supported the call for the suffrage, but the turbulent and, at one stage, violent actions of the Chartists soon led to the withdrawal of support from all but a very small number of Members of Parliament.

The Chartist petition was presented to Parliament three times by sympathetic MPs. In all three cases it was overwhelmingly rejected. But the collection of signatures was only a small part of the activity which occupied the Chartists. At the political level they organised a series of conventions, or anti-parliaments, whose delegates were elected by mass votes at monster meetings. They organised these meetings, often simultaneously at centres throughout Great Britain, and tens of thousands of men, women and children attended to hear Chartist orators as well as bands of music and sometimes-dramatic performances. In Chartist centres schools were established for children and for adults, cooperative stores were tried out and it was a group of Chartists in Rochdale who finally hit on the successful trading formula of 'dividend on purchases' which was the foundation of a century and a half of successful trading. The early cooperative stores also supported educational work and in some cases cooperative workshops. As the journals demonstrated, Chartist workmen and women wrote poetry and songs and performed them at political and social events, as well as performing dramas as varied as Shakespeare plays, Cobbett's one drama, and works especially written for the occasion such as the popular version of the trial of Robert Emmet. To an extent, in the twenty-odd years of its existence, Chartism in the strongest centres offered a kind of counterculture, an attempt to go ahead even before the achievement of the vote with the establishment of schools, honest trading centres, halls for education and entertainment, and the land scheme.

Ideological historians of the Labour movement have presented the land scheme either as a backward-looking peasant-inspired movement which turned its back on the irreversible process of industrialisation or as an attempt to establish freeholding settlements which would entitle their occupants to the vote. Neither of these motives was uppermost in the minds of the organisers or of the originator of the scheme, Feargus O'Connor. His idea was that spade husbandry could support families and could provide a rational basis for the evaluation of a reasonable wage. If a network of land colonies could be built throughout the land, men and women who wanted to leave factory labour could earn enough to live by honest industry off the land. This would prevent the absolute debasement of factory earnings by providing an alternative, and would also help to establish a standard by which industrial wages could be set. It may be argued that this argument was no more intellectually satisfactory than the often-alleged idea of the return of all workers to the land, but it was a very different view and one which was shared by many industrial workers. O'Connor's land scheme did not involve the freehold ownership of land by the individual tenants, and since the franchise after 1832 was only open to leaseholders of quite considerable status, none of the holdings came anywhere near providing a franchise before the law was reformed later in the century. The land scheme was a form of social self-help by which an alternative to town and city dwelling was to be opened for Chartists and their supporters, just as their schools and recreational buildings were providing leisure and training facilities which they hoped more enlightened regimes might support when universal suffrage was achieved and there was a Chartist bench in the House of Commons.

Chartism, then, was a diverse and many-sided movement organised around the idea of the vote as the right of the citizen, as the means to ensuring that the interests of all members of society were considered when laws and regulations were passed. It was also a movement of self-help in which working people organised for themselves and in which they gained the confidence to take part in many forms of public service including local government and school and poor law boards. It also laid the foundations for the unions of skilled workers and the cooperative stores and building societies which enabled the regularly employed working families to protect themselves against the vagaries of the free market ideology of the second half of the century.

Note on Sources: I have written a standard work on The Chartists (1984). This gives, to some extent, a narrative account of the movement and a description of its membership. In the bibliographies mentioned below there is a vast selection of work on aspects of the movement. I am therefore only noting here things which I actually mention in this piece.

1) Bibliography of the Chartist Movement, Harrison and Thompson 1978; The Chartist Movement: a New Annotated Bibliography. Ashton Fyson and Roberts 1995.

2) For a discussion of the way in which the writing of the history of Chartism has been affected by the politics of the writers, see my essay 'Chartism and the Historians' in Outsiders (1993)

3) Felix Holt, the Radical. (1866)

4) Bronterre's National Reformer, 4 Feb. 1837

5) For further discussion of the interaction between Irish nationalist politics and British radicalism see John Belchem 'English Working-Class Radicalism and the Irish 1815-1850 in Eire-Ireland' vol XIX No. 4 1984, and my 'Ireland and the Irish in KD English Radicalism before 1850' in Outsiders.

6) For an account of one district, see James Epstein 'Some organisational and Cultural Aspects of the Chartist Movement in Nottingham' in (eds) Epstein and Thompson The Chartist Experience 1982.

Further suggested reading: *The Chartists* by Dorothy Thompson.

CHAPTER THREE

The Birth of the Dream 1845-1847

THE NATIONAL LAND COMPANY was formed in April 1845 at a sparsely attended Chartist conference held in London. It was this conference that was to sow the seeds for the founding of the first estate at Heronsgate, and other estates were to be bought and built in quick succession. It was Feargus O'Connor's idea and led him into conflict with the other Chartist leaders. Following the rejection of the Charter in 1842 O'Connor had been thinking for some time that there were only two ways for the working classes to gain political power. One was to ally themselves with the middle classes who had the vote through their property qualifications, but the middle classes were not interested in such an alliance; the other was to settle workers on the land with each man holding freehold property of the value of forty shillings, the minimum qualification for a county vote.

O'Connor's plan was simple. A sum of £5,000 would be raised by selling 2,000 shares at £2 10s each. The money would be used to buy 120 acres of good arable land at the price of the day, which was about £18 15s per acre. This would provide 2 acres each for 60 landholders and leave £2,250 to buy houses and stock. These two-acre plots and houses would be let by the National Land Company in perpetuity for £5 per year. Other leading Chartists were angered by O'Connor's scheme, saying that Chartism was for political ends and not the economic emancipation of the working classes. However, O'Connor was determined to continue with the scheme and he spent the rest of 1845 travelling and studying the management of land in smallholdings. He even visited France and Belgium and met Marx and Engels who were against the private ownership of land. O'Connor said his scheme had nothing to do with socialism but was concerned with 'individuality of possession and cooperation of labour'.

Despite the adverse criticism, subscriptions began to pour in from all over the country and in January 1846, for instance, £200 a week was recorded. Chartist branches collected threepence or sixpence a head towards the shares. 'The Northern Star' kept making announcements about the registration of the company and every week the paper covered news of smallholding management; O'Connor's book on small farms was recommended.

In March 1846 O'Connor bought the Herringsgate Farm near Rickmansworth for £1,860; the price had been £2,344 but three annuities of £20 each were subtracted from the original price. This was the first Chartist estate and was the cheapest in price, costing just over £18 per acre. Later,

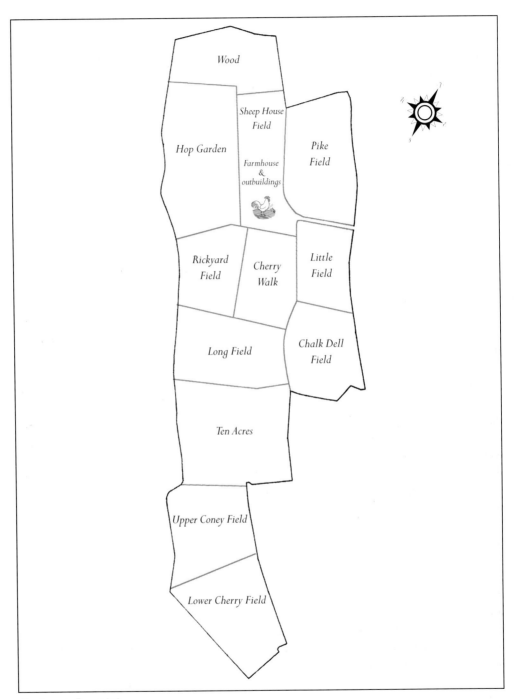

Wood

Sheep House
Field

Hop Garden

Pike
Field

Farmhouse
&
outbuildings

Rickyard
Field

Cherry
Walk

Little
Field

Long Field

Chalk Dell
Field

Ten Acres

Upper Coney Field

Lower Cherry Field

Herringsgate Farm 1838

O'Connor was to pay in the region of £50 per acre for Lowbands, £36 per acre for Minster Lovell, £45 per acre for Snigs End and £36 per acre for Dodford. Why did O'Connor choose Herringsgate Farm in rural Hertfordshire for his first estate? The price per acre was cheap and it was available. Land near the industrial cities from where the potential allottees came was for the most part owned by the aristocracy and the new industrial magnates. Further, O'Connor believed that a move from the industrial North and Midlands to the South of England would be attractive. When news of the purchase of Herringsgate Farm was announced, more Chartist branches were opened and subscriptions poured in. When the time came to pay for the farm, the Land Company had not been registered as an official organisation due to political and economic considerations (as explained further in chapter 7). This meant that the Land Company did not exist in the eyes of the law and therefore could not hold property; thus O'Connor signed the contract and became the owner of the property. As the result, the ballot winners, or allottees as they were referred to later, did not become the freehold owners of their properties due to the difficulties of setting up the Land Company and the original settlers were leaseholders. As Dorothy Thompson writes, 'The O'Connor land schemes did not involve the freehold ownership of land by the individual tenants, and since the franchise of 1832 was open only to leaseholders of quite considerable status, none of the holdings came anywhere near providing a franchise before the law was reformed.'

Thus an important aim behind the founding of the Land Company, the acquisition of the county vote, had failed at the very beginning. Interestingly, another property of 130 acres was purchased at Carpenders Park near Pinner station, and this was sold at a profit soon after Herringsgate farm had been bought.

The ballot for the allotments at Herringsgate was held at the Old Manor Court Room, Nicholas Croft, Manchester, on Easter Sunday the 20th April 1846 and everyone who had paid up on their shares of £2 10s was entitled to take part. At this time 1487 people were eligible for a chance to win one of the 35 cottages and allotments. According to the system now agreed those 157 people who held two shares were eligible for the 13 four-acre holdings. 580 people held one and a half shares and were eligible for the five three-acre holdings and 750 held one share which made them eligible for one of the 17 two-acre holdings. Excitement was running high and hundreds made their way to Manchester. Some walked all night to get there, only to find that the hall was full and they had to stand outside. Feargus O'Connor spoke of the grass and trees on the Estate, the clear unsmoked sky over it, the birds no freer than they would be themselves.

The draw was made first for the four-acre sites, then the three-acre sites and finally for the two-acre sites. Holders of the plots can be seen on the map page and appendix, but it should be noted that George Hearson of Leeds was replaced by Charles Smith of Halifax; Charles Brown of Halifax was replaced by Charles Tawes of New Radford; and Joseph Mills was replaced by Alfred Barker both of Ashton-under-Lyne. It was announced that the rent for the plots would be about £6 a year for a two-acre plot and £11 10s for a four-acre plot. Each owner would be given a cash loan to start him off with £15 for two acres, £22 10s for three acres, and £30 for four acres.

A few days after the ballot, O'Connor and a London builder Henry Cullingham, who was a skilled worker and an enthusiastic supporter and speaker for the Chartists, moved into the existing farmhouse. They worked hard laying out the four main roads of the Estate. Each was nine feet wide with a total length of about one and a half miles. They gathered together every bit of timber and building material they could find on the Estate and went to Watford and Uxbridge to get estimates from contractors to build the houses. But these proved too expensive, so O'Connor decided to hire labourers and craftsmen to do the work and purchase the material required himself. Cullingham was in charge of the carpenters and masons and dealt with the outside suppliers. By June 1846, two hundred men were at work on the site, and roads and houses were to be seen rising all over the Estate. The houses cost about £100 each to build, being much cheaper than the £230 each quoted by outside contractors. The houses were built to a very high standard and were constructed of the best materials.

When O'Connor bought Herringsgate Farm in 1846 he would have found the surrounding area totally different to what we know today. It was basically farmland with estates owned by Lord Grosvenor and occupied by tenant farms. Long Lane connected Herringsgate Farm to the surrounding areas; to the south it joined the Rickmansworth to Maple Cross Road and to the north Shire Lane. There is evidence (confirmed by an aerial survey of 1957) of an old Roman road from St Albans to Silchester. This road ran across the Chess Valley, along the line of Green Street, and on to Chalfont St Giles. At some time in early history, Long Lane joined the Roman road. There was a beer shop on Long Lane and opposite it a fine country house (now Oakhill) owned by Lord Grosvenor; further up Long Lane was a farriery, known as Mumfistells (now Long Lane House). The Swillett, as it is now called, consisted of a few cottages including Tinks Cottage and Beechwood Cottages.

In regard to the original farm, the name Herringsgate Farm was used when O'Connor bought the Estate. Maps of the 18th century and early 19th century refer to 'Herring Gate'. Deeds in the hands of the Formosas (Oakhill) dating back to 1739 refer to 'Herringers' and 'Herringsgate'; in 1599 'Heryngarste' and in 1656 'Herrigat' was used. At times locals called it 'Herrings Farm'.

The immediate farms in close proximity were Bullsland Farm, Hill Farm, Kings Farm and Long Hill Farm. To the south was Woodwick (Woodoaks) and to the west New Land Farm. These were typical farms of the day, producing crops such as wheat and oats; and rearing cattle – both for milk and beef – and sheep. The census of 1841 revealed that the population of Chorleywood parish was 938 with the estimated number of hereditaments 200, compared with a population of 447 at the beginning of the century. By this time the manorial lands with the system of open fields was in decline, enclosures were taking place and new estates were appearing. Most of the commons or greens had been enclosed including Quickley Green, but Chorleywood Common survived and still survives today. And so when the allottees moved into O'Connorville they found a small rural population, although the town of Rickmansworth was growing.

O'Connor and later the allottees and the locals and some from further afield established a working relationship. Henry Cullingham became not only O'Connor's foreman, but also a speaker at local meetings, explaining the land plan and Chartism and defending O'Connor against local suspicions. Cullingham was busy, workers had to be employed and contracts made. He found an overseer for the labourers in Mr Thomas King. Joiners, smiths and bricklayers were under a second

24

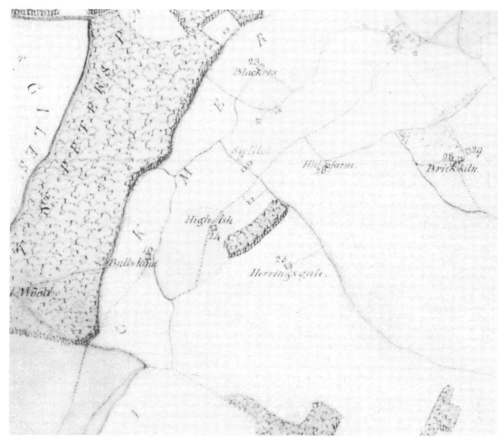

The area surrounding Herringsgate Farm, 1805

man, and horses and field workers under another. The search for contractors to build the cottages was more difficult. The contractors of Uxbridge and Watford proved to be too expensive but Messrs Beeson of Rickmansworth were contracted to build three cottages. In June 1846 there were 200 men at work helping to create the O'Connorville Estate; carpenters, sawyers, bricklayers, sand-diggers, wall-builders, plasterers, road-makers and carters. Most were locals from Chorleywood, Rickmansworth, Watford or Uxbridge, whilst some came from the north, having read in 'The Northern Star' about work in O'Connorville. They worked from five in the morning to seven in the evening in gangs of six, constructing the roads and building the houses. Over a five-day period a gang of six could earn £3.

Mr King, the overseer of the labourers, is worth commenting on here, since he bought Laburnums (plot 18) in 1857. He was the great-great-grandfather of Monty McCulloch, a current Heronsgate resident. Miss Fanny King who ran the epileptic centre at Laburnums was another descendant.

Feargus O'Connor was conscious of public opinion and of the need to improve the image of the working class as being capable, responsible, civilised and good. To consolidate local relationships,

25

O'Connor arranged several events. The first was on the 6th July 1846, when he declared a half-holiday for his Estate workers and organised a cricket match to be played on Chorleywood Common. A tent was set up and local people came to watch the cricket which began at one o'clock and went on until seven in the evening. A team of bricklayers captained by O'Connor beat a team of carpenters and sawyers by 28 runs. After the umpires had drawn stumps, sixty men from the Estate sat down to a meal in the tent. This may have been the first cricket match played on the common as the Chorleywood Cricket Club was founded later in the century. The first cricket match the 'Watford Observer' recorded was between Rickmansworth and Chorleywood in 1868.

The second event was a public meeting on Chorleywood Common on a Sunday afternoon in July 1846. About 600 people attended and listened to speeches by Cullingham and O'Connor, and although both spoke well, the crowd was not convinced it was possible to get a living from two acres. A Mr Gay of Rickmansworth invited O'Connor to continue the debate on a piece of open ground known as The Fortune in Rickmansworth. Despite Gay's antipathy to the land scheme, local working class people were not put off and a branch of the National Land Company was opened at Chorleywood. However, nobody from Chorleywood was amongst the original settlers.

The third and most important event was the demonstration planned for the 17th of August 1846 when there was a procession from London to O'Connorville, billed as 'Labour's Procession to Labour's own Land, purchased with Labour's own money'. The purpose of the event was to show off the new Estate. The main procession started from Marble Arch at seven in the morning, a four-horse stagecoach came from Reading, and vans arrived from Oxford, Yorkshire, Lancashire, Exeter and Plymouth. The day was a huge success. One of the visitors wrote that the cottages were substantial, roomy, airy, well lit, with oak floors and good cast iron grates. The London contingent left at seven in the evening. Throughout the day there had been no accident, damage or bad behaviour. The Northern Star of the 22nd August 1846 reported the event:

'CHARTIST JUBILEE
GRAND DEMONSTRATION TO THE PEOPLE'S FIRST ESTATE. "O'CONNORVILLE"
On Monday morning, August the 17th, at Sunrise, the "Great Metropolis", East, West, North and South, was in a state of joyous excitement; vehicles of all descriptions, from the "four-in-hand" down to the "one-horse chaise", were in requisition, with their banners and streamers "fluttering in the breeze", each bearing a suitable inscription, "the Charter and the Land" being most conspicuous, all hastening to the place of rendezvous, Hyde Park Corner, Oxford Street; which, shortly after seven o'clock, presented a most animated appearance. The various vehicles extending from Oxford Street to Bayswater, were freighted with joyous-hearted men and women, all animated with one spirit, all inspired with the human-ising determination of rescuing their fatherland from political and social bondage, and all journeying to view, with their own eyes, their - our - "First Estate"; to place their feet on that "foot of earth", which they hope will enable them to redeem the soil for the whole people. As the cavalcade proceeded, persons of all grades thronged the doors, windows, and thoroughfares to witness this truly novel spectacle, "Labour's Procession, to Labour's own Land, purchased with Labour's own Money!" On arriving at the far-famed town of Uxbridge, (rendered famous in history by an attempt to wrest a "Charter" from the tyrant Charles, and in which town, near the bridge, still stands, the Treaty house, now used as a Public House,

the Crown Tavern, in which that conference assembled, the long room or parlour being pointed out as the identical room in which it held its deliberations) the street was literally wedged up with people, and every place from which a view could be obtained was crammed with persons anxious to obtain a glance at the passing scene. Here, and all long the line, prospectuses and every other document giving information relative to the Chartist Co-operative Land Society, was sought for with avidity.

On arriving at O'Connorville, at twelve o'clock, we found a vast number of persons had preceded us by other routes; the "Ordnance" nevertheless, greeted this new accession of strength, by a roar of thunder from its "Iron throat". We had ocular demonstration that this demonstration was no mere metropolitan pleasure excursion, but "A National Jubilee", in favour of the "Universal Rights" of man, each county appearing to have at least a fair share of representatives present; even from Yorkshire and Lancashire in the north; and from Exeter and Plymouth in the West.

Among other vehicles, we noticed one van that came loaded from that seat of learning, the City of Oxford, a distance of forty miles; and a splendid "turn out", a four-horse stage coach, from the town of Reading, Berks., bearing an elegant silk banner, inscribed in the letters of gold, "Reading district of the Chartist Co-operative Land Society". The vehicles altogether numbered nearly two-hundred.

On entering the gates, the band played "The Chartist Land March". (The words and music of this march may be had of Mr Whitmore, through Mr Wheeler.) The first object that met our view, was a huge tri-coloured banner floating, high above an immense chestnut tree, bearing the inscription, "O'Connorville"; and secondly, Rebecca, the Chartist Cow, like the Sacred Cows of old, clothed in her vesture of tri-colour, rendered holy by popular voice, which is the voice of God; next, the immense Dancing Booth, erected for the accommodation of our Chartist friends, attracted the attention of every one. The remaining booths, for refreshment and amusement, were also of a very elegant character. Several "Wandering Minstrels" attended, and earned the patronage of the visitors by singing "The People's First Estate". The following was also sung by several friends, and much admired; the lines are the composition of a district secretary of the Chartist Co-operative Land Society, Mr William Dallibar.

BEAUTIFUL VILLAS
(Air, Land of the Free)
Those beautiful Villas how stately they stand,
A national honour to this our land,
Triumph of labour itself to employ,
And industry's fruits fully to enjoy;
Let fame on thy founders her laurel bestow,
And history's page their true value show;
We have seen many schemes, none can rival thee,
Thou beautiful Villas, the pride of the free.
Beautiful Villas, homes for the brave,
What solace you give the system-bound slave;
"Knowledge is power", no longer despair,
Is the great moral lesson that you declare;
I have seen many homes, none can excel thee,
Thou beautiful Villas, homes for the free.'

O'Connor said that no one was to move in until he said so, but John Walwark, a two-acre owner, and a weaver from Ashton-under-Lyne arrived on the Estate in August 1846 and O'Connor let him stay. He and his wife settled down and he sold gingham (cotton cloth with stripes or checks) to the locals which he wove on the hand loom he had brought with him.

Rosecot (plot 6), 1880s

By the end of September 1846, most of the outdoor work was finished with all the plots laid out and the land ploughed and harrowed. Tools and seed had been purchased and a dung heap was ready by each gate. Feargus O'Connor had ordered ten boatloads of London stable dung at 60 tons a load to be delivered to the Grand Junction Canal wharf at Rickmansworth, three miles from the Estate. Work on the school at O'Connorville, as it was now called, continued during the winter months. The school cost £500 and the schoolmaster, when appointed, was to pay this cost. The schoolmaster's salary would be paid by the parents of the children attending the school.

At this time O'Connor purchased 170 acres at Lowbands near Gloucester for another estate; when he returned from Lowbands in February 1847, he found three more families had moved in. O'Connor tried unsuccessfully to get them to leave. One of them, William Oddy, with his wife, his boy aged 12, and his girl aged 14, said they had never been so happy.

In the spring of 1847 carrots, turnips, swedes and potatoes were planted and the official notice of settlement from the 1st of May 1847 was issued. The settlers from the south and west were instructed to go by the Great Western Railway to West Drayton and through Uxbridge to O'Connorville, and the settlers from the north were to go by the Birmingham Line to Watford and then via Rickmansworth to O'Connorville.

Newspapers provided communication for the working classes. The Chartist press, in particular 'The Northern Star', was an important vehicle in presenting Chartist ideals and principles. The Northern Star was founded by O'Connor and through its editions presented the views of O'Connor and the purpose of the Land Company. However, the paper was also quite prepared to present another point of view and criticism against O'Connor.

The government from the early 19th Century had tried to price newspapers out of the working people's reach by the imposition of a heavy stamp duty. In 1836 a Stamp Act was passed which, although it reduced the duty from fourpence to one penny (prepaid) on all newspapers, greatly increased the penalties for producing or possessing unstamped newspapers. The Chartist press had overcome this by publishing and selling cheap periodicals without the necessary stamp and accepting the punishment of fines and imprisonment.

The Northern Star was founded in 1837 and by 1847 charged fivepence per copy. This was a considerable sum for a working man, but it went from strength to strength and was a credit to O'Connor and his editors. O'Connor was fortunate in that 1837 saw the introduction of new machinery and techniques in printing, but it was his own energy which ensured its success. In Ashton-under-Lyne, for instance, 1330 copies were ordered weekly during February 1839. In 1839, 42,077 copies were printed in the period April to June and sold throughout the British Isles. In Dublin over 400 copies were sold weekly in 1842. This was the circulation of The Northern Star at its peak, but it must be noted that its readership was far in excess of its circulation, and a very large printing continued until 1849. The enormous number of newspapers caused circulation problems. Mail coach companies and the postal authorities had to hire extra carts or wagons for the initial distribution to other towns. The newspapers were then collected by agents and the paper was eagerly picked up by coffee and beer-house keepers and local subscribers.

Saturday evenings, Sundays and Mondays were the days on which it was read aloud to waiting groups by people like Gabriel Redfearn, a blanket weaver of Littletown in the Spen Valley who would read the newspaper for hours at a stretch in the summer to sizeable audiences or in the winter to more select groups around his fire. The paper appealed to a working class, perhaps more literate than we might expect and its content is a compliment to its journalists and editors. The quality of the staff was very high and included men like G.A. Fleming, and Harvey and Ernest Jones. It was literary in content and included satirical and comical poetry and the ballad. Thus a considerable percentage of the people of the British Isles knew about Chartism, the Land Company and O'Connorville. In comparison, these days few people know about Heronsgate.

The Northern Star spoke of the departure of William Howse from Pershore in Worcestershire in the following terms; he was to live at The Limes (plot 12).

'Pershore, Worcestershire - Departure of AN ALLOTTEE FOR O'CONNORVILLE

Friday last, the 30th ult., was a high day with the Chartists of this locality. Mr William Howse, one of the fortunate allottees at O'Connorville having determined to leave his "cold quiet home" for "the land of promise" on the above named day, the members of Pershore branch of the National Land Company resolved that the public, both friends and foes of the cause, should be fully apprised of the happy change that awaited our friend Howse; accordingly, before five o'clock in the morning, a coach and four horses, decorated with laurels, evergreens and flowers, and having a full load of staunch Chartist working men, preceded by an excellent band of music in an open vehicle, and headed by the splendid banner of the Cheltenham branch of the National Charter Association, and other colours waving in the morning breeze, proceeded to the residence of Mr Howse, situated at the pleasant little village of Pensham, about a mile and a half from this town. Arrived there, he was saluted by a few hearty cheers which made the welkin ring, and aroused from their slumbers the few remaining rustics who had not yet escaped from the hands of Morpheus, and who came, gaping open-mouthed, to the scene of action, scarcely believing the evidence of their own senses, having to the last moment been assured by the farmers, their employers, that this Chartist Land plan was all a humbug, and that it was only a deep laid scheme of Feargus O'Connor to get hold of the people's money. Here, however, was a coach and four, which vehicle had never before been seen in Pershore, in the memory of the eldest inhabitant, really come for the purpose of carrying off in triumph their neighbour Wm. Howse, who had been duped by that Feargus O'Connor into a neat little house and two acres of good land, and had, even without consulting the feelings of the Pensham £50 tenants-at-will, been transmogrified, through the exertions of that very self-same Feargus O'Connor, the enemy of the working man, from a hard-working eight-shilling-a-week labouring serf into a worthy and independent freeholder of the county of Hertfordshire. Mr Howse having taken his seat, away went the merry company, followed by the hearty and lusty cheering of the astonished villagers, with the band playing merrily, the morning sun smiling cheerfully on us, and our friend Howse standing in a conspicuous place on the top of the coach, (the observed of all observers,) and holding in his hand a coloured plate of O'Connorville, framed; we entered Pershore about six o'clock, where, notwithstanding the early hour, hundreds of the inhabitants had already congregated in the streets waiting the arrival of the Chartist farmer, and although some few grumblers were occasionally heard to express their disapprobation, yet the great majority appeared pleased that the plan had so far succeeded, and their hearty good wishes followed the hero of the day. After parading the town we halted, and giving three cheers for the Charter, three for the land, three for Feargus O'Connor, and three for Farmer Howse, we proceeded with colours flying to the Defford Station of the Bristol and Birmingham Railway, three miles from Pershore; where, on the arrival of the train, Mr Howse took his seat for Birmingham, and amidst the puffing of the engine, the enlivening strains of the band, and the cheers of his friends our first Chartist Farmer departed for O'Connorville. This demonstration has put the working men on the qui vive, and as the result, we expect a large accession to our ranks. Wm. Conn, Jun., Sub-Sec.'

The great day arrived and The Northern Star dated 8th of May 1847 reported:

'The settlers arrived at Watford… and while the sun was still high, the travellers being all seated in vans, in readiness for the occasion, the band struck up "See, the Conquering Heroes come". The road for the whole distance presented the appearance of a Gala Day and never was such a merry May Day seen in Hertfordshire or in England before. At the entrance to the Holyland (O'Connorville) the first settlers were met by many old friends and well wishers and all were conducted to their respective abodes, all anxiously inspecting their castle and their labour field…'

The allottees were amazed and thrilled by what they found. There were ten pairs of semidetached houses making 20 houses. 18 of these houses had two rooms upstairs and two rooms downstairs, with a kitchen built out on the side and a courtyard behind with a separate privy and washhouse.

The remaining semidetached house providing two dwellings was similar but had only one room upstairs. 15 houses were single-storey with a kitchen, bedroom and sitting room.

Alice Hadfield in her book, 'The Chartist Land Company' published in 1970 says there were 13 pairs of semidetached houses with two rooms upstairs, five houses with three downstairs rooms and one above and 17 were single-storey; but research does not support these figures. I believe her figures to be based on the size of the allotments in that there were 13 four-acre plots, five three-acre plots and 17 two-acre plots including plot 11 which in fact was larger.

> 'Feargus O'Connor appeared at ten o'clock and found the women even more delighted than the men. In the kitchens were a table and a wall dresser (an example can be seen in the outhouse of Crowthorne (plot 4), now used to store garden necessities and tools); in the living rooms were some shelves and a chimneypiece. Apart from this the houses were not furnished and the settlers had to provide the remaining furniture and food. After a midday meal, they all met at the schoolhouse which was nearly finished and was empty except for a few carpenters' benches. Feargus O'Connor spoke and said they could buy the freehold of their lots at the price of 20 years rent but none did so. He exhorted them to work hard and have good family lives, and warned them against the dangers of drink and religious controversy.'

The Northern Star of Saturday May 8th 1847 reported O'Connor's speech to the occupants of O'Connorville in full:

> 'My Dear Friends,
> Saturday last was a proud day for me and an auspicious one for you. Your class have frequently been led to expect great benefits from extravagent promises, and have been as frequently deceived. Such, however, was not the case with you on Saturday, as it was my pride to hear one and all declare that every promise, however extravagant, had been more than fulfilled, and every expectation more than realized. You are now placed in the most honourable situation that man can possibly aspire to, in a situation in which, by wholesome and moderate labour, you may be independent of man's caprice and fortune's frowns; in a situation which will enable you to lay up a sufficient store in the days of youth and health to live upon in your old age, or when sickness may overtake you. What a sensation of delight you must have experienced on last Sunday morning, when, for the first time in your lives, you awoke to the cheering thought, that your day's employment did not depend upon foreign markets or domestic tyrants; when you were enabled to survey your labour-field from your castle window, and, to know that, if tired, you may lay you down and rest in your own bed, attended by your own wife, and surrounded by your own children. Having placed you in that honourable and enviable situation, let me now counsel you and implore of you to attend to my advice. There is a beer shop adjoining your land; avoid it, I beseech you, as a PESTILENCE, for if any enemy can be the means of ousting you from the lovely spot on which it was my pride to locate you, it will be man's greatest, most vicious and inviting enemy, drunkenness. I have earned a right to address you on this subject, because it is my boast to say that I have NEVER BEEN TIPSY in my life, and if I had been addicted to that base destroyer I never should have had patience, never health, strength, or constitution, to have redeemed you from starving, and, therefore, I pray you to worship sobriety as a great and adorable friend and Deity. Drunkenness is the first step to poverty, to crime and disgrace. You never see a teetotaller being convicted of crime, you never see a teetotaller starving, or his family in misery; and what possible pleasure can the supposed enjoyment give you? Next, I would caution you, not against the sin - for it is

no sin, nor yet crime - of poaching, and I do so, because you are in the neighbourhood of poachers, and because I know the fascinations that the pursuit has for the young and thoughtless. Do not become poachers, because the practice will inevitably lead to drunkenness, to idleness, to neglect of your land, to disgrace. Do not take the first step, for that is the most dangerous step; if you do you will be marked and watched, and your otherwise good character will be blemished by that one propensity. Do not allow your schoolhouse to be turned into a discussion-room as to which is the best form of religion, and, above and before all, either attempt to force your creed on others, or allow preachers of any denomination to disturb your simple society; for, so sure as you do, so sure will feuds, and quarrels, and dissension, and strife, be the result; and those who come amongst you to cast out devils will make a hell of your paradise. Avoid religious controversy as you would avoid a plague, and worship your God each after the dictates of his heart; but do not frown upon those who worship in a different manner. Now, disputes as to what is most acceptable to the Creator have been the principal cause of poverty for the industrious, and plenty for the idle; for, believe me, that those who profess so much solicitude about your souls are mainly actuated by a love of gain. A murderous, plundering, adulterous king changed the religion of this country to gratify his lust, and to enable him to rob the poor for the purpose of bribing the rich; and the whore-monger and drunkard, George the Fourth, had the matchless effrontery to order new prayers and to make alterations in the prayer book, so that you are now Protestants by Act of Parliament, whereas your forefathers were Catholics; and if the beast Harry had wanted to marry a Jew you would have been all Jews. So I pray you not to allow cunning preachers to disturb your minds, that they may live upon your fears. Again, if a religious man, or a solicitor, should come amongst you, except our own poor man's LAW SEEKER, Mr Roberts, turn him from amongst you, for he comes to strip you and then to laugh at you. Avoid grumbling for it leads to ruin. Love your wives and your children, because it ensures respect and makes your children respectful, loving, and dutiful; and, above and before all, take care and attend to their education in youth; for, bear in mind, that, with the ready means of instruction at command, your children's ignorance would be a brand upon the negligent parent. It will give me great pleasure to visit you frequently, to encourage and instruct you, and help you - that is, those who deserve it - and my displeasure will be a warning to your neighbours to doubt you; for, indeed, you may be happy if you are only prudent, and always bear in mind, that your failure would be a censure upon me, and would harm our watchful enemies with food for slander, as they would ascribe your failure to the fallacy of the principle, or to anything to wound me; they would pass over, nay praise, your crimes, if they enabled them to stab me. I am very sanguine in the hope, that before September twelve-month I shall be able to place ONE THOUSAND more in your position, and to go on still more rapidly each succeeding year, in proportion as the blessings of the system are felt and developed. Indeed, if the working classes only willed their own emancipation, and were not possessed of the notion that they would pay up today, and be located tomorrow, I would make a paradise of England in less than FIVE YEARS, and would cheerfully slave every hour of the day for such a noble purpose; but I can scarcely blame their haste, as, truth to say, the transition from perfect slavery and dependence to perfect freedom and independence, is a charming thing. If those with money would lend it at three and a half per cent., on the best security in the world, I would change the whole fact of society in TWELVE MONTHS from this day, and locate thousands on their own land; but Labour has always been our greatest enemy. Now, my friends, wishing you God speed, health, comfort, and happiness, and assuring you that I shall frequently visit you, and, promising you a letter upon what your next operations should be in next Saturday's Star, I take my leave for the present, and am, Your sincere and affectionate friend, FEARGUS O'CONNOR'

An open day was held at Whitsun. The big event of the day was a communal dinner in the schoolhouse provided by Mr Toovey of Watford. At eight o'clock the festivities were over and there was a scramble to get to Watford Junction where there was a huge train to take the crowds back to Euston. The Northern Star of May the 29th 1847 amongst other things reported the whole event thus:

'THE LAND! THE LAND! THE LAND! GRAND DEMONSTRATION AT O'CONNORVILLE
On Monday, the 24th of May, 1847.

Whit-Monday of the present year presented to the eye of the agrarian reformer indubitable proofs of the great, growing, and almost universal interest felt not only by the masses who toil, but by many who live by the labour of others, in that great and noble work, so well begun by the Chartist Convention of 1845 - the placing of Labour's sons and daughters in the possession of house and home; The making them the possessors of their own freeholds, and the tillers of their own soil, for their own sole use and advantage. The several roads leading to "The People's First Estate, O'Connorville" on this auspicious morn, presented a gay and animated appearance, the villagers dressed in their holiday attire appeared at door and window to give a hearty welcome to the "pilgrims" journeying from the metropolis to O'Connorville. The villagers for miles around the People's Land appear to have formed a deep attachment to Chartism, and to have imbibed a strong desire to have Chartists for their neighbours; a decisive proof of this was given as we passed through the village of Pinner. On our vehicle stopping to refresh the "cattle", a catalogue, announcing the sale of some freehold land, situated adjacent to that village, was given to us, and a fervent hope expressed that Mr O'Connor might become the purchaser. Nearing Rickmansworth, at an angle of the road, and by the side of the famous Moor Park, one of the residences of the noble lord, one of the members for Middlesex, we obtained a bird's-eye view of "The People's Farm". The flag floating from the summit of that noble building - the school - was distinctly visible. Our fellow travellers immediately gave three long and loud cheers for "The Happy Homes of Honest Industry".

Having at length arrived, and set our feet upon Freedom's happy land, we found the visitors pouring in from all parts. Amongst the earliest arrivals were three handsome vans, heavily freighted, bearing a banner with the inscription in front - "Men of Marylebone" and a second very handome tricoloured banner bearing the inscription - "The Land the People's birthright". These were under the very able management of Messrs Packer Goodwin, and Vincent Pakes, and a more happy party it was never our lot to witness. The Westminster vans immediately followed, ably piloted by the Messrs Witmore, whilst every train tended towards the depopulation of the "Great Wen", and the peopling of O'Connorville. Nor were the towns or villages of the provinces at all behindhand. Scarcely a town or village, east, south, north, or west, but was represented at this celebration. In walking round "South's Field", we noticed vehicles of all descriptions from St Albans, Luton, Cheddington, Uxbridge, Aylesbury, Hertford, Wycombe, Great Marlow, Beaconsfield, Amersham, Watford, Chenies, Woburn, Harrow, Pinner, Chesham, Maidenhead, Windsor, Slough, Colnbrook, Brentford, Leighton Buzzard, Hemel Hemstead and every place within twenty miles of the much favoured spot; whilst Manchester, Stockport, Chorley, Leeds, Nottingham, Derby, The Potteries, Merthyr Tydvil, Bristol, Bath, Devizes, Cheltenham, Birmingham, Reading, Horncastle, Torquay, Maidstone, Woolwich, Greenwich, Kingston, Croydon, Brighton, Coggeshall and numerous other towns and districts throughout the United Kingdom, had their representatives present; and not the least noticeable were the farmers of the neighbourhood on their thorough-bred steeds. The secretary of the Labourer's Friend Society, held in Exeter Hall, and Mr Charles Cochrane, the candidate for the representation of Westminster, were present and appeared to take a deep interest in the proceedings of the day. The extreme fineness of the weather - the sun shining resplendently; the great influx of visitors, their countenances beaming with joy; the gay holiday dresses; the galaxy of female beauty present, together with the sight of the homesteads and bounteous crops, tended to make all feel that O'Connorville was one of the loveliest spots in all creation. As the various parties arrived on the ground, each appeared to have their particular place of rendezvous; the Westminster district making for Mr Richardson's (plot 20), the Tower Hamlets' district going to Mr Mitchell's (plot 15), and the Somers' Town lads and lassies making for Mr Gambell's (plot 33); whilst many of the provincials made direct for Friend Wallwork's, all of whom provided bountifully for their visitors, whilst each allottee had his private party. There were several large public booths erected on the "Chartist Land", to supply refreshments to the very numerous company. Several small parties were seen in all directions closely scanning the elegant Chartist villas, the growing crops, the Chartist pigs, etc.

THE CROPS consist chiefly of barley, peas, broad beans, cabbage and potatoes; the whole presenting a very healthful appearance, and bid fair to be more than an average crop. Mr Richardson, who, for many years, was a disciple of the late William Cobbett, and who has much profited by the instructions of that great master, has his ground ornamented with very many gooseberry, currant, raspberry, and dwarf apple trees, and is altogether tastefuly set out and well cultivated for his brother allottees. The pigs looked healthy and thrifty, and when we consider the very short time the allottees have had possession, the appearance of the Estate does them great credit, and must have inspired the visitors with hopes amounting to a certainty of ultimate success.

THE PUBLIC MEETING

Half-past two o'clock having arrived it was announced that the public meeting would commence forthwith. The people, therefore, proceeded to the hustings, a waggon placed on an eminence in "South's Field", closely approximating to the "Estate". On the motion of Mr Stallwood, Mr Cooper, of Manchester was unanimously called to the chair, and said, all persons visiting O'Connorville to-day must come to the conclusion that the people had taken a right view of their own interests (Hear, hear). He was convinced that, were there more of such estates, it would be of the greatest advantage to the working classes. (Loud cheers). The allottees must not expect at the onset everything from the land; on the contrary, at the beginning the land would expect everything from them - (Hear, hear,) - and in the end would afford them a heavy interest on their labour; then let them work on harmoniously in the good work, persevere, and their efforts could not fail to be crowned with success. When he entered O'Connorville he was not prepared to see such an exhibition of beauty and utility combined. Mrs Hemans and other poetesses had often given to the public beautiful poetry, but here was poetry and reality practically combined. (Much applause).

Mr Christopher Doyle rose amidst considerable cheering, and, in allusion to the school on their Estate, said it had been erected that therein there might be instilled in the minds of the children, not bigotry and prejudice, but the principles of liberty, truth and justice. (Loud applause.) They had heard much of education lately, they had heard of Lord John Russell and the minutes of council. Lord John was a very great man and possessed a great mind, (Laughter) and never swerved from his principles (Roars of laughter). They seemed incredulous, but it was a fact (Renewed laughter). He never had any to swerve (Applause). He (Lord John Russell) had talked of education, but he denied the right of any to it, unless they held certain theological dogmas or were taught a certain description of catechism, yet he wished

34

the nation to pay for it. (Hear, hear). Now he (Mr Doyle) had not the least objection to national education, but he demanded that when all had to pay, that all should be enabled to be partakers, and that, too, without prejudice. (Loud cheers). The newspapers confirmed the report of Mr O'Connell's death. Looking at the present awful state of Ireland, he could not help saying he thought it would have been well for her had she possessed a different set of leaders for the last half century. (Cheers) And when he looked at O'Connorville, his thought was, were Feargus O'Connor, her leader, she would be in a much surer path for the obtaining liberty, plenty and happiness. (Vehement cheering).

(Mr O'Connor at this moment entered the meeting and was greeted with the most hearty plaudits). Mr Doyle then announced that some china, earthenware, etc. with the O'Connorville Estate wrought on it, had been sent by their friends in the Potteries, and would be at their office in Dean Street, for sale at moderate prices. This would be another means of carrying out the great principle of co-operation. (Great applause).

Mr Feargus O'Connor now rose amidst loud, long, and hearty cheering, which having subsided, he said, (pointing to the "villas" on the "People's First Estate") when he erected those cottages he felt sure that though mute, they would more eloquently proclaim the march of Democracy than all the speakers and lecturers had or could set forth (Loud cheers). The strength of other plans consisted in such support as a venal Press could give them, and that withdrawn, they burst like a bombshell over the heads of their supporters (Cheers). But he had received no such support; he had received the confidence of the people, he had performed all he had promised, and now rested on the hearts and affections of a grateful people; and he defied all the opponents in the world to destroy him or his plan. (Loud cheers). William Pitt had founded his system on the National Debt – he (Mr O'Connor) had established the National Land Company, and bound its members with a brazen link, and no government could break them asunder (Much applause). Other plans had been put forward, but when their promoters had been asked to define their principles, they had failed to do so. He had been asked to define the ulterior measures of Chartism – "There they are," said Mr O'Connor, pointing to the Estate (Loud cheering). He had often told them that they had fools and knaves amongst them - they said "Why buy the land when it is ours already?". He answered it as an Irishman, by asking another question - "Why buy a leg of mutton when 'tis yours already?" (Loud laughter.) When he first came to Herringsgate Chartism was unknown; now every labourer called himself a "charterer" (Laughter) and, when, their mistresses asked what they meant by "charterer", they responded "House and Land, if you please, marm," (Loud laughter, and great applause.) He recollected once hearing a man speaking of another whilst driving him up from Watford, and he said, "He's a great radical sir." He (Mr O'C.) asked him what he meant by "a great radical?" "Oh!" said he, "he's a terrible drunkard, and be smashing all the glass and crockery" (Roars of laughter.) Their prejudiced neighbours had, however, come to understand Radicalism since the cottages were built. (Cheers.) At Lowbands, too, Chartism was unknown, but now the villages around it sent up as much as £30 per week for the Chartist Land Company. Yet there were some knaves or fools who asserted that he had started the Land plan to sink Chartism. There was one Jemmy O'Brien, he did not know in which class to place him, whether knave or fool; however, England did not appear to be large enough for him (Loud cheers). He (O'Brien) called two, three and four acres of land "mere patches." He did not think if "Jemmy" had thirty acres, ten for horticultural, ten for agricultural, and ten to grow malt, it would be enough for him; he would starve then and require two acres more to grow cabbage. (Laughter.) Jemmy said to the members

35

of the Land Company, when they subscribed any more funds, "Place them in the hands of Richard Oastler, he will take greater care of them than Feargus, and spend them better for you". Now he (Mr O'C) believed were the kingdom polled from end to end, that an immense majority would be found in favour of vesting the funds in the hands of Feargus O'Connor. (Vehement cheering.) Now he would just tell them what his share in the company was, and he could not illustrate it better than by placing that day's work before them. He rose at four o'clock that morning and came ten miles to Gloucester, from thence by the Great Western Railway to Slough, and from thence by gig here. That was his share, and all he ever would have. (Hear, hear.) He had created a great and enduring public opinion and if all the bishops, archbishops, aristocrats, merchants, princes, and all the candidates that would appear on the hustings shortly, were to combine and shout – "Free Trade", "Poor Laws", "Ten Hours' Bill", they would be met with an over-whelming shout of – "House and land." (Tremendous cheering.) He had often said there was a philosophy in idleness, and, acting on it, he had bided his time as regarding political agitation; but when the disso-lution took place, as they were determined to have a few good men in the house, Feargus O'Connor, like bad luck, would be everywhere. (Great applause.) He pointed to the Estate as a model for future reforms. He liked not to hear people complain of oppression, when they had the means of redemption in their own hands (Loud cheers.) Two omnibus loads of people had come yesterday from Stourbridge to Lowbands, and he had been engaged in the occupation of going from door to door looking for lodgings for the visitants – (loud cheers) – and had called at every door except that of the parson. He had omitted his, as he was sure he would not concede the rites of hospitality. (Hear, hear.) Experience told him never to expect a good Samaritan in a parson – (Loud cheers.) – yet for engaging in such a holy work on a Sunday he was denounced as an infidel, whilst the parson was regarded as the servant of God. (Hear, hear.) But he called the parsons devils nothing else. (Loud cheers.)

He admired rural life, and believed "God made the country, the devil the town"; and he believed between this and next summer he would locate over two thousand men – (Loud cheers) – as it was far cheaper to build by wholesale than retail. (Cheers.) Let them resolve to spend their money in land, instead of the gin shops, and it could and would be done. (Great applause.) They were becoming powerful and ultimately the government must take up the question, and do nationally what he was doing locally. (Loud cheers.) Johnny Bright had sent a flogged soldier to Herringsgate, and he had traduced, slandered and vilified the Company; but the letters in the Manchester Examiner had had the effect of setting people inquiring who previously knew nothing of the Land Company. He (Mr O'C) had done his share; he trusted they would do theirs, and continue until every working man, woman, and child, were brought to share the blessings of peace, liberty, and happiness – the objects of the National Land Company. (Tremendous cheering.)

Mr Stallwood said he had much pleasure in moving a vote of thanks to the chairman, for his able conduct in the chair. The motion was seconded and carried unanimously amidst loud cheers. Mr Cooper briefly acknowledged the compliment, and the meeting dissolved. At the close, Messrs Stallwood and O'Connor having announced that dinner was ready, numerous friends proceeded to the schoolroom, which was tastefuly decorated with green boughs for the occasion.

The Public Dinner was then served up. Mr Cooper presiding, and Mr T. Clark officiating as vice-chair-man. At the cross table we observed Feargus O'Connor, Esq, Charles Cochrane, Esq, T. Allsop, Esq, – Biggs, Esq, and the secretary to the Labourer's Friend Society. At one of the side tables were seated

Messrs T.M. Wheeler and C. Doyle, two of the directors of the Land Company, with numerous active friends of the movement. Several ladies also graced the table with their presence. The viands were, as the occasion demanded, of a substantial kind, consisting of roast and boiled beef, veal, lamb, meat pies, salads, etc. The dinner was furnished by Mr Toovey of Watford, and did the purveyor great credit. The bracing air of O'Connorville caused the guests to do ample justice to it – the tables having been cleared.

The Chairman said without any circumlocution he would proceed to the toast of the evening, merely remarking that the Labourer's Friend Society and the Field Garden System had shown that the Land Plan was perfectly practicable. (Cheers.) The toast he had the honour to submit was as follows: "Prosperity to the Allottees on the O'Connorville Estate, and may the whole population speedily enjoy the blessings to be derived from a Free Soul."

The sentiment was given with great applause, and Mr O'Connor rose to respond amidst reiterated acclamations. He said he was gratified beyond measure to respond to the sentiment, but no eloquence of his could equal the impression created by the appearance of the "People's First Estate", and, although it was a meagre outline of the full length portrait yet to come, it was yet sufficient to convince them of the certainty of that prosperity to which the toast alluded, and which must fill their hearts with joy, and cause gladness to resound throughout the length and breadth of the land, whilst it must ultimately confer freedom, contentment and unalloyed bliss on the whole human race. (Vehement cheering.) As an inducement to the allottees to become good agriculturists, and good general cultivators of the soil, good fathers, and good husbands, he had resolved to award out of his own pocket three separate prizes of the relative value of £7, £5, and £3. But let them not suppose that the man who grew the best cabbages, or had the finest crop, the most beautiful flowers, or the cleanest ground, would carry off the premiums. Other things must be associated with these. Whilst he held out this inducement to emulation, he wished to see social comfort combined with plenty in his home colonies. (Loud cheers.) His test would be ability, ingenuity, sobriety, and affection for wife, children, and happy homes. (Tremendous cheering.) The Chairman had alluded to the allotment system; he (Mr O'Connor) was a great enemy to the allotment system. He would tell them why. The allotment system set them toiling for others all day, and after they were spent with a day's toil for others, allowed them to work an hour for themselves in the evening. (Hear, hear.) He did not like such a system. He did not think the people should be treated worse than brute beasts. (Cheers.) Why should the industrious man be subject to be turned out of his house at a month's notice? (Hear, hear.) Why should they lay eggs to be sucked by another. (Great cheering.) He infinitely preferred that each man's house and land should be his own freehold, secured to him in a way that no one could dispossess him thereof. (Reiterated cheering.) But "Jemmy O'Brien" had asked why not insert all their names in the conveyance? Simply because it would cost a million and a half of money to do so. There must be a holder or landlord for the nonce, and, without egotism, he believed he might say that there was none in whom the people had so much confidence for that purpose as himself. (Loud cheering.) He was fond of the land that he had bought a farm (and paid for it too). What would "Jemmy O'Brien" say to that? (Laughter.) Sir R. Peel had once told him that he (Mr O'C.) had royal blood in his veins. (Hear, hear.) He believed he came of a good family and stock, but he had a much greater honour conferred on him than that. He had been promoted from the ranks of the Aristocracy to the ranks of the Democracy. (Enthusiastic cheering.) How many people had attended here today who were without principle, or who were a kind of mongrel Whig and Tory, a kind of half-bred between a donkey and a mare, (laughter) but who would now return converted into thoroughbred Chartists. (Loud laughter and great applause.) Some of his family for serving the people had been called traitors, and but barely escaped the gallows, and had suffered banishment from their native land. (Shame, shame.) But if it was treason to love and faithfully serve the people, then he gloried in the name and trusted he should live and die a "traitor". (Vehement cheering.) Some little medical quack had written to "the Manx man" and said, "See what a sensation Feargus O'Connor has caused by pretending to give land". Well, he supposed putting the people in the possession of house and land at O'Connorville was a pretence, and that building a pigsty in the moor was a reality. (Loud laughter.) There is a building reformer for you! (Laughter.) He had always preferred a man working for himself for one pound a week, to working for a master for thirty shillings, because he was more independent. There was a great pleasure in his present occupation, much more pleasure than could attend the chariot races of the Queen of Spain, or even a Madrid bull fight (Laughter.) He had been a fox-hunter, a race-man, a dinner-man, a party-man, and had been well received by all, but none had afforded him so much pleasure, so much real gratification, as did his present pursuit of buying land, and building houses for the people. (Loud cheers.) He trusted his plan would be thrust upon the government, and that the government would be made to do that nationally which he could only carry out locally. (Loud cheers.) This one hundred and three acres had originally been cultivated by three men and a boy. What vast support they must have afforded to the shopkeepers in the neighbourhood! (Laughter.) But now the same land was made to support thirty-five families. What a revolution! He was sorry to see that some had been induced to leave the land, but was happy to find that they had been amply compensated, as they had sold for sums of £40, £78, and £90; whilst one had been offered as much as £120 for his farm. (Loud cheers.) But still he said stick to the land – (Hear, hear) – and when he came here in August next, he felt assured that he would find himself amply rewarded, by finding the allottees in possession of a bountiful harvest, peace, contentment, and lasting prosperity. (Great applause.) He might say he had been almost universally abused, and had rested for support entirely on the poor and despised working classes, against the united forces of the middle and upper classes to whom he owed his great success. (Loud cheers.) He had seen the beginning, and might he never see the end, until such time as every man, woman, and child was in possession of his just right – the Land – and all the blessings it so bountifully yielded. Mr O'Connor resumed his seat amidst tremendous applause.'

The dream of Utopia had begun well. At the end of the summer of 1847 there was a feeling of 'freedom, happiness and contentment' amongst the allottees. The cottages had been splendidly built, relationships with the locals from the surrounding areas were amicable, the crops planted in the spring of 1847 had flourished, the livestock were healthy and the network of lanes had been soundly constructed.

The new inhabitants of O'Connorville in the late summer of 1847 were for the most part very happy. Crops of carrots, turnips, swedes, barley and vegetables had been harvested and stored, new outbuildings were built to store the crops and house the animals and barns were erected. An example of a barn dating back to those days can be seen at Chartist Cottage (plot 25). Pig farming was popular and most people had at least two hogs, some had many more; some had Berkshire sows which produced big litters – William Mitchell (plot 15) had 14 pigs. A few allottees had cows; one called Rebecca had been on the Estate since 1846 and was named Rebecca after the Rebecca riots (1842-43) over tollgates in South Wales. There were also horses, a donkey, goats, ducks, fowl and rabbits in abundance.

Rosecot (plot 6), 1880s, looking north along Nottingham Road South

The building of the school had been completed, but the schoolrooms had not yet been fitted out nor a schoolmaster appointed. However, all were interested in when the school would open, what subjects would be taught and how much the fees would be. By now, all the cottages had been furnished, often only sparsely and most were content with their lot. Some land had been fenced. They had roots, firewood and old posts for burning in their fireplaces and ovens, they had smoked bacon, duck and chicken eggs to eat, they baked their bread and cooked stews and faggots. They picked rose hips and crab apples and other fruits for jam, sweetening and eating; they used rabbit skins to line their jackets and breeches and told stories and sang songs by their fireplaces at night. Life was much better in O'Connorville than in the factory towns.

Charles Tawes (plot 9) was offered £50 for his two acres, but he refused the money. George Ramsbottom (plot 14) said he had never been so happy and would never leave. David Watson (plot 25) was happy now that he no longer had to look after his father. He had five pigs and had killed one weighing 32 stone; 448 pounds of ham, bacon, lard, pig's head brawn, black puddings and bacon bone soup. John Lambourne (plot 2) was thankful to see his children so healthy; William Mann (plot 4) and his wife had never been so happy; Thomas Smith (plot 30) was very proud of the manglewurzel of 32 inches in circumference, which he had grown. George Richardson (plot 20) had harvested the finest onions 'you ever saw' and said about his wife that 'she doesn't know what it is to be sick now, but was always poorly before'. Michael Fitzsimmons (plot 3), the Irishman from Manchester was also very happy. Feargus O'Connor had created a fine new settlement, but he knew winter was coming and difficult times lay ahead.

39

 CHAPTER FOUR

Feargus O'Connor (1796-1855) by James Epstein and the Author

How should we judge Feargus O'Connor? Was he a rogue or was he a philanthropist and gentleman leader? Historians in the years since his death have varied widely in their assessment. Early historians such as R.C. Gammage who wrote a 'History of the Chartist Movement 1837-1854' in 1854 and later historians, such as Donald Read and Eric Glasgow who wrote 'Feargus O'Connor Irishman and Chartist' in 1961 and Alice Hadfield's 'The Chartist Land Company', paint a picture of a man brought up in County Cork in a landowning family, not well off but with extreme radical ideas. They tell us that O'Connor was a tall, strong, ginger-haired fellow with a bulging forehead that made his eyes look sunken and emphasized his turned-up nose, and that he was an expert with horses, cards, a crowd of fellows and a scene. As O'Connor's land plan emerged in 1842 it was regarded as a distraction of energy from the main political drive of the Chartist movement by the majority of Chartist leaders and led to his quarrelling with all the leaders. He is portrayed as a dangerous man, blown up with his own conceit and dallying with communism, and his dilatory methods involved no central account keeping which were to lead to accusations of fraud. A select parliamentary committee was set up in 1848 under William Hayter, the judge advocate, to enquire into the legality and dealings of the Land Company and the potential burden to the poor law boards in the parishes of the inhabitants of the estates. Mr W.H. Grey the government accountant, reported:

> 'From the frank and open manner in which everything had been submitted to my inspection, and from the readiness with which every enquiry of mine has been met, I am thoroughly satisfied, not only that the whole of the money has been honourably appropriated and is fully accounted for, but also that several thousand pounds more of Mr O'Connor's own funds have been applied in furtherance of the views of the National Land Company.'

This report did not prevent the winding-up of the Land Company. O'Connor's bad press from early historians and his confrontations with parliament lay in that what he was trying to achieve was too early and too controversial for the governing classes of the British Isles and of the mid-Victorian era. He had fallen foul of the authorities as early as 1843 when, with 58 other Chartists, he appeared at the Nisi Prius Court, Lancaster, on charges of sedition, conspiracy, tumult and riot. Early historians branded him as a heavy drinker being particularly fond of brandy, a womaniser who was alleged to have fathered two children by a local woman whilst lodging at the now named Hope Lodge (plot 20), and that he was insane as early as 1847. The first two accusations seem strange as he constantly spoke of the dangers of drink and the importance of family values; but that he died with signs of insanity seems probable.

More recently, historians such as James Epstein have been recalling O'Connor in a much more favourable light. James Epstein is a lecturer in history at Vanderbilt University in Nashville, Tennessee, U.S.A., and recently he published a book 'Feargus O'Connor, the Lion of Freedom'. He presented his views on O'Connor to the residents of Heronsgate in 1997 at the 150th anniversary of O'Connorville's opening, and here is a transcript of his talk under the title 'Feargus O'Connor and the Cult of Gentlemanly Leadership':

O'Connor was the founder of the land plan and Chartist leader after whom O'Connorville was named. I wish to help you understand his enormous popularity among plebeian radicals, both men and women, in the 1830s and 1840s – i.e. the Chartist period – particularly around the theme of the gentleman leader.

He was born probably in July of 1796, son of Roger and Wilhelmina (née Bowen) O'Connor of Connorville, County Cork, and nephew of Arthur Feargus.[1] He came from a family of wealthy Protestant, Anglo-Irish landowners, although both his father and uncle changed their surnames from Conner to O'Connor. They also both became United Irishmen – revolutionaries of the 1790s linking Irish nationalist independence to large aspirations inspired by the French revolution.

Feargus' father was exiled from Ireland in 1801 for his involvement with the United Irishmen; his uncle Arthur was tried for high treason and eventually became a general in Napoleon's army, never returning to Britain. Feargus first attended school in London after his father's exile from Ireland in 1801 and when his father was allowed to return in 1803 was subsequently educated at several schools near Dublin. He probably went to Trinity College, Dublin, but did not take a degree. He lived on his father's Dangan Castle estate in County Meath where as a young man Feargus pursued a keen interest in horse racing. Around 1819 he was admitted to the King's Inn, Dublin and in 1826 joined Gray's Inn, London; in 1830 he was admitted to the Irish Bar, but practised law only briefly. Previously, in about 1820 Feargus had inherited the estate of Fort Robert, County Cork, from his uncle Robert Conner. O'Connor was a reforming landlord and in 1822 he published his first political tract, 'A State of Ireland', in which he denounced corruption in local government.

The Irish context is important in a number of regards. Firstly, O'Connor grew up in a highly politicized household and family; he was introduced to radical and revolutionary politics early. His father was in touch with radical politics in London and was a close friend of the patrician radical and MP, Sir Francis Burdett. His uncle was one of the leaders of the bloody Irish rising of 1798. His family connections were important to his own introduction into English radical politics, winning him an instant audience among plebeian radicals. It is well worth remembering how important Ireland was to British politics: Ireland was England's first colony, its pre-famine population was one third that of Great Britain, and a large pre-famine Irish population had settled in London and through-out industrial England. So the first point is that rather than separating or distancing Feargus from radical politics in England and Scotland, his Irish background and family made him a hot item – it

FEARGUS O'CONNOR, ESQ^R.

Barrister at Law.

Feargus O'Connor

served to connect him to pressing issues of the day. Secondly, although the predominantly Protestant leaders of the United Irishmen of the 1790s tended to come from urban areas, either Dublin or Cork, Feargus grew up as a landowner, an Irish squire, a reforming landlord and a fine horseman. His rural, gentlemanly background was, as I will argue, also quite crucial as he emerged and sustained his status as a popular leader.

It was during the reform agitation of 1831-32 that O'Connor first publicly came forward as an advocate of Irish rights and democratic political reform. At this time his extraordinary talents as a public speaker first became evident. After the passing of the Reform Bill, O'Connor stormed the country registering the new electorate and he was returned head of the poll for County Cork. He was also returned as a supporter of Daniel O'Connell and pledged to the repeal of the Union (1801) between England and Ireland. He soon allied himself with London's popular radicals and was involved in various campaigns, including those for a free (untaxed) press and the return of the transported Dorchester labourers (trade unionists transported in 1834). However, Feargus quickly clashed with O'Connell over the 'Liberators' refusal to move a motion for the repeal of the Union. And although O'Connor was re-elected for County Cork in 1835, he was unseated in June 1835 owing to his lack of the necessary freehold property qualification. Fort Robert was not freehold but was held on a very long lease. It was at this point that O'Connor embarked on a career primarily as a leader of English popular radicalism, although he continued to bring Irish issues to the fore.

As an independent agitator O'Connor did more than any single leader to lay the groundwork for Chartism, organizing radical associations in London and the North of England and in Scotland. During 1836 and 1837, he agitated around issues such as universal male suffrage, repeal of the newspaper stamp, abolition of the new Poor Law and shorter hours for factory workers. In November 1836 he became an honorary member of the London Working Men's Association, the society that drew up the People's Charter with its famous six points.

Increasingly, however, Feargus turned his attention to the industrial districts of England and Scotland. Most significantly, in 1837 he established 'The Northern Star', a weekly newspaper, published in Leeds. Within four weeks of the publication of the first number, on the 18th of November 1837, the paper was making a profit and within a year it was the most widely circulated provincial paper in the land. The Northern Star became, in effect, Chartism's official journal, publishing not only O'Connor's weekly letter addressed to the 'unshaved chins, blistered hands, and fustian jackets', but a wide range of local Chartist news. In the columns of O'Connor's paper adherents became aware of the movement's national scope. The establishment of 'The Star' coincided with the height of the anti-Poor Law agitation in which O'Connor joined Richard Oastler and the Reverend Stephens at huge rallies characterized by violent rhetoric, burning torches, and the firing of guns.

O'Connor was crucial in spring 1839 to the coming together of Chartism. It was O'Connor who committed the forces of northern radicalism to the Birmingham Political Union's national petition, the People's Charter drawn up by the London Working Men's Association, and to plans to hold a national convention, seen by many as a rival to Parliament. He had attended nearly all the

44

huge demonstrations from the late summer of 1837 through the winter of 1838 which elected delegates to the Convention. He assumed the role of national leader coordinating and unifying the agitation, although his identification with the lawless tone of northern radicalism and his refusal to dissociate himself from recommendations for popular arming, alarmed moderate leaders.

At the Chartist Convention which assembled in February 1839, O'Connor was from the beginning the chief figure, declaring the body to be 'the only constituted authority representing the people of this country'. The Convention faltered over the question of what to do once Parliament rejected the National Petition, failing to devise a strategy of decisive action. In July 1839, however, after the Convention had at last committed the movement to a 'National Holiday', or general strike, O'Connor's opposition was crucial in reversing this decision on the grounds that Chartists were not yet prepared for a showdown with government authorities and in substituting a token three-day strike.

O'Connor almost certainly knew something of the secret plans afoot for armed insurrection in autumn 1839, although he was not involved in the preparations for the Newport rising on the fourth of November when a body of Welsh Chartists staged an unsuccessful rising. In March 1840, O'Connor was found guilty at York Assizes of seditious libel for speeches, his own and those of others, published in The Northern Star and was sentenced to eighteen months imprisonment in York Castle. Despite his relatively good treatment in prison – class distinction extended to prison – he fully exploited the popular image of the patriot martyr. Ever the populist showman, he emerged on his release wearing a suit of working man's fustian to signal his allegiance to the people.

I don't intend to give a blow by blow account of O'Connor's entire political career up to his death in 1855. Suffice it to say, that at least until 1848 he was Chartism's most prominent and easily its most popular leader.[2] He again faced trial in March 1843 at Lancaster along with 58 others on charges of seditious conspiracy arising from the Chartist strikes that swept the industrial districts of the North and the Midlands the previous summer, and although convicted on one count of endeavouring to excite disaffection by unlawfully encouraging a stoppage of labour, he was never brought up for sentencing due to a procedural error. In 1847 he was again elected to Parliament, becoming the only Chartist MP. Sometime in 1851, however, O'Connor suffered the onset of serious mental illness, perhaps the final stage of syphilis. In June 1852, he was admitted to Dr Harrington Tuke's asylum at Chiswick where he remained until just before his death. 'The Times' reported that fifty thousand persons attended his funeral on September the 10th at Kensal Green.

So what are we to make of this man and his remarkable political career? In the aftermath of Chartism, and especially by the later 19th century, O'Connor's reputation had gone into steep decline. By this time millions of working people had shifted their allegiance to popular Liberalism; William Gladstone, a very different sort of gentleman leader, had won the hearts of the people. O'Connor seemed to embody so much that Liberalism had set itself against: violence and the divisive rhetoric of class, passion in place of reason, and a backward vision of life on the land as opposed to industrial progress.

Indeed, the first historians of Chartism saw O'Connor as the destroyer of a movement born of the idealism of moderate and enlightened London artisans – men like the cabinet maker William

Lovett of the London Working Men's Association; O'Connor was pictured as the quintessential representative of the northern masses, of the 'unshaved chins, blistered hands, and fustian jackets' that he had so often addressed in his weekly letters and speeches. Mark Hovell, the movement's first significant historian, characterized O'Connor's supporters as, 'A great, vague mass of desperate, excited, and uneducated labourers … crying out for leaders … He came forth to lead them he knew not whither, and they followed blindly.'

The image of O'Connor as a vainglorious, self-seeking rabble-rouser became part of the orthodoxy of British political history. Needless to say, this is an inadequate characterization. For the rest of my talk, I want to suggest a rather different way of viewing O'Connor and his relationship to Chartism, the 19th century's largest and most sustained mobilization for democratic rights. Leadership implies a relationship: a relationship between leaders and followers or leadership and led. Yet these very terms present loaded categories, suggesting a one-way process: leaders lead and followers follow.

In approaching the subject of radical political leadership and the relationship it implies, it is necessary, therefore, to start with some appreciation of the political culture that sustained, set certain limits on and, to a considerable extent, defined leadership. It is important to recognize Chartism's more distinctive characteristics: namely, its national dimensions, its openness, its democratic practice and striking capacity in towns throughout the country to generate a leadership from within labouring communities themselves. The movement drew upon an experienced and articulate core of plebeian activists and a long-standing political culture. Many Chartists could have echoed the words of the weaver poet Samuel Bamford when he wrote 'I was born a radical'. For it was in the weaving communities and burgeoning factory towns of the North that radicalism and its culture remained most firmly intact, stretching back to at least the 1790s and the period of the French Revolution. If Chartism took its name from a document produced by London artisans, it took its early tone from the smaller, more closely-knit communities of the industrial North and Midlands.

That said, we are left with a problem: most of Chartism's major national leaders were drawn from outside the ranks of the labouring classes. Above all, the movement's presiding leader, its champion and hero, was an obscure Irish squire. What are we to make of this?

In fact, one of the distinctive features of nineteenth century British popular politics more generally was the central role played by the gentleman leader, particularly by the gentleman of the platform, the great public orator. In an era that witnessed the emergence, establishment and eventually the limited acceptance of the working class political presence, the importance of gentleman leaders may seem at odds with notions of working class independence and collective self action. Radicalism's reliance on gentlemen leaders such as Sir Francis Burdett, Lord Cochrane, Henry Hunt and Feargus O'Connor would appear to compromise independent working class politics. While such leaders 'knew the forms and language of high politics' and could 'belabour the Ministers in their own tongue', their appearance before 'Huzzaing crowds' seems to undercut the reform movement's rhetoric of equality, stirring older responses of deference rather than democracy.

46

What sort of impression did O'Connor make? Looking back almost half a century, the radical John Vallance recalled O'Connor's first visit to Barnsley, Vallance's home town, in the winter of 1835:

'His figure was tall and well proportioned, and his bearing decidedly aristocratic. He wore a blue frock coat and buff waistcoat, and had rings on the fingers of each hand. In a graceful manner, and in emphatic language, he told the Radicals of Barnsley that he had sold off his horse and dogs, greatly reduced his establishment and come weal come woe, he would henceforth devote his whole life to promote the well-being of the working classes. ... The language of O'Connor, to ears accustomed to little else than the Barnsley dialect, as spoken by pale faced weavers and swart cobblers, sounded like rich music.'

Georg Weerth, a young German revolutionary, also remembered his first sight of O'Connor a decade later in Manchester.

'I shall never forget the moment when I first set eyes on him at a meeting. The audience had been waiting for a long time and the hall was full to overflowing. ... There was an uncanny silence. O'Connor's appearance was awaited with the solemnity and anxiety which is felt at the approach of a thunderstorm. Suddenly a wild uproar arose outside the door; a wave of intense excitement passed through those in the front; they stretched their necks to right and to left; elbows dug into other people's ribs; all were drawn by a magnet in the direction whence the hubbub came.

O'Connor had crossed the threshold into the hall. Flanked by a group of his friends, he made his way through the crowd, shaking hands with many, calling some by name, greeting everyone heartily like a father greeting his children on his return home.'

Together Vallance and Weerth capture much of the style, excitement and recurrent images surrounding the gentleman leader. The exotic distance that seemed to separate aristocratic speaker and working class audience was mediated by declarations of personal sacrifice, singular devotion to working people, familiarity as well as unmistakable touches of deference: a father returning home to his children. O'Connor was simultaneously of the people and not one of them. He was a gentleman set off from his own social background, a liminal figure: at home on the platform but otherwise moving outside and beyond any given local community.

The gentleman leader's lack of attachments was one source of grave suspicion. Contemporary novelists, for example, summoned the danger posed by such leaders. The figures of Slackbridge, the trade union leader and mob orator in Dickens' 'Hard Times' (1854) and O'Flynn - modelled on O'Connor - in Charles Kingsley's 'Alton Locke' (1850) warn readers of the people's vulnerability to the designs of self-appointed leaders, unknown men operating outside their communities. Novels such as 'Hard Times', Disraeli's 'Sybil' or 'The Two Nations' (1846), Mary Gaskell's 'Mary Barton' (1848) and 'North and South' (1855) reframe contemporary anxiety about where and how legitimate social and political leadership and authority were to be found and exercised. Nor were such anxiety and suspicion restricted to the propertied classes. Plenty of working class radicals harboured doubts about such leaders' motives and their independence.

In extending politics beyond community and other boundaries, O'Connor, like Henry Hunt before him, drew upon ambivalent traditions. He drew, firstly, on the gentlemanly tradition of high-class rabble rousing. Throughout the eighteenth century, flamboyant figures, such as the rakish John Wilkes or Charles James Fox, had exploited the space made available to the fickle crowd to wreak havoc. No less theatrical than these earlier leaders, O'Connor also sought to attract people to the spectacle and fun of radical politics. His commitment and purpose were, however, altogether different, seeking as he did, to establish a permanent movement and challenge to elite rule. While offering play and amusement, a chance to ridicule and reject authority, his very character as a gentlemanly leader underwrote the independence, virtue and integrity of the radical mass platform.

As the personification of the radical cause, the gentleman leader's independence cut two ways. On the one hand, freedom from financial dependence meant that he was less prone quite literally to sell out the movement, accepting paid employment from rival movements or organizations or making a career of politics (trading in politics); on the other hand, it was difficult for the radical movement to hold a leader like O'Connor accountable, particularly with regard to specific policies. The highly ritualized declarations of allegiance to the radical democratic movement and recitations of personal suffering in the people's cause recognized O'Connor's need to establish an exclusive and reciprocal sense of personal attachment. The mutual flattery of the platform was a stylized form of bonding. Thus by appearing, as promised, in a fully tailored fustian suit, O'Connor reaffirmed his exclusive attachment to working class democracy.

Such gestures had more than a touch of the romantic and charismatic about them. Men like O'Connor were larger than life figures; men who lived on the edge, beyond ordinary constraints. This was true of their personal and sexual as well as their public lives. O'Connor who never married toured the country for a while with the renowned actress Louisa Nisbet, notorious for appearing in breeches, a role that connected her with the erotica of the 1840s. The political platform and the stage complemented one another: radical orator and actress were both something less than socially respectable. O'Connor's reckless personal life was in marked contrast to the bourgeois probities that characterised the public images of Liberal leaders such as John Bright's and Gladstone's personal lives. O'Connor conveyed a very different image of manliness, more closely aligned with the eighteenth century gentlemanly libertine.

With their intriguing blend of legitimacy and licence, radicalism's gentlemanly leaders proved great crowd-pullers. O'Connor deployed his star status to considerable effect: his itinerant performances encouraged local democratic endeavour while coordinating local and regional activity into a national movement. Gentlemanly patriot and showman, it was O'Connor who mobilized the people. Radicals needed both to ridicule establishment pageantry and to outmatch it, offering not just misrule but more attractive forms of public ceremonial. O'Connor and the Chartists recharged the mass platform with its own ritual and tradition, enabling the radicals to challenge the establishment for control of public space. Assembling in carnival atmosphere behind banners and bands in trade, local, family, ethnic and other groups, the crowd joined together in proud display as the excluded but sovereign people, demanding their constitutional rights 'Peaceably if we may, forcibly if we must'. A blend of disciplined display, conviviality and menace, this popular format owed much to the character of its gentlemanly leaders.

48

Spokespersons who were drawn to popular radicalism from outside the boundaries of the working poor tended to be mavericks, men who became more or less detached from associations and identities beyond the movement itself: disgruntled gentlemen like Major John Cartwright, Hunt, O'Connor and Feargus' successor, Ernest Jones. The fact that they were displaced gentlemen, that they were not middle class employers or men of business may have been part of their attraction to working men and women. The gentleman's heroic stature stood against the middle; it was organized around a mythic unity of sentiment between high and low: gentleman and people. In contrast, middle class politicians who attempted to win some measure of working class support during the Chartist period – men like the banker Thomas Attwood of the revived Birmingham Political Union – failed precisely to the extent that they refused to accept popular radicalism's cultural style, its modes of mobilization, organization, and leaders.

Popular radicalism remained stubbornly independent of compromising extra parliamentary alliances, as well as from party and parliament: indeed, this was the oft-repeated advice of O'Connor. The independence of the gentleman leader, committed only to the programme and forces of radicalism, mirrored radicalism's own independence and reliance on the support of an oppressed and excluded 'people'. During the 1840s, O'Connor laboured to translate the independence and energy of the mass platform to the National Charter Association, often regarded as Europe's first independent working class party.

Recruiting members on his tours, defending the need for a paid executive if Chartism was to have independent working class, national leaders, and seeking to give the movement organizational permanence, O'Connor campaigned to make the association the party of all true Chartists.

It is also important to understand the class nature of the demand for what was termed 'universal suffrage'. From as early as 1817 and Hunt's commitment of the radical platform to universal suffrage until the Chartist years, democratic citizenship acquired an increasingly distinct class meaning. Those attracted to Chartism came overwhelmingly from the ranks of men and women who either worked for wages in some form, or provided labour necessary for the reproduction and maintenance of those working for wages. Moreover, the programmatic demand for full manhood suffrage was increasingly associated with the contested right of working people to move within and to lay claim to public space. O'Connor attended the great outdoor meetings out of which Chartism was born; he also attended the torchlight meetings initially convened because certain factory masters would not allow their workers to attend the 'monster' demonstration at Kersal Moor which was held on a Monday. Space and time are inseparable from relations of power and authority. The refusal of factory owners to give their workers the day off to attend the Kersal Moor demonstration re-emphasized the factory's disciplinary regime, particularly as it was now set off against the licence of the moor. The decision to take by night what had been denied by day, to move from the town's edge into its centre, after parading the town's periphery with thousands of torches, was a gesture of class defiance: a challenge to the authority of factory, town and national government.

O'Connor's attendance at these meetings beside the Revered J.R. Stephens and his defence of Stephens' language of 'War to the knife' against moderate and predominantly middle class critics is crucial to understanding the widespread support that O'Connor forged among working people.

Thus Feargus associated himself with popular radicalism's threatening edge, and risked putting himself on the wrong side of the law. The public meeting was in itself a challenge to authority: the massive occupation of public space transgressed elite views of order and legitimate participation. It was uncertain if such assemblies were legal; whether the authorities would allow them to meet; or whether meetings would be banned (as they were during the French wars, 1817 or the 1820s by Seditious Meetings Acts) or would perhaps be attacked. As late as summer 1848 Chartists arrived at meeting places to find them occupied by troops; on the famous tenth of April 1848 they faced not only thousands of middle class men enrolled as special constables but troops and cannon under the command of the Duke of Wellington. Above all, the gentleman leader was an orator. To speak within such contested social and legal space, demanding justice in the language of the popular constitution or primitive Christianity, was to confront authority and power as they were constituted and to suggest a reordering of political authority.

Where then, finally, does the land plan and O'Connorville fit into this account and the cult of the gentleman leader? After Chartism's tempestuous early years, O'Connor increasingly stressed the importance of working people's alienation from the land. As early as 1841, he declared: 'Lock up the land tomorrow, and I would not give you two pence for the Charter the next day.' In 1843 a National Charter Association conference at Birmingham approved his proposal for establishing Chartist land communities, although it was not until April 1845 that the Chartist Co-operative Land Society was established. O'Connor's scheme was to buy agricultural estates, divide them into smallholdings and let the holdings by ballot. O'Connor elaborated his agrarian vision in his book 'A Practical Work on the Management of Small Farms' published in 1843. After 1845 much of O'Connor's energy was absorbed by the land plan, raising money, trying to register the company as a friendly society, buying land and supervising the building of cottages. On May Day 1847 settlers moved into O'Connorville, the first of five Chartist settlements.

The land plan is best understood in terms of longstanding, popular, radical interest in, and ideas on, the land and notions of collective self-reliance. The vision was one based on the independence of the self-employed worker – the weaver, farmer, or craftsman. As the independence of the skilled, male artisan came under increasing pressure, the populist image of the yeoman farmer, the small settlement on the land, became increasingly attractive to urban workers and their families. The importance of the land in exorcising the monster of urban civilization was not just an escapist fantasy, but offered a counter ideal: a normative vision opposed to modern industrial civilization.

O'Connor, himself an independent gentleman raised on the land, captured this desire for manly independence: 'I am a beef and mutton, a pork and butter and bread and milk and honey Radical. I am an open-air, a work-when-I'm-able and work-for-myself-and-my-family Radical.' I want to conclude with a short quotation from the speech that Feargus made on the opening day of the O'Connorville Estate: 'What I now witness is but a feeble outline – a meagre unfinished sketch of that full length portrait of freedom, happiness, and contentment which will eventually result from the novelty I have ventured to propound. While joy fills your hearts here, the song of gladness resounds throughout the land.'

Of course, the sketch remains unfinished or at least the modern world painted a very different portrait of the future; that said, the utopian energy expressed here, the commitment to imagine the world ordered differently, still offers perhaps a powerful counterpoint to urban civilization and its modern discontents.

1. This section draws on my entry for the 'New Dictionary of National Biography', forthcoming (Oxford University Press).
2. This section draws on John Belchem and James Epstein 'The nineteenth century gentleman revisited', Social History, 22 (May 1997) pp. 174-93.

James Epstein

Another assessment of O'Connor is to be found in a book entitled 'Chartism' written by Eva H. Haraszti who was the wife of A.J.P. Taylor. The following quote from 'The New York Daily Tribune' of May the 3rd, 1853, page five, appeared in her book.

'Marx quoted at the same time from "The People's Paper" Jones' appreciation of O'Connor, "Here was a man who broke away from rank, wealth and station; who threw up a large fortune, not in private self-denial, but in political self-sacrifice; who made himself an eternal exile from his own country, where he owned broad acres and represented one of its largest counties; who was hated by his family because he loved the human race; whose every act was devotion to the people and who ends almost destitute after a career of unexampled labour .... utter prostration, of disunion, doubt and misery, he gathered the millions of his country together, as men had never yet been gathered. O'Connell rallied the Irish, but it was with the help of the priests; Mazzini roused the Italians, but nobles and traders were on his side; Kossuth gathered the Hungarians, but Senates and armies were at his back; and both the Hungarians and the Italians were burning against a foreign conqueror. But O'Connor, without noble, priest or trader, rallied and upheld one downtrodden class against them all! Without even the leverage of national feeling to unite them! La Fayette had the merchants, Lamartine had the shopkeepers, O'Connor had the people! But the people in the nineteenth century, in Constitutional England, are the weakest of all. He taught them how to become the strongest"'.

The reader should make their own judgement of Feargus O"Connor.

CHAPTER FIVE

The End of the Dream 1847-1860

THE SPRING AND SUMMER of 1847 passed. Interest in the O'Connorville experiment was kept alive through articles in the press expressing anxiety about the fate of the agriculturally unskilled city settlers. They were expected to live throughout the winter without money and there were concerns the produce of the summer would soon run out. In November 1847 O'Connor visited the Estate and spoke to most of the inhabitants. There were already seven newcomers. O'Connor said he would pay the rent for O'Connorville out of his own pocket from next May, when it became due, until November. The rent could be paid back by degrees.

The spring of 1848 was a bad one for farming and the allottees lost some of their stock by sickness, and their crops suffered. Mrs Entwistle, who lives in Chorleywood, had a great-grandfather, Mr Turney, who was a farmer and he tried to advise and help the settlers with their land and livestock. The Turney family are, of course, well known in Chorleywood today.

By March 1848 most of the allottees had now been resident on the Estate long enough for them to qualify for relief under the new Poor Law and this, coupled with the serious doubts as to the legality of the Land Company fuelled by those in authority (Parliament), caused the Poor Law commissioners in London to send an inspector, John Bevans, to judge whether the settlers were likely to become a burden on the local parish rates. This could be an expensive possibility for the local population if the settlers needed support or relief.

Mr Bevans' report was pretty damning. He ignored the fact that the settlers had been in residence only a short while. He described the allotments as being unable to sustain those who worked on them. He said the crops were inferior, there was little livestock – only four cows and a few pigs and, with the exception of a few vetches (peas), there was no food for the animals, no hay, no straw and consequently no means of making manure. Likewise there were no farm implements – even the ploughs belonged to neighbouring farms. And some of the farmwork was done by the employment of local farm labour. This was not surprising, Bevans said, as the settlers were unaccustomed to the management of farmland. Furthermore, the wives were unused to dairy work and could not make bread.

A more favourable account appeared in the London Journal of the 3rd of June 1848:

'Mr Williams, the occupant of a four-acre allotment received the author with every attention; after a while we entered into conversation with him on topics connected with O'Connorville and with agriculture. By his fine, healthy countenance and familiarity with agricultural subjects, he led us to suppose that he had obtained a practical knowledge of what he spoke upon … He told us that as yet he had not derived much profits from his farming … He did not gain sufficient earnings to provide against an evil day … He had already purchased off a previous occupant his allotment for the sum of £80 and had bought a cow, a couple of pigs, and had made some alteration to his dwelling since his residence at O'Connorville. As his farming was not of such a flourishing nature as one would have been led to anticipate … we begged him to refer us to some of his companions, who were practically acquainted with the culture of the ground. He told us that the majority had come from the manufacturing districts, and knew more about the loom and the spinning jenny than the spade and the plough. But he directed our attention to a man busily occupied harrowing at about a hundred yards distance from us. "There's a man," said he, "who has been a field labourer a-farming all his life". We went to the person pointed out to us, and questioned him as to his idea of the efficiency of the system at O'Connorville. He said that he had an allotment only of two acres, but that he found it answered his purpose. Whilst he had saved nothing from the new system of life that he had adopted, he seemed satisfied with his lot; and what was more, determined to be so. From other enquiries that we made, we found that nobody at O'Connorville had as yet saved money, but nearly all had got through the year comfortably enough and without incurring expenses. We therefore came to the conclusion that Mr O'Connor in his description of what a man can do with a small allotment of two, three or four acres of land, had considerably coloured the picture of a brighter hue than a sober and dispassionate judgement might approve of.'

It is important to note that Mr Williams could not have stayed at O'Connorville long for there is no mention of him among the original allottees in 1846 and no mention of a Mr Williams in the 1851 census. It is difficult to ascertain how much say and cooperation the O'Connorville settlers had in the management of the Estate, but it does not seem that it was run as a cooperative since each allottee owned and worked his or her smallholding individually. And, despite the fears of the local poor law authorities, a check through the minute books of the Watford Board of Guardians for 1847-8 does not show any allottees applying for relief.

However, the end of the Estate as O'Connor had envisaged it was near. In May 1847 only three plots out of the original 35 allottees had changed hands. But the census of 1851 shows that six plots were unoccupied and 22 had changed hands. The average age of the head of the family was 46.7 years and it seemed that women headed two allotments: plot 15 found Elizabeth Newsome as head of the family. Aged 45, she was described as a gunmaker's wife born in Middlesex with two daughters; Elizabeth aged 12 and Emma aged ten and a son John aged six. However, the sale particulars of 1857 show the plot holder is Charles Newsome. And at plot 21 (now Little Aymers) Elizabeth Blakeborough, aged 19, is described as the head of the house. She was a farmer's daughter with a baby girl aged ten months; but in the 1857 sale details the holder is Stephen Blakeborough. No doubt the men were away when the census officer came in 1851. The allottees were starting to find different ways of supporting themselves other than just depending on the land. According to the 1851 census, James Purvil aged 36 and his wife Harrieta were silk painters; James Burnett aged 53 is described as a hand loom weaver. Edward Bukhock aged 60 was both grocer and farmer.

Within five years of the census of 1851 there were only seven of the 35 allottees left and it can be concluded that the allottees now regarded their plots as a prize won in a raffle, which enabled them to move in and change their way of life and after a time to sell up and move on, using the money to improve their situation. I have tried to find out where the original allottees went to. In consultation with Dorothy Thompson and from other records, I have concluded that most of the allottees returned to their former home towns, but it is possible some moved to nearby villages and towns and there is scope for further investigations into this topic.

In June 1848, Parliament set up a select committee to investigate the Land Company and in July their findings were announced. They were that the National Land Company was an illegal scheme and should be closed down in its existing form and a better designed company started if the directors so wished. The Estate of 103 acres and 35 homes was valued at £8,700.

Between 1848 and 1851 the national interest in Chartism started to fade, and the allottees of O'Connorville and the other Chartist estates – Lowbands (Gloucestershire and Worcestershire borders): bought in October 1846 and opened in August 1847; Mathon (Herefordshire): bought in February 1847 but project abandoned in February 1849; Snigs End (Gloucestershire): bought in June 1847 and opened in June 1848; Minster Lovell - Charterville (Oxfordshire): bought in June 1847 and opened in May 1848; Great Dodford (Worcestershire): bought in January 1848 and opened in July 1849 – argued with O'Connor over what rent they should pay. From this period on, it is sad to say, the behaviour of Feargus O'Connor became more and more irrational and in the summer of 1852 he was sent to a clinic for the insane at Chiswick. He stayed there until August 1855 when his sister removed him to take care of him at her house, where he died on 30th August 1855 and he was buried at Kensal Green.

In August 1851 the Winding-Up Act was passed by Parliament and the Chartist estates were then administered by Chancery. A Mr William Goodchap was to be in charge. These were anxious days for the allottees. They had come from the industrial towns of the North of England and the Midlands and from other parts of the British Isles with high hopes and great expectations of a better life free from the mill and factory to start a new life. Now reality faced them. Their smallholdings were difficult to farm, the soil was not always very fertile and many of them knew little about farming. They could just about feed themselves, but there was not enough left over to sell to pay for the pleasures of life, and in any case the surrounding farms supplied the bulk of the food requirements of the locals. Some of the original allottees had already left O'Connorville, but many wanted to stay on.

But what did the future offer? Employment in the neighbouring villages and towns was not easy to find. Would the Winding-Up Act mean the allottees' leases were invalid and they would lose their properties? They already knew they were not freehold owners. What would the government do, concerned as it was about a sizeable settlement in a rural area? And who was Mister Goodchap? Would he act like their former hated factory and mill owners? O'Connor was sick, but still they looked to him for help and guidance. In fact, whilst Parliament was preparing for the Winding-Up Act (1851) the allottees had held a demonstration in O'Connor's favour and had sent him an address of sympathy and gratitude. There is no evidence of any leadership qualities emerging from any of the allottees themselves, nor was there any sign of cooperation amongst the allottees to deal with their problems as a unit. They were not rebels; they were quiet, decent people. Was this indeed the end of their dream?

In August 1851 after three years' deliberation the National Land Company was ordered to be wound up. In October of that year Joseph Humphries, Master in Chancery, gave powers to William Goodchap under Court of Chancery to be the accountant and official manager and to sell allotments and houses to people who could prove title to them by virtue of residence or of previous purchase. Mr Goodchap held his enquiry into the O'Connorville Estate at the Swan Inn in Rickmansworth in August 1852. Goodchap then went round the Estate to settle rents and convey the longed-for leases. Goodchap was keen to display a charitable attitude to the population of O'Connorville, now numbering 170. He found that most allottees could prove their title. He also found that the cottages were mostly in reasonable repair, but the produce of the land was poor. The allottees said that they were unable to live off the allotments because of the poor soil and the isolated position of the Estate, three or four miles from any town or transport. Some also said it was impossible to live on three or four acres, but they all wished to stay on the Estate if they could have leases and be let off back rents. Mr Goodchap found that the amount of rent already paid and the money allowed for improvements more than covered liabilities of past unpaid rent, and the leases could be sold either to existing tenants or new tenants. Fee farm rents were planned to be sold by auction later.

Mr Goodchap's tour of inspection of the Estate in 1852 revealed that there were 20 semidetached cottages of two storeys: 12 of these cottages were on four-acre sites (nos 23 and 24, 25 and 26, 27 and 28, 29 and 30, 31 and 32, 33 and 34) two of three acres (nos 18 and 19) on the western side of Nottingham Road and the remaining six cottages (nos 2 and 3, 4 and 5, 6 and 7) were on two-acre sites on the eastern side of Nottingham Road. Fifteen cottages were single storey; Bradford Road had three single-storey cottages with plot 35 being four acres, plot 20 was three acres and plot 12 was two acres and the schoolhouse (plot 36) was two acres and 31 perches. On the eastern side of Nottingham Road were five single-storey cottages on two-acre sites (nos 1, 8, 9, 10 and 11, although plot 11 was three acres and 11 perches). Halifax Road had seven single-storey cottages of which five (nos 13, 14, 15, 16 and 17) were on two-acre sites. Plots nos 21 and 22 were three acres. This added up to 35 cottages and a schoolhouse.

Mr Goodchap found that the school had closed by 1851 and was occupied by a James Lindon; Goodchap, himself, was to purchase it in 1858 before selling it on to William Prowting Roberts. In 1848, M.D. Graves MCP was appointed to be the schoolmaster from the many applicants who applied for the post. He called the school O'Connorville College. It was his intention to run an agricultural, horticultural and model farm school, and also to provide a good education. Children of grocers and cheesemongers would be boarded and educated. The fees would be 16 guineas per year, but this sum did not include the cost of stationery. Mr Graves placed an advertisement in The Northern Star of the 1st July 1848 for pupils, and the school was to open on 10th July 1848. It is not clear how many pupils actually attended the school nor whether many from O'Connorville itself attended the school. No fees were mentioned for day pupils. However, a sampler beautifully drawn and written by Ann Dawson has survived to this day (see colour plate). Ann Dawson was not a Heronsgate resident and the date 1847 was before the school had opened, but the school had been built by 1847. The other estates all had schools with the exception of Dodford where there was not enough money for the schoolhouse.

'MrsWoodwards', an original O'Connorville single-storey cottage (probably plot 15)

The O'Connorville schoolhouse had a two storey centre with a gabled sloping roof. Downstairs there were three rooms: the back two both had fireplaces – one was the kitchen and the other the sitting room. In the large front room was a staircase that led to a landing, off which there were two bedrooms with fireplaces. Built on to the sides were the classrooms – to the right the boys' classroom, where O'Connor and the allottees and the guests had first met, and to the left was the girls' classroom. The McMurtries who until recently lived at The Grange, believe that the boys and girls were segregated, but Hugh Norwood who has been studying the Chartist architecture suggests that this was not the case. There was no need for the pupils to enter the centre part of the building by the front door, for each classroom had its own door. The overall design was thus similar to the rest of the cottages on the Estate, with the master's house in the centre being not too different from two semidetached cottages; and the classrooms, at least on the outside, bearing architectural comparison with the single-storey cottages. On the roof of the school there was a bell, which was used to summon the pupils to class and assembly; it was later transferred to Sherwood (plot 14) by Mrs Felkin. In the grounds were outbuildings for the school animals and the land was used for agricultural and horticultural purposes.

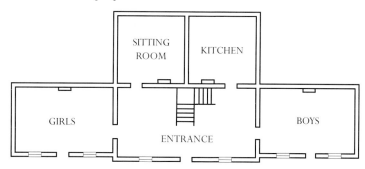

The School – Ground Floor

A closer inspection of the cottages would have shown that all of them had been expertly constructed. The cottages were of a common design with the exception of the semidetached houses on plots 4 and 5 (Crowthorne and Laurel Cottage). All houses were built with brick and covered with stucco. Each had a kitchen with a tiled floor, an iron grate with an oven and a boiler for hot water and a built-in dresser. In the two storey semidetached cottages the kitchen was built at the side; entry was through the kitchen into the two living rooms. Stairs led up to the two bedrooms on the first floor, with the exception of Laurel Cottage and Crowthorne which had only one bedroom (see colour plate). Rooms were 12 feet square, boarded and papered, with oak floor boards and built-in cupboards, but the bedrooms were smaller because space was taken up by the stairway. The single-storey cottages had three rooms: a central kitchen, a living room on one side and a bedroom on the other. All the cottages had narrow, six, eight or nine-paned opening windows, and chimneys which marked each end of the roof. Alice Hadfield says the roofs sloped down at the back to a lower level and here were to be found the outbuildings: a dairy, wash house, cart shed, cow and pony shed. Joining the house on one side were a privy and pig sties, each pig sty had a small yard, and on the other side of the yard was a wood shed and fowl shed. These outbuildings were constructed with brick and roofed with slate. A low wall joined the two sets of small buildings at the end with a gate into each allottee's land. Between the outbuildings was a good-sized yard for the house and here the well was often located (see diagram).

A look at the 1854 survey map of the O'Connorville Estate by Edward H. Burnell of 32 Bedford Row, London, who was acting for the government when the settlement was being wound up (see colour plate), does not entirely support the theory that all cottages had a regular pattern of outbuildings as outlined in the previous paragraph. Some did and into this category can be put plots

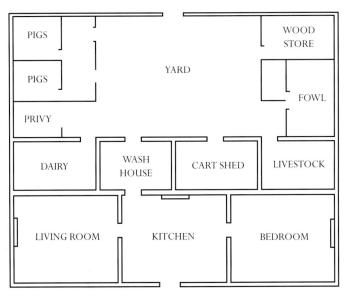

A single-storey cottage with outbuildings

4, 5, 18, 19, 31, 32, 33 and 34; others had a more informal pattern of outbuildings built later by the allottees themselves. In the case of the other estates of Lowbands, Snigs End, Minster Lovell and Dodford, O'Connor offered the allottees the opportunity of having three-roomed single-storey cottages with outbuildings or four rooms with no outbuildings. The allottees chose to have three-roomed single-storey cottages with outbuildings.

It can be concluded from this that it had proved both expensive and time-consuming to build his first Estate at Heronsgate and on no other estate did O'Connor construct two-storey cottages. He, in fact, kept to a pattern of three-roomed single-storey cottages with outbuildings. Laurel Cottage and Crowthorne are interesting in that they were the only two-storey cottages with one bedroom upstairs and the shape of their lower sloping roof bears similar characteristics to those on other estates such as Minster Lovell and Dodford.

In 1853 after his enquiry into the O'Connorville Estate and his tour of inspection in 1852, William Goodchap started to sell the land and plots. Some plots were sold to existing tenants and some to new buyers and by 1858 all plots had been sold. The schoolhouse had been bought by Goodchap who was to sell it on a short time later. When Heronsgate plots were sold between 1853 and 1858, fee farm rents were a separate issue and were payable to his Chancery office. The question of rents has caused considerable concern throughout the history of Heronsgate, but more particularly in the early years of the Estate.

When the winners of the 'lottery' in April 1846 learned that they had won a plot in O'Connorville, they were also informed by O'Connor that there would be a rent. It would be about five per cent of the cost of building a cottage and preparing the allotment, and, as previously stated, O'Connor said that this would be about £6 a year for the two-acre man and £11 10s for the four-acre man. O'Connor had plenty of outgoings: each man would be given a cash loan to begin with – £15 for two acres, £22 10s for three acres and £30 for four acres. Also in the sales notice of Herringsgate Farm of 1846 it was stated that, 'tithes have been commuted, and the rent charges apportioned on this lot in lieu thereof as £17 3s and £5 8s 6d per annum'. And the lot was to be sold 'subject to three annuities of £20 each, payable to the Putnam family and the exclusive right of sporting over this Lot is reserved during the life of a gentleman, named Thomas Ayres, aged 58 years'. A land tax of £2 16s 2d per annum and a quit rent of £1 16s 10d per annum to the Lord of the Manor of Rickmansworth was also to be paid.

O'Connor paid the rent charges, the annuities, the land tax and the quit rent as mentioned in the sales notice, but he had great difficulty in getting any rent himself out of the allottees and many of them were uneasy about the tenure of their holdings. When O'Connor first envisaged the Land Company it was his intention that the allottees should hold the freehold rights to their properties and thus be entitled to a county vote; but the difficulties involved in establishing the legality of the Land Company meant that the estates were acquired in his name and the directors of the Land Company acted as trustees and the allottees were not in law recognised as freehold owners. Thus no allottee in the period 1847 to 1853 had been eligible for a county vote. Members of Parliament at this time were elected by their boroughs, towns or counties. Changes of ownership were effected through the Land Company which kept a record of plot owners.

View of O'Connerville, early 1880s, looking north from Nelson House (plot 2)

The winding-up was to be completed by disposing of fee farm rent incomes at auctions at The Swan Inn, Rickmansworth on Wednesday the 27th of May 1857 and Monday the 31st of May 1858 by Abraham Booth, auctioneer of 1, Carlton Hill Villas, Camden Road, London. The annual income from the fee farm rents was valued at £280 for 35 allotments and a brick built schoolhouse of two acres 0 rods and 31 perches was described as freehold land. In fact the capital needed to buy out a rent was equivalent to what the house was worth at the time – about £114 – and the existing tenants were unable to buy out their rents at these auctions. Thus the auctions of 1857 and 1858 were unsuccessful. The fee farm rent sale was finally achieved on the 30th of May 1860 when William Prowting Roberts, the Chartist solicitor from Manchester and original signatory of Herringsgate Farm, acquired all the rent rights. This is confirmed in the deeds of Heronsgate houses that I have seen. Also the Stevenage Land Registry of the 30th of May 1860 records conveyance between William Goodchap, Francis Edward Williams and William Prowting Roberts for all the fee farm rent charges of the O'Connorville Estate for the sum of £18,020.

The sum of £18,020 seemed excessive and the name of Francis Edward Williams was a new and unknown name. Eventually this mystery was unravelled. The £18,020 W.P. Roberts paid was not just for the fee farm rents of O'Connorville but also for fee farm rents of some of the other Land Company estates. The Masters of the Court in Chancery in 1854 had authorised William Goodchap to raise £6,000 on any of the Land Company estates either by sale or mortgage to cover costs of the winding-up of the estates. Goodchap borrowed £6,000 at five percent from F.E. Williams of Warwickshire offering the O'Connorville fee farm rents incomes, the schoolhouse and unconveyed land as security. These were conveyed to F.E. Williams on 27th January 1855. In March 1859 Master Richard Richards of the High Court in Chancery ordered that the remaining freehold land and rent charges of the estates of the Land Company should be sold in four lots. It has already been pointed out that the auctions at The Swan Inn, Rickmansworth in 1857 and 1858 had failed to produce buyers and so had auctions at the other estates.

O'Connorville was to be sold as Lot 3 and Snigs End and Lowbands were two of the other lots, but it is uncertain which was the fourth lot. Was Snigs End sold in two halves or was Lot 4 Minster Lovell (Charterville) or Great Dodford? Charles Fitzgerald, historian and great-great grandson of W.P. Roberts believes that in fact Charterville was the fourth lot.

On 18th May 1859 the four lots were duly put up for auction at the London Auction Mart but none reached their reserve price. The income generated would have been: £617 for Snigs End from 76 rent charges plus meadow, four messuages, 11 acres of land and the schoolhouse; £280 for O'Connorville, from 35 rent charges plus the schoolhouse and its land; and £300 for Lowbands from 43 rent charges plus the schoolhouse, two messuages and four acres of land. If Charterville was the fourth lot, the income from its rent charges would have been £256.

Finally, on the 30th May 1860 William Prowting Roberts' offer of £18,020 was accepted by the Court of Chancery and a document issued by the Lytham District Land Registry confirms this. When W.P. Roberts came to pay his £18,020 the money was distributed as follows: £5,861 16s 8d to F.E. Williams to buy out the mortgage on O'Connorville, £10,000 as deposit to the Court of Chancery, £1,500 payment to Goodchap and the Chancery solicitors (Tucker, Greville, Tucker);

£500 payment to Master Richards of the Court of Chancery and to James Tucker and the balance £158 3s 4d, to the Court of Chancery. On the 30th May 1860 William Prowting Roberts became the owner of the fee farm rent charges plus the schoolhouse (then unoccupied) and its two acres of land in O'Connorville plus the rent charges of other estates.

So the Estate finally had a new receiver for fee farm rents and was now in a very good pair of hands. Prowting Roberts was a fine Chartist and was ideally suited to watch over O'Connorville.

 CHAPTER SIX

Dodford

WHAT WAS IT LIKE living in one of these cottages? A visit to a Chartist cottage at Dodford in the late 1990s would be illuminating. It would enable one to envisage what it would be like to live in a Chartist cottage in the 1840s.

If Mr Goodchap were to be reincarnated, no doubt he would want to visit Dodford to see Rosedene, the Chartist cottage purchased by the National Trust in October 1997 (see colour plate). He would be greeted by the many Chartist enthusiasts amongst the current Dodford residents and they would talk enthusiastically about Rosedene, saying it was in almost its original state. Amongst them, Diana Poole a keen historian, would tell Mr Goodchap:

'The three rooms along the front are as they should be. The bedroom fireplaces are believed to be original. The floors of the bedrooms have wide boards and are not in too bad a state considering the general condition. One interesting point is the ceiling on the left bedroom, it has narrow diagonal boards going from corner to corner.

They may be present in the other two rooms and are just covered by plasterboard or paper. In fact paper was peeling off the boards in the left bedroom. We have seen this diagonal boarding in another cottage in the main room, where it has been painted as a feature. The windows to the bedrooms are not original but the front door and side windows are. The range is original, with oven and pothook. The cupboard is thought to be original, and again we have seen it elsewhere. We believe we can see the shadow outline of a dresser on the wall, but that could be the eye of faith! The floor is made of large red quarries thought to be original.

The living room is a mystery. A brother and sister who lived here in the 1920s say it was once the dairy with solid slab work surfaces, earth floor, steps down (as it should be), and no windows. We are not sure about the cupboard. It seems "original" and we wonder if it was moved from somewhere else. The kitchen behind it was where their mother did the washing. They called it the brewhouse, a term used in the Black Country for a wash house. There was the one cold tap, put in in the 1950s, and no drainage except to a field drain.

The wall between the hall and pantry was probably put in by their father, but there is some argument about that. It could have been the wall between the pantry and the back bedroom. They insist that they used to sit in the hall area which they called the kitchen and which had what seems to have been a portable iron stove. The pump is still there above the well, which has been cemented over. In wet weather you can hear water running in. Alfred Crisp, the father was a builder as well as a market gardener. He worked for the firm which built the church in 1907/8. The back bedroom was a store with an earth floor and was used for storing chicken food etc. When the third child was born their father put in a wooden floor and a window and made it into a bedroom. This floor has fallen in, so that says something for more modern timber. The privy is original and was still used up to last November. The barn is thought to be original. There are others like it in Dodford.

The four acres now contain a lot of fruit trees, mostly plum, but in rather poor condition. In fact no maintenance or alteration was done for at least 30 years. The two of them remember it as strawberry fields, and they recall picking the strawberries and sending them to Birimingham very early in the morning by horse and cart. It was the nearness to Birmingham that saved Dodford. Indeed it is that which makes the properties valuable today. I feel certain that all Dodford plots were four acres. By the way I have almost completed my search for all the original plot holders.'

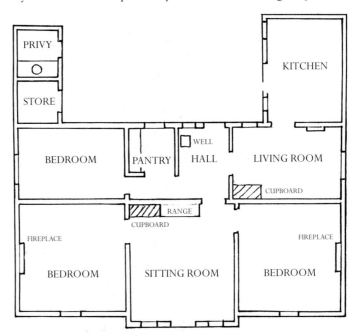

Rosedene: as lived in up to November 1997

The reincarnated Mr Goodchap might reply, saying:

'I am interested in what you say. However, in the late 1840s and early 1850s, the middle of the three front rooms was usually the kitchen, which may also have been used as a sitting room. Generally, the two rooms on either side were bedrooms, but one sometimes was used as a living room. The cupboard next to the range is the original one and the range is a beauty. Each cottage had a dresser and it is very likely that it was where you think. The other cupboard in the living room which you think may have come from elsewhere is something which I cannot comment on. The

64

The original range at Rosedene

rooms at the back and to the sides were outbuildings, one of which as you rightly say was a privy, but the others were used as a dairy, or wash house, or cart shed, or for animals, or to store wood. Some of the earliest settlers both here and in Heronsgate, did indeed build barns. It is nice to see that the first builders did such a good job and that the original lathe and plaster walls and ceilings and some of the windows and the front door still survive in their original state.

Rosedene incorporates many of the features to be found in the single-storey and two-storey cottages of the Heronsgate Estate, but it is more easily recognisable as one of O'Connor's cottages. Its sloping slate roof and chimneys compare with Crowthorne and other Heronsgate cottages, which I remember from my inspection tour of 1852, as does the brickwork. (These features can be seen in the colour plates and other pictures in the book.) Incidentally, as I entered Rosedene, I noticed the Trefoil above the door. Snigs End also had Trefoil vents. The other estates had air vents called Pediment vents; each estate had its own style of vent which became a symbol by which the estate could be recognised. O'Connorville had no such symbolic vents, but had its own symbol, a rolled version of the charter. O'Connorville had these symbols at the front, nearest the road along the divide of the semidetached cottages. Single-storeyed cottages had the symbols both at the front and the sides. Below are some examples of these vents. I can confirm that all Dodford plots were about four acres and it is pleasing to see that the grid pattern of the lanes of the estate remain, although I cannot remember there being a church or a pub. I am delighted that the National Trust under the guidance of Claire Norman plans to restore Rosedene and its approximate four acres to create a feel of what it was like to live on one of O'Connor's plots and I hope they will be more successful than the original settlers.'

Trefoil vent: Dodford and Moat Farm area of Snigs End

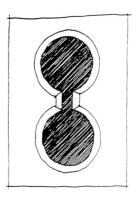

Double circle vent: Lowbands Estate

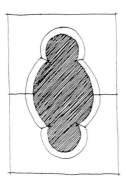

Quatrefoil vent: Snigs End Estate, except Moat Farm area

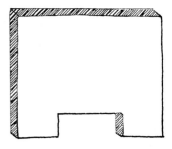

Rolled Charter: O'Connorville Estate

CHAPTER SEVEN

The Years of Uncertainty 1860-1880

WPROWTING ROBERTS was to play an important role in Heronsgate's history. But what was his background? He had been associated with O'Connor from the earliest days and we will look at some of his earlier involvement with the land scheme.

W.P. Roberts was born in 1806 and died in 1871 at Heronsgate House (plot 36). He was a founder and leading member of the Chartist movement. He was the first lawyer to campaign on behalf of labour and to use the judicial system to defend workers' rights. His efforts on behalf of the miners earned him the title of 'the miners' attorney' and, according to Fredrick Engels 'the name of Roberts became a terror to the mine owners'. In the 1840s and 1850s his fame throughout the North of England made him the subject of popular ballads. Though he was never a socialist, he acted as solicitor to Marx and Engels. Roberts throughout his life campaigned for working people to have greater control over their own destiny and thus he was a supporter of cooperatives, the formation of friendly societies and the acquisition of smallholdings where the downtrodden town dweller could start a new life. He became treasurer of the Chartist Land Company.

W.P. Roberts belonged to the professional middle class. His father, Thomas, was vicar of Chelmsford, Essex and subsequently he became Master of the local Chelmsford grammar school. William Prowting Roberts was Thomas's fifth son and he was sent to public school at Charterhouse. He began his working life in insurance in the City of London but soon he decided to train as a solicitor. He undertook in-service training under a qualified solicitor, a Mr Deville, who was after a number of years able to report that W.P. Roberts had reached a satisfactory level of competence; he was placed on the Law Society's register and was able to practise law. Roberts began his legal career in Bath and he married Mary Moody in 1829; she bore him two children (Thomas born 1831 and Mary 1834) but she died in June 1837 and nothing else is known about the marriage.

It is not in this book's remit to trace in detail the working life of W.P. Roberts, but suffice it to say that it is from the late 1830s onwards that Roberts becomes very active in Chartist affairs and the improvement in the situation of the working class. His influence spread from the backwaters of the West Country to the industrial North and, in particular, to the mining districts of Northumberland and Durham and also in 1845 to Manchester where he had an office at 59 Princess Street and where the first concept of the land plan took shape. The land plan led Roberts into close association and friendship with Feargus O'Connor. Soon they were seriously considering the legality of setting up a land company. There were four possibilities within the law: one was to set up a friendly society; another was to use the framework of the Joint Stock Companies Act of 1844 which laid down basic business conduct and account keeping; a third was to acquire a royal charter and the last alternative was to secure a private Act of Parliament.

All these presented problems and extra expense and, even more importantly, the strong possibility that Parliament would reject the immigration of large numbers of Chartist colonists into a small area. So O'Connor decided to set up his own organisation with W.P. Roberts as treasurer and Thomas Wheeler as secretary. The directors were O'Connor, Philip McGrath, Christopher Doyle and Thomas Clark. Two East London tailors, James Knight and William Cuffey, were the auditors. Most of these men were to own properties in Heronsgate at one time or another. It was O'Connor's decision to go it alone – which, strictly speaking, was outside the law – that was to lead to trouble. There is no evidence of financial fraud and it is clear both O'Connor and Roberts spent considerable amounts of their own money to keep the land scheme afloat. However, records were not kept as conscientiously as might have been hoped.

W.P. Roberts' position in the Land Company caused him to visit Heronsgate on many occasions. On the failure of the completion of the winding-up of the Estate in 1857 and 1858, as we have seen, he purchased the fee farm rents. He wanted to retain an interest in the settlement and, if possible, to preserve its Chartist character. Thus in 1860, having purchased Heronsgate House on the site of the old schoolhouse, he moved in with his second wife, Mary Hill Hopkins. She was from a family of considerable financial means and by all accounts the marriage was exceedingly happy – they had two sons and two daughters and descendants speak of their mutual devotion. She refers to him as 'My beloved husband'. She may never have agreed with, or even understood her husband's politics, but she always stood by him throughout his many tribulations, and she played a large part in his life.

As a family the Prowting Roberts played an important role in the continuing development of Heronsgate. They invited Chartists from all parts of Britain and overseas to 'O'Connor's Paradise'. On one occasion, a Polish-Hungarian band played at a special commemorative party for 'the victims of 1848' in front of a large number of people. In Heronsgate itself the family took a keen interest in the church: for instance in 1865, they subscribed £47 to the Chapel fund and in 1886, although the Roberts family by that time no longer lived in Heronsgate, Mrs Roberts donated a lectern and Miss Roberts donated a Glastonbury chair.

The 1871 census, the year of William Prowting Roberts' death, revealed that the many residents of Heronsgate House were: William Prowting Roberts, solicitor, aged 64 from Chelmsford Essex; Mary aged 50 from Bath; Charles aged 20, unmarried undergraduate; William aged six, who was to enter the church and is mentioned later in the book in connection with fee farm rents; and Eliza, an unmarried sister from London. In addition to the family were Constance Finn aged 19, a visitor from Jerusalem; Mariona Stanford aged six, a visitor from the Cape of Good Hope; Elizabeth aged 22, an unmarried housemaid from Amersham; and Ellen Mason aged 20, an unmarried cook. The Roberts family lived in comfortable circumstances but after W.P. Roberts' death, Mary eventually found Heronsgate House too big and too expensive to maintain, although she had also purchased plot 11 in 1876. She moved to 14 Powis Square, Bayswater, London in 1880. Heronsgate House, was leased for a while to Captain MacLean and in 1884 William Marshall Hutchison purchased it for £2,500, a considerable sum for those days. Also in 1884 Mary Roberts sold Holly Lodge (plot 11) to William Robert Petheridge for £150 plus an annual fee farm rent of £10 13s 6d. The Prowting Roberts' residential link with Heronsgate had ended, but not their association and interest in the Estate. Five years later Petheridge was compelled to sell Holly Lodge mainly because he was unable to pay the fee farm rent – this is the only case I have unearthed of this occurrence.

Let us now look in some detail at what happened in the years between the winding-up of the O'Connorville Estate and 1880. It is recorded in 1855 that seven of the original householders dating back to 1847 were still on the Estate. These householders were Thomas and Ann Merrick (Meyrick) from Worcester and their three children – they lived at plot 23 (Bircham Cottage); Martin Griffiths and his son Martin, who also came from Worcester and lived at plot 26 (Wood Weye); John and Hannah Lambourne from Reading lived at plot 2 (Ladywalk Cottage); Michael and Ann Fitzsimmons from Manchester and their three children lived at plot 3 (Whitegates); Philip and Mary Ford from Gloucester with their six children lived at plot 5 (Laurel Cottage); Richard Evison lived on his own at plot 8 (Cherry Tree Corner) and William House and Murin from Worcester lived at plot 12 (The Limes).

The census of 1861 reveals that Philip Ford, Tom Merrick and Martin Griffiths were still in residence while William House had sold plot 12 (The Limes) in 1857 and by 1858 had bought plot 19 (The Hop Garden). It should be pointed out that the census officer spells House 'Howse' and that his wife was called Murin.

In 1851 Edward Whitmore (plot 4), Joseph Burnett (plot 6), Thomas Heaton (plot 9), Aris Hore (plot 11), Elizabeth Blackborough (plot 21), Thomas Meads (plot 22), Thomas Bailey (plot 31) and John Surgeon (plot 34) were in residence and they, or a member of their family, were still in residence in 1861, although Joseph Burnett had moved to plot 33. Thus in 1861 there were 17 new residents and according to the census seven unoccupied cottages - plots 3, 10, 18, 20, 28, 29 and 36. However Prowting Roberts had already bought the schoolhouse (plot 36) in 1858 and Michael Fitzsimmons was definitely in occupancy of plot 3. Thus it is clear the winding-up of the O'Connorville Estate did not mean that the original houses were left empty; many remained in the hands of families who had lived on the Estate since the 1850s or even earlier and some were bought by new residents. By 1861 all the occupants held freehold rights but paid fee farm rents to Prowting Roberts, quit rents to the Lord of the Manor of Rickmansworth and annuities to the Putnam family.

The 1860s were a quiet period in the development of Heronsgate and, with the exception of Prowting Roberts, the residents were largely involved with working their own land and labouring on the nearby farms. The first major change was the building of the Anglican church.

The church, known as St John the Evangelist (George Bastin writing in 1970 says the chapel built in 1865 was dedicated to John the Baptist) was founded by 1865 and a record of subscribers to the Heronsgate School Chapel with the Reverend A. Scrivenor as the incumbent at Christ Church, Chorleywood and the Reverend W.F. Clements as curate of Chorleywood can be seen in the vestry.

One of the principal subscribers to the Heronsgate chapel was J.S. Gilliat, whose great nephew was to become the vicar at Chorleywood in the 1950s. Gilliat had become a Member of Parliament

St John's in 1885 before construction of the Chancel

and was to play an influential role in the area for many years. John Saunders Gilliat came to Chorleywood in 1860, aged 31. He was recently married and purchased The Cedars as his home. He was head of a mercantile house founded by his grandfather. Their trade was tobacco: they not only bought the tobacco, shipped it and sold it, but also financed the planters who grew it. J.S. Gilliat travelled widely through the southern states of the U.S.A. and was well known. He earned the reputation of being rich, religious and respectable. J.S. Gilliat married a Babington, whose family was part of the Clapham Sect. The members of the Clapham Sect were philanthropists. The group which included the Thorntons, the Babingtons, the Stephens and the Willberforces initiated reforms to help the poor and needy, to wipe out slavery and to evangelize the world. Lord Macaulay's mother was a Babington and when Gilliat married into the Babington family he became a member of the social elite of England. After Gilliat had moved to The Cedars in Chorleywood he took the leading position in the parish and was to play an important role in the further development of Heronsgate. R.M.S. Gilliat was another descendant of J.S. Gilliat who gained a cricket blue at Oxford and played for Hampshire after the Second World War.

Other important contributors to the chapel fund were Prowting Roberts (W.P. Roberts) - £47, Mrs Bristow - £50, Lord Ebury - £5, the Bishop of Rochester - £5, Viscount Malden - £2 and Miss Burdett Coutts - £10. Angela Georgina Burdett Coutts is another interesting figure. She was born in 1814 and never married. She was the heiress and granddaughter of Thomas Coutts, the banker and in 1837 inherited two million pounds from his estate. She is remembered as a philanthropist and donator of gifts to Church of England buildings, and it is known that she was friendly with J.S. Gilliat and the Clapham Sect. It should also be noted that Miss Burdett Coutts was a relative of Sir Francis Burdett, the radical MP and friend of Feargus O'Connor's father. She would have been aware of the Chartist settlement in Heronsgate and it can be assumed that J.S. Gilliat easily persuaded her to subscribe to the St John's Church fund. The only Heronsgate residents to make a contribution, apart from W.P. Roberts, were Mrs Heaton, Joseph Barnett and the Abrook family who moved into Heronsgate in the late 1870s.

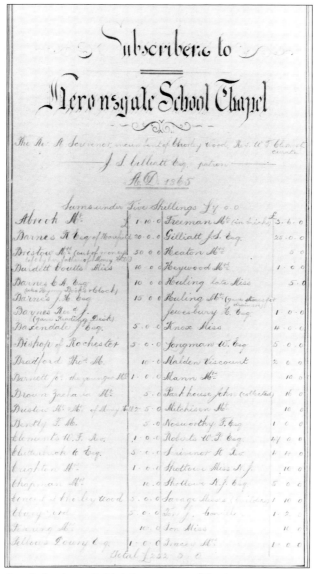

List of subscribers to St John's (a transcription follows)

Subscribers to Heronsgate School Chapel A.D. 1865 Total £252 3.0	
Abrook Mr	Freeman Mr (in bricks)
Barnes R. Esq of Harefield	Gilliatt J.S. Esq
Bristow Mrs (out of monies left by her father of Money Hill)	Heaton Mrs
Burdett Coutts Miss	Heywood Mrs
Barnes C.A. Esq (also Hymn Books & Clock)	Huling late Miss
Barnes J.H. Esq	Huling Mr (gave stones for drains etc)
Baynes Rev'd J. (gave Reading Desk)	Jewesbury H. Esq
Baxendale J. Esq	Knox Miss
Bishop of Rochester	Longman W. Esq
Bradford Thos M	Malden Viscount
Barnett Jos the younger Mr	Mann Mrs
Brown Zacharia Mr	Parkhouse John (collected)
Bristow Mr & Mrs of Money Hill	Mitchison Mr
Bently F.M.	Nosworthy F. Esq
Clements W.F. Rev	Roberts W.P. Esq
Clutterbuck E. Esq	Scrivenor A. Rev
Crighton Mrs	Shottowe Miss N.J.
Chapman Mrs	Shottowe N.J. Esq
Concert at Chorleywood	Savage Messrs (builders)
Ebury Lord	Ton J. Councillor
Fenning Mrs	Ton Miss
Fellows Dowry Esq	Tracey Mrs

A transcription of subscribers from the previous page

Was this money used to build the church in 1865 or was it used to enlarge an existing building? The latter at first seemed very possible as the church bell, a turret bell, was cast in Salford, Manchester by a John Bailey probably between 1857 and 1865 when Bailey worked for himself as a bell caster, having previously worked at the Albion Works, Salford.

Tom Killick, a keen historian and resident of Heronsgate for over 45 years, states that St John's was built as a Chapel at Ease for Christ Church, Chorleywood. The Chorleywood church dates back to 1845 as recorded on one of their bells. According to Geoffrey Dodds in a 'A History of Chorleywood', there was a public subscription for the enlargement of St John's in 1860 by patrons of Christchurch for their daughter church at Heronsgate. J.R. Lewis in his book, 'The Village School', says: 'A new school and chapel were built near the entrance'. These facts suggest St John's may have been built prior to 1865.

It is interesting to note the church was called the school chapel although the school had closed by 1851. To find out if it is possible the church is older than 1865, I wrote to the vicar at Christ Church, Chorleywood and the archivist for the Diocese of Rochester, as Heronsgate was in the Parish of Chorleywood and the Diocese of Rochester until 1875. The administrator at Christ

Church replied that, 'Many of the parish papers were buried when the old vicarage was demolished to make way for the school'; and the archivist for the Rochester Diocese answered my letter by saying, 'No trace has been found of any reference to St John's Church, Heronsgate, Hertfordshire'. However, I followed the matter further. In 1875, Heronsgate with Mill End, was transferred to the Diocese of St Albans and the administrative assistant at the St Albans Diocesan Board of Finance gave me the following answer:

'I am afraid we do not have any record of the founding of St John's Church, Heronsgate. If it was founded in 1865, this would have been before the creation of the Diocese of St Albans and so it is possible the records remain in the Diocese of Rochester .....'

A possible explanation in regard to the naming of the church and its date is that Prowting Roberts, the owner of Heronsgate House, the driving force behind the subscription, planned to re-open Heronsgate House as a school and wanted a chapel both for the residents and his proposed school and hence the name the school chapel. The school never re-opened. The most likely explanation is that the close proximity of the new chapel to the old school caused it at first to be called the school chapel, and it was built in 1865.

To return to the residents of O'Connorville. The 1871 census shows an almost complete change of owners. It shows six houses to be unoccupied, but this figure could be exaggerated as the owners could have been out when the census man visited; almost certainly this was the case with plot 3. Plot 29 (Rosemary Cottage) was supposedly unoccupied in 1851 and 1861, but had found an owner by 1871 in J. Burnett or J. Barnett who also owned plot 33 (Croft House).

Fifteen houses had changed hands in the years from 1861 to 1871, and the 1871 census figures show that there were 117 residents in Heronsgate. Of the original cottages 25 were occupied by married couples; the other nine were variously occupied by single men (Crump - plot 4 and Taylor - plot 32), single men with lodgers (Howard - plot 7 and Buckson - plot 16), a single woman with a young child (Mary Halliday - plot 4), a widow (Murin Howse - plot 19), a single man with a servant (Cartwell - plot 20) or a single man with a married lodger and four children (Woolley - plot 25) and a retired single woman living with her brother and sister (Watson - plot 28). There were two unoccupied cottages (plots 17 and 27) in one of which a tramp was found sleeping.

Mr Peddle, the census officer, found that there were 39 residents aged 50 and over, 40 aged between 21 and 49 and 38 aged 20 and under. Families remaining from the 1851 census were Michael Fitzsimmons and his wife, Martha, Philip Ford and his wife, Mary and their two children (plot 5), J. Burnett who had moved from plot 6 to plot 29, W. Hore (plot 11), Murin Howse who had moved from plot 12 to plot 19, and Thomas Merrick and his wife Ann (plot 23).

It must be pointed out that Mr Peddle, the census officer, had very bad handwriting and there are also inconsistencies in his spelling of names and other details. Later in the century the Peddle family were to establish a funeral service business along with their decorating and general repair business in the High Street, Rickmansworth.

Peddle lists the occupations of the residents as being: fifteen farmers, one retired officer, one solicitor, four carpenters, two market gardeners, one coachman - Reuben Harding from Great Missenden (Little Aymers, plot 21), one cowman, one millwright, one shopkeeper, three agricultural labourers, one butcher, one gardener, one jeweller, one decorator, one railway secretary, one baker and Sarah Armstrong, a schoolmistress, who was the daughter of Frederick Armstrong the millwright at plot 31. Thus the majority's main interests still lay in working the land. The new residents of 1871 were not from the industrial cities of the North; they came from the the country areas of Cambridgeshire, Ireland, Wales, Essex, Kent, Wiltshire, Northamptonshire, Gloucestershire, Worcestershire and the local counties of Hertfordshire, Buckinghamshire and Middlesex.

'The Land of Liberty' public house (a Harman's pub)

74

The census of 1871 shows that the beer shop had now become a licensed premise named The Land of Liberty, Peace and Plenty, so named for the first time because of its proximity to O'Connorville, the Chartist connections with liberty, and the inherent hope of the settlement of land ownership with peace and plenty. The original settlers were not encouraged by O'Connor to visit the beer house and there is no evidence that they did so. The Ordnance Survey map of 1822 shows no beer shop in Long Lane. In all probability, the beer house came into existence just after 1830 as a result of the Beer House Act of 1830 which allowed any householder on payment of two guineas to obtain from the excise a licence to sell beer for consumption 'on' and 'off' the premises. Most importantly, while the fully licensed houses were controlled by the magistrates, the beer houses were not and as a result, their numbers increased rapidly. Many gained a bad reputation, some being considered little better than brothels; consequently they earned themselves the nickname 'Tom and Jerry houses'. This would have been another reason for the original settlers to avoid the beer shop on Long Lane. However, in 1869, the Wine and Beer House Act was introduced and beer houses also had to apply to local magistrates for a licence. These were granted to 'old beer houses", but it was difficult for new beer houses to obtain a licence. Full licences in the 19th century were generally granted only to coaching inns which offered stabling and accommodation. The 1869 Act did not grant a full licence to the Land of Liberty – this was not achieved until after the Second World War and therefore only beer, porter and wine could be purchased until that time. However, the Land of Liberty had become respectable, and the census of 1871 reveals that John Swain and his wife, Ann, who were in their early thirties were in residence with their four children and that William Beckley, a tramp from Buckinghamshire, was asleep in the pigsty at the back of the premises.

The photograph on page 60 with St John's church in the foreground, taken pre-1886 and the addition of the chancel, shows The Pines (plot 22) and Oakhill to the left. To the right in the background is The Grange Lodge, Waterfield House and The Land of Liberty public house. By this time, The Land of Liberty was a building much as we know it today, but without the bay windows which were added at a much later date.

CHAPTER EIGHT

Fee Farm Rents 1847-1997

In an attempt to clarify the situation in regard to rents and freehold ownership, we shall look back at the earliest days of the O'Connorville Estate. O'Connor had always intended that there should be a rent on the cottages and land which the first settlers had won by ballot. To enter the ballot, prospective settlers had to buy shares. Each share cost £2 10s; one share gave the prospect of acquiring a two acre plot, one and a half shares, a three acre plot and two shares a four acre plot. Shares could be bought in weekly installments of 3d. The plan was that the plots would be let in perpetuity and the amount to be paid was dependent on the acreage of their plots and varied between £6 2s and £10 15s 6d. These rents came to be called 'Fee Farm Rents' which was a term used since medieval times for describing the rent of agricultural land. At the very outset, O'Connor announced at the May Day 1847 meeting that the allottees could buy out the fee farm rents of their lots at the price of 20 years' rent, but none did so.

Also, it was planned that the ballot winners should have freehold rights to their cottages, but because of legal difficulties, none did so. The early settlers were leaseholders and did not begin to acquire freehold ownership until after the Winding-Up Act of 1851. For instance, Thomas Bradford, in 1854 wanted to buy the freehold rights to Plot 13 (Herons Lodge). He was able to prove his title to the plot and having paid up money owing on past fee farm rents, William Goodchap the government manager of the Estate allowed him to buy the freehold rights subject to a fixed fee farm rent of £6 2s payable to the Chancery office. Other settlers bought their freehold rights at the same time.

Between the years 1851 and 1857, William Goodchap was keen that the fee farm rents should be bought by the plot owners, but none could afford the money which was in the region of £114. Also his attempts to sell the fee farm rents at auction in 1857 and 1858 failed (some historians have said that it was the freehold rights which were auctioned in 1857 and 1858). Once again, the inhabitants of the cottages had the opportunity to buy the fee farm rents but none were able to afford the money. As mentioned earlier, it was William Prowting Roberts who bought the fee farm rents in 1860. The annual income from the Heronsgate rents was £280 or an average of £8 per plot. Plot owners were also required to contribute to other rents. These included three annuities payable to Edward Putnam, Samuel Putnam and Elizabeth Putnam the wife of William Humphreys. The Putnams were the landowners from whom William Hunt had purchased Herringsgate Farm. William Hunt died in 1846 and his solicitor sold the farm to O'Connor. There was a quit rent (dues) which was payable to Thomas Ayres, the Lord of the Manor of Rickmansworth and there was a land tax. By the 1920s quit rents were paid to the Chorleywood Urban District Council.

Rents and in particular fee farm rents continued to be a factor in Heronsgate life until towards the end of the 20th Century. On the death of William Prowting Roberts in 1871, the income from the fee farm rents went to his wife Mary and when she died in 1892, the Reverend W.J. Roberts their son of Salisbury Vicarage, became the beneficiary of the income. Thus, from 1860 until the early years of the 20th century fee farm rents were paid to the Prowting Roberts family. But gradually, the rents would be bought out by Heronsgate dwellers.

It is worth noting here that in 1884 one William Robert Petheridge bought Holly Lodge from Mary Roberts for £150 plus an annual fee farm rent of £10 13s 6d. Although Mary had by this time moved away from the Estate her interest and associations with O'Connorville were still strong. By 1889, Petheridge was compelled to sell the property mainly because he was unable to pay the fee farm rent. This is the only case I have unearthed of this occurrence. As the years went by and Heronsgate owners became more prosperous, fee farm rents were bought; some for individual plots, for example, by R.J. Parsons and J.F. Marchant, and some in blocks of plots, for example, by Frank Pope.

A look at the conveyancing schedule of plot 17 in 1912 refers to a freehold property known as Herons Court, where the fee farm rent was £6 8s. The property was subdivided: Wiverton the original Chartist plot paid £1 15s 6d and Herons Court paid £4 12s 6d which reflected the land size of the properties. These rents were paid to the Reverend W.J. Roberts. In 1920 R.J. Parsons bought the fee farm rents for both properties for £124 and subsequently Wiverton was required to pay its fee farm rent to the owners of Herons Court. This purchase by R.J. Parsons was part of a large attempt to sell off the fee farm rents when the question raised its head again in 1920.

On Wednesday the 30th of June 1920 Swannell and Sly offered for sale fee farm rent charges amounting to about £178 9s 6d per annum on various properties which were held under separate conveyances. Swannell and Sly proposed the sale by auction in lots. There were 22 lots in this sale and they were as follows:

Lot 1   Herons Lodge (1 acre, 3 rods 75 perches) - with a fee farm rent charge of £6 2s.

Lot 2   Sherwood (1 acre 3 rods 36 perches) - a rent charge of £6 8s.

Lot 3   The Bungalow - similar charge and similar area.

Lot 4   Herons Court and The Nook (2 acres 0 rods and 2 perches) - a rent charge of £6 8s,

Lot 5   The Pines (3 acres 0 rods 1 perch) - a rent charge of £6 8s.

Lot 6   Herons Nest (2 acres) - a rent charge of £6 8s.

Lot 7   The Limes (2 acres 0 rods 4 perches) - a rent charge of £6 8s.

Lot 8   Glenthorne (3 acres 3 rods 36 perches) - a rent charge of £10 5s 6d.

Lot 9   The Nest (3 acres 3 rods 33 perches) - a rent charge of £10 15s 6d.

Lot 10   Laburnums (3 acres) - a rent charge of £8 12s 6d.

Lot 11   Cherry Tree (2 acres 0 rods 10 perches) - a rent charge of £6 8s.

Lot 12   Walnut Tree Cottage (3 acres 3 rods 35 perches) - a rent charge of £10 10s 6d.

Lot 13   Daphnes, Woodcroft and Bowood (4 acres 0 rods 7 perches) - a rent charge of £10 10s 6d.

Lot 14   Crowthorne and Sherwood Cottage (2 acres) - a rent charge of £6 8s. The Ordnance Survey map of 1914 shows Sherwood Cottage and it can be concluded it was erected sometime between 1898 and 1914.

Lot 15   Lawrence House (Whitegates) (2 acres 0 rods 4 perches) with a rent charge of £6 2s.

Lot 16   A similar charge secured on the outbuildings and grounds of the property at one time known as Nelson House (Ladywalk Cottage) having an area of about 2 acres. Nelson House was burnt down in 1919.

Lot 17   The Hut (1 acre 3 rods 30 perches)

Lot 18   Rosemary and Homeland (4 acres 0 rods 6 perches) - a rent charge of £10 5s 6d.

Lot 19   The Plain Cottage and Bush Cottage (4 acres) - a rent charge of £10 5s 6d.

Lot 20   Oak Cottage (3 acres 8 rods 6 perches) - a rent charge of £10 5s 6d.

Lot 21   Holly Cottage (3 acres 3 rods 38 perches) - a rent charge of £10 15s 6d

Lot 22   St Cecilia (4 acres 1 rod 22 perches) - a rent charge of £9 15s 6d.

Some examples of conditions of sale were:
- There was a reserve price for each lot and no bidding could be retracted.
- A ten percent deposit was required.
- Each purchaser on completion was entitled to the rent charge.
- The title to the rent charge commenced with the will of Mary Prowting Roberts who died in 1892 and left the right to rent charges to her son, Reverend William Prowting Roberts.

An example of one of these sales has already been mentioned in this chapter: Lot 4 - Herons Court and The Nook (Wiverton) - was bought by Reginald John Parsons for £124 with a deposit of £12; the agreement was signed by Messrs. Swannell and Sly as agents for the Reverend William Prowting Roberts and Frederick Arthur Toynbee, the vendors and R.J. Parsons of Herons Court. Similar purchases of the lots were made but some remain shrouded in mystery.

However, it is worth pursuing the matter of fee farm rents further. In June 1925 as a result of a conveyance between the Reverend William Prowting Roberts and F.A. Toynbee to Mr Frank Pope, fee farm rent charges were bought by Frank Pope totalling £911 8s. The rent that would be produced for Mr Pope added up to £76 12s 6d for the following properties:

Plot 1   (Amberwood and Sunnyside) - with an annual rent of £6 2s and owned by Mr W. Fitzsimmons and Mr David Ford respectively.

Plot 14   (Sherwood) with an annual rent of £6 2s and owned by Mrs Felkin.

Plot 8   (Cherry Tree Corner) with an annual rent of £6 8s and owned by Mr B. Harrower.

Plot 12   (The Limes) with an annual rent of £6 2s and owned by Mr Daniel Ford.

Plot 13   (Herons Lodge) with an annual rent of £6 8s and owned by the Young Women's Christian Association.

Plot 15   (Chorheron) with an annual rent of £6 8s and owned by Mr David Ford.

Plot 22   (Breve House) with an annual rent of £8 6s and owned by Mr L.A. Nicol.

Plot 23   (Bircham Cottage) with an annual rent of £9 15s 6d and owned by Mr H.F. Clempson.

Plot 25   (Chartist Cottage) with an annual rent of £10 15s 6d and owned by Mr W.J.F. Giffard.

Plot 26   (Woodway) with an annual rent of £10 5s 6d and owned by Mr B.P. Haigh.

Thus some fee farm rents were now paid to men like Frank Pope and R. J. Parsons. Many others had been bought out by 1925, but some were to cause problems at later dates.

Fee farm rents, the quit rents and the annuities (who paid annuities to the Putnam family anyway?) were by now a minor irritant. For example, Herons Lodge ceased paying its quit rent of 9d to the Chorleywood Council in December 1930 when Anne Louise Mulholland paid £254 for it. There is no recording of Herons Lodge or, indeed, any Heronsgate properties having paid any of their share of the £20 annuities to the Putnam family. The fee farm rents had not increased since O'Connor's time, but men like Frank Pope still hoped to make money from them.

Although many households had either bought them or ceased paying them, fee farm rents were to continue to be a factor until the 1990s. The last mention of fee farm rents I have been able to trace dates back to 1992 and concerns Michael Bowler. By the mid 1950s Frank Pope had sold the fee farm rents of Cherry Tree Corner, The Limes, Chorheron and Breve House and on September 29th 1954 he sold the rights to Sherwood, St Cecilia, Chartist Cottage and Wood Weye to Mr Armstrong. In March 1956 conveyance between Frank Ronald Pope (no relation to the Popes of The Limes and Sunnyside) to Laura Maud Armstrong gave her the right to rent charges on Herons Lodge and The Beehive plus Sunnyside at £6 2s per annum for the sum of £146 8s. Thus these fee farm rents had also fallen into the Armstrong family's hands. The right to Sunnyside's fee farm rents were bought out shortly after, but those for Herons Lodge continued to be paid to the Armstrong family.

Michael Bowler had bought Herons Lodge from his father's estate in May 1974 and in 1976 he started to try to buy out the fee farm rent of £6 2s from the Armstrong family. There followed a difficult period of negotiations. Michael Bowler's father had bought the Whitegates field with its deep litter chicken houses from Jimmy Ross to add to the Herons Lodge smallholding area. Pigs were already kept in the Herons Lodge orchard. Smallholding was a tax efficient method of offsetting gardeners' wages. It seems that Jimmy Ross passed on the notional quit rent payment with the Whitegates land. When negotiations with the Armstrong lawyers began they demanded fee farm rent for Whitegates field, which was, they said, the rent being paid; there was no rent being paid for Herons Lodge. Eventually in 1992 it was proved Whitegates' fee farm rent had been bought out in 1920 and Michael Bowler was able to prove the freehold on Herons Lodge land. This was the last of the fee farm rents paid by a Heronsgate owner.

It is perhaps appropriate that this chapter concerning, in particular, fee farm rents should end with my chance meeting with May Stuart Fitzgerald, the great granddaughter and her son, Charles Fitzgerald, the great-great grandson of William Prowting Roberts. We talked about the fee farm rents and Charles Fitzgerald confirmed that his great-great grandfather had bought the rights to all the rents in 1860 for Heronsgate, Lowbands, Snigs End and he believes, also for Charterville. This would end the controversy about which was the fourth estate. He mentioned that the children of one of W.P. Roberts' daughters by his second marriage, and the great grandson of W.P. Roberts' eldest son Charles, received the rents for Snigs End until the 1950s when they were bought out.

CHAPTER NINE

The Dream Renewed 1880-1918

THE YEARS 1880 TO 1918 saw remarkable development in the character and housing of the former O'Connorville. No doubt the proximity to London, the extension of the railway network to the Rickmansworth/Chorleywood area from the mid-19th century onwards, and the attractive environment played their part. In 1852 the first railway came to Rickmansworth from Watford and in 1874 the Harrow line was extended to Rickmansworth; in 1889 a branch line running through Chorleywood was opened. Coach and horse travel remained an important source of transport to and from Heronsgate until the next century, but Heronsgate was becoming more accessible.

The 1881 census shows that 23 houses had changed hands since 1871 (or almost 2 in every 3). Three houses were inaccurately shown as unoccupied (plots 6, 18 and 24) and Thomas Merrick (more generally spelt Meyrick, plots 23 and 27) and James Wood (plots 7 and 8) as occupying two houses. George Virge occupied one of the three supposedly unoccupied houses with his wife and four children, but I cannot trace which one. The census shows a far wider spread of occupations and a greater variety of skills which can be broken down as follows: There were 121 residents of whom three were farmers, three were labourers, one was an accountant, one was a market gardener, one was a carpenter, one was a farm bailiff, six were retired or unemployed, one was a coal merchant, two were widowed, one was a nurse, seven were servants, two worked in London, one was an Inland Revenue officer, one was a blacksmith, one grandly called himself a 'gentleman', and there was one military man - Captain Allan MacLean, a captain in the Dragoons, who lived at Heronsgate House with his wife and four servants: Mary Roberts had moved to Powis Square, London and rented Heronsgate House (plot 36) to Captain MacLean.

The register of baptisms between 1875 and 1890 in the parish of Mill End, of which Heronsgate was part, shows occupations of the fathers of the 46 births registered to be working class as either craftsmen or unskilled labourers; but that three fathers were gentlemen and all three of them lived in Heronsgate.

The change in background and skills was reflected in the considerable activity of this period. The first development was the extension to St John's Church which was built by a local contractor Mr Darvell. On Saturday the 24th of July in 1880 the first stone of the new chancel was laid by John S. Gilliat MP and the Church was reopened on the 16th of October 1886, when the Lord Bishop

A view of the Church and The Pines (plot 22) in the early 1890s. Note the Chancel has been built

of St Albans preached the sermon. These occasions were reported in the Watford Observer in 1880 and 1886. Here are some extracts:

'CHURCH EXTENSION AT HERONSGATE: On Saturday afternoon, the foundation stone of a new chancel to the chapel of ease at this place was laid by Mr J.S. Gilliat, MP in the presence of a numerous assembly. The officiating clergy were the Reverend C.W. Neild, vicar of Mill End and Heronsgate; the Reverend A.E. Northey, vicar of Rickmansworth, and the Reverend J. Aitken, vicar of Chorleywood. Among the visitors were Mrs Neild, Mrs Hutchison (the wife of the new owner of Heronsgate House), Mrs Harvey Fellows and Miss Fellows, Miss M.A. Fellows, Mr Lance, Mr and Mrs Kingham (Daphnes), Mr and Mrs Ridding, etc. A short service of hymns and prayers having been held, the stone was lowered, and after the usual formalities, declared by Mr Gilliat to be well and truly laid in the name of the Trinity. Mr Gilliat then addressed those present in a few well chosen words, and alluding to the first establishment of the Church of Jerusalem, touched upon its gradual but sure development, and the innumerable blessings that have followed thereupon. Speaking of church expansion in the surrounding vicinity, the hon. gentleman referred to the period when the parish church of Rickmansworth was the only and mother church of the district, but was now able to look complacently and admiringly at her lately nestling daughter churches of Mill End, West Hyde, Croxley Green and Chorleywood running alone, and in the hands of their respected vicars doing good work.

Mr Gilliat gratefully testified to the deep spiritual blessings he had received from the ministrations at these churches throughout his life, and calling to mind the hard struggles for existence by the old settlers in the place they were now standing, when known by its old title of O'Connorville, spoke of the increasing arrivals of well-to-do residents and their friends, to whose assistance they were indebted for the contemplated improvement they were inaugurating. He hoped ere long the sacred means of grace would be administered upon the spot they were now gathered. A collection was then made for the building fund, and placed upon the stone. After the benediction pronounced by the Reverend C.W. Neild, the proceedings terminated.' (1880)

'HERONSGATE MISSION CHURCH: On Saturday afternoon last, the Lord Bishop of St Albans dedicated the new chancel of this mission church and delivered on the occasion a most eloquent sermon. The Reverend C.W. Neild, vicar of St Peter's, Mill End, who is also vicar of the Mission Church, and others of the local clergy took part in the ceremony. Despite the extremely wet state of the weather, a numerous congregation was present. The sacred edifice was beautifully decorated with corn, fruit, flowers, and vegetables, as the harvest festival services were also held on the same day. At the evening service the Reverend J.B. Shackle, curate of Farnham Royal, Bucks, preached the sermon. On the following Sunday afternoon the sermon was preached by the Reverend C.W. Neild. The offertories at all the services were in aid of the fund for enlarging and improving this mission church.' (1886)

Many people gave generously to the church extensions. The east window built by Messrs Clayton and Bell was presented by Mrs Lance. This stained glass window with three lights contains the inscription: 'Behold the Lamb of God which taketh away the sin of the world. To the Glory of God in memory of his mercies.'

Mrs Roberts late of Heronsgate House donated a lectern and Miss Roberts donated a Glastonbury chair. C. Wallace Neild, vicar of Mill End was also vicar at St John's; whilst William Kingham acted as the warden. Principal donations to the chancel and porch were Mr Morgan - £50 and Gerald Williams - £21. It is to be noted that more Heronsgate residents are in the 1886 list of subscribers including the warden William Kingham, a draper, and Misters Bond, Hutchison, Gill and Ford.

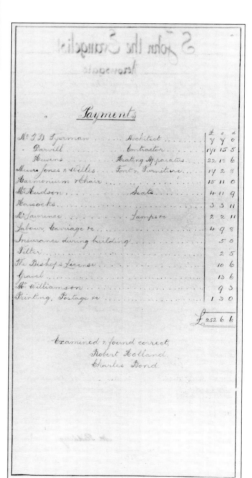

List of subscribers and expenses for the construction of the Chancel (a transcription of the subscribers follows)

S. John the Evangelist Heronsgate   Funds raised for building the Chancel 1886
Total Receipts £252 6s 6d

By Donations

Mr	Morgan		Miss	Cartmell
	Gerald Williams		Mrs & Miss Young	
	Morrison		Mr & Mrs Daniel Ford	
	Lance		Miss	King
	Woods			Holland
Lord Ebury				Osborne
Mr	Bond			Eva Bond
	Hutchison			Minnie Bond
	Clutterbuck		Mrs	Burbridge
	Birch			Timms, Senior
	Gilliatt			Saunders
Rev	C. W. Neild		Mr & Mrs Burchfield	
	J. Aitken		Mrs Richardson	
Mr	Howard Gilliatt		Mr & Mrs Emott	
	Holland		Mr & Mrs Timms	
Rev	A. E. Northey		**By Offertories**	
Mr & Mrs Kingham			Laying 1st Stone	
	Gill		Harvest Festival, S. Peters 1886	
	Bond, Junior		Opening Services Oct 16, 1886	
	Alfred Holland			8 a.m.
Mr & Mrs Emmott				3.30 p.m.
	Burchfield			7.30 p.m.
Mrs Holland				Oct 17
Mr & Mrs Philip Ford			Harvest Festival, S John's 1887	
By Cards			**By Societies**	
Mr	Gerald Williams		Diocesan Ch. Building Socty	
	Arthur Lance		Incorporated Building Socty	
Miss	Olga Lance		Proceeds of Entertaining	
Mr	Tom Lance		per Miss M. A. Fellows	
			Mr Ridding	

A transcription of the subscribers from the preceding page

In December 1884 a Wesleyan chapel was built on part of plot 19 (Hop Garden) on the instructions of John Proctor of Woodoaks Farm. John Wesley had founded the movement in the 18th century and it had grown in popularity in the 19th century. Wesleyanism had grown out of an antipathy to the working conditions of the new industrial era and it allowed the development of talents and freedom of expression that was denied elsewhere. Many clergy of the Established Church paid little attention to the social evils of the time (the Reverend Neild was not in this category), but Wesleyans pursued an enthusiastic study of the bible together with its strong moral values; Wesleyanism's conservative, non-violent political aspirations appealed to John Proctor of Woodoaks Farm (often now known as Findlay's Farm) and to many Heronsgate residents, particularly those in the inner regions of the Estate. The Reverend William Hirst of Poplar preached the opening sermon in December 1884 and about 100 people attended the public tea which followed. At first the Wesleyan Chapel was to be well attended by Heronsgate residents and it lived happily side by side with St John's.

The Wesleyan Chapel built 1884

During this period the Estate became known as Heronsgate; in 1886 J.S. Gilliat refers to 'Heronsgate', but the 1891 Ordnance Survey map calls it 'O'Connorville' or 'Herringsgate'. However by 1914 the Ordnance Survey map refers to 'Heronsgate'.

In association with the activities already mentioned and with the advent of new occupants, the years 1880 to 1914 saw bigger and new houses appear and the old cottages improved. Exact dates of new buildings and developments are often difficult to ascertain, but a study of the Ordnance Survey maps of 1891, 1898 and 1914 shows major changes taking place. The following comments are based on a study of the above-mentioned Ordnance Survey maps, a study of local records, a study of deeds and documents of residents and numerous discussions and interviews. However, it must be pointed out that the 1891 map was first surveyed in 1871 and later in 1875 before being finally published in 1891, and that the map of 1914 is based on the surveys of 1871 and 1876 with revisions carried out in 1897 and 1913. It is the revision carried out in 1897 and the Ordnance Survey map produced in 1898 which provide the evidence of considerable building in the years 1891 to 1898. Records were not properly kept until the Town and Country Planning Act of 1947, and even then inaccuracies are seen to occur.

By 1914 there had been considerable development and activity on the properties bordering Long Lane. In 1892 Miss Annie Nutter Price bought the property now known as Herons Lodge from James Leeming. In those days it was recognised as plot 13. James Leeming had bought the property in 1886 from the Fitzsimmons family. Leeming also owned plot 2 (Ladywalk Cottage) and was responsible for the demolition of the Chartist two-storeyed double cottage and the erection of Nelson House (Ladywalk Cottage) on a new site in 1890. Lawrence House (Whitegates) was built later in about 1895 on plot 3.

Miss Price's intention was to use her acquisition for the work of the Young Women's Christian Association. She had the original single-storey Chartist cottage extended into two storeys and a matching two-storey section was added to the front, separated by what became stairs and corridor. New bricks were laid outside the original Chartist cottage, and thus today there is no external evidence of the different periods of building, but inside can be seen the original arched door shape. A foundation stone on the front extension says: 'This stone was laid by Annie Price and Florence Richardson in October 1892'. Florence Richardson is believed to be a relative of the Miss Richardsons who ran the school at The Firs (High Holly) in the 1920s.

At the same time a small two-roomed brick cottage was built for the superintendent of the YWCA hostel. The term superintendent was given to the warden 'who with earnestness and love would manage the household'. By 1897 the YWCA archives refer to plot 13 as Peace Cottage –Holiday Home, 'This haven of rest for workers'. In 1898/9 Peace Cottage was listed in a report on YWCA Hostels and Institutes. It stated 'Peace Cottage (Holiday Home) offers 10 beds with full Board and Lodging at 10 shillings per week or 2s 6d Saturday to Monday am'. Train fares from London to Chorleywood were 1s 6d return and those eligible to use the Holiday Home were Business Assistants, Students and Teachers.

The YWCA started its Holiday Homes and Hostels in the 1860s; at first in London and the provincial towns and later at seaside resorts and in the tranquillity of the countryside. Their aim was to provide attractive board and lodging in a friendly, Christian atmosphere.

In 1897 Miss Price sold Peace Cottage to Baron Kinnaird. Arthur Fitzgerald Lord Kinnaird succeeded his father in 1887 and became the 11th Baron. It was his mother The Honourable Mrs Arthur Kinnaird (née Mary Jane Hoare) who was the founder of the first women's Hostel in London in 1855 for Florence Nightingale's nurses en route to or returning from the Crimean War of 1854 to 1856. From this grew the YWCA Hostel movement. In 1877 the YWCA Hostel movement joined with Miss Emma Robart's Prayer Circles (also founded in 1855) to form the YWCA as we know it today. Its main objectives were work and prayer in accordance with the word of God. Its aim was to break down artificial barriers of class or circumstance and it was to be completely non-denominational, respecting all people's religious beliefs. Peace Cottage was one of many Holiday Homes; from 1897 to 1912 Miss Fitzgerald was its superintendent and then Miss Goodman, having obtained the lease, became the superintendent until just after the First World War.

A lot of work was done at Sherwood in the years 1891 to 1898. It is probable at this time that the property was called Herondale; at a later date it acquired the name Sherwood possibly after the Nottingham constituency which O'Connor represented as its MP in 1847 or due to the fact that Frederick Felkin came from Nottinghamshire. A driveway was constructed from Long Lane to a coach house built for horses with stables, accommodation for a groom, a hayloft and a harness room. Fireplaces were built to keep the groom and horses warm. In the main house there were cellars, a laundry, a butler's pantry and small cramped living quarters for the servants. Each of the six principal bedrooms had its own fireplace and downstairs in the living rooms were beautiful marble fireplaces. Vegetable gardens, rose beds and orchards were laid out and cedars planted along the drive. Soon after 1903 on the death of Frederick Felkin at Heronsgate House, Mary Elizabeth Felkin moved into Sherwood where she lived until her death in 1928. In 1905 a splendid new sitting room was built. The bell which now sits on the roof of Sherwood is the old school bell which Mrs Felkin brought with her from Heronsgate House. Mary Felkin was the youngest daughter of George Foster whose only trace I could find at first was in Gilham's shoe ledger in 1908 and 1911, and on the memorial plaque in St John's Church to Frederick and Mary Felkin. Later it was concluded that George Foster was the Professor George Foster who bought Ladywalk in 1900 from T. Wilks, the tanner of Mill End.

William Marshall Hutchison purchased Heronsgate House (the old schoolhouse now named The Grange) for £2,500 in 1884 from Mary Prowting Roberts, who by this time was living in London. It was not long before William Hutchison was making his mark on Heronsgate. Between 1884 and 1898 he built a driveway to Long Lane and planted it with Corsican pines. On the present croquet lawn he planted a monkey puzzle tree which grew 50/60 feet high. A lodge now called Grange Cottage was constructed for his servants, and the original Chartist cottage on plot 11 was demolished. William Hutchison also extended the house by additions to the sides and back, enlarging the servants' quarters, building two large cellars – typical of the Victorian era – and adding a stable block for two horses to the right of the house. The name 'Jackanapes' can still be seen above one of the feeding troughs in one of the stables. It is not certain how much time William Hutchison spent at Heronsgate House but the deeds show a Mary Moor (1884-1898) and a Mrs McOstrich (1903-1913) as being co-owners and it is known the Felkin family lived in the house for a while before Mrs Felkin moved to Sherwood. In 1913 Madam Kirkby-Lunn, the well-known opera singer bought Heronsgate House and she lived there until the end of the war.

The development in Long Lane continued. In the 1900s Home Close was built as a second house on the original Chartist plot 16. The other building on that site is now called The Grey Cottage. Herons Court was built in the 1890s and Oaklands at the turn of the century. White Lodge, Fernhill, Athelstan and Hillside, now considered as part of Heronsgate, were built in the period 1896-1914.

To look in greater detail at these developments we shall start with Herons Court which was built on the Wiverton site. Wiverton, at this time called The Nook (and previously known as The Retreat), was purchased in 1891 by Charles Bond the London hairdresser and perfumer and he was responsible for the erection of the first building on the site now called Herons Court. Charles Bond died in September 1909 and left his estate including Herons Court to his son George.H. Bond (also a London hairdresser) and Ada Maria Davey and Alfred Frederick Prechtel subject to the rent charge and quit rent. In 1912 G.H. Bond, sold Herons Court to R.J. Parsons and so Wiverton and Herons Court became separate properties. The present house was built by R.J. Parsons in 1914 with his architect Bertram Haigh, who also lived in Heronsgate. When R.J. Parsons bought from G.H. Bond, the abstract of the title dated 20th July 1912 refers to the freehold property known as Herons Court and to rent charges. Bond, Davey and Prechtel sold for £1,350 that parcel of land to R.J. Parsons containing about one and a half acres situated at Heronsgate and forming part of an allotment of land containing two acres and two perches which was number 17 (Wiverton); together with the messuage and buildings erected thereon and known as Herons Court; and it was separated from the rest of the allotment of land by a hedge or fence, and on the south east side by a hedge forming a boundary with the allotment known as Home Close.

The sale was subject to a perpetual fee farm rent charge of £4 12s 6d payable on the 25th of March and the 29th of September in every year being a proportion of a perpetual annual rent charge on the whole property of £6 8s secured by Indre dated the 17th of July 1854 made between William Goodchap and J.H.J. Wolfe and also subject to an annual payment of sevenpence being a proportion of the annual quit rent charged upon the whole of the Heronsgate Estate.

The schedule also refers to conveyance between Thomas Martin Wheeler to J.S. Woolfe in 1853. Wheeler was the Land Company secretary and was not an original settler. Was he exploiting his position out of the winding-up of the Estate? In 1913 George Bond sold Wiverton to H.J. Taylor and T.M. Swales.

Other plots further north along Long Lane had been divided. In November 1898 the following for sale notice appeared in a local newspaper and at local hostelries where it could be seen by travellers:

> 'Also for sale the valuable enclosure of freehold building land with four roomed cottage, having a frontage of 300 feet to Long Lane, 300 feet to Halifax Road, and 300 feet to Stockport Road, the whole subject to a rent charge of £8 5s 6d. This offers a splendid site for a Gentleman's residence, commanding extensive views. The site may be viewed by permission of the respective tenants, and further particulars and conditions of sale had at the usual Inns of the neighbourhood, and at the offices of Messrs Rowell and Lomas, solicitors, Rickmansworth, and of the auctioneer, High Street, Rickmansworth and Chesham'.

The land was bought by Charles Bond; a fine Edwardian House, at first called Hillmorton and later known as Oaklands, with sitting rooms, dining hall, reception area and stabling on two acres of land was to result from this sale. The original Chartist cottage (Little Aymers plot 9) was to remain, mostly unaltered on a site of about one acre until much later when alterations took place.

Finally, at the northern end of Long Lane was The Pines (plot 22), which underwent major extensions in the 1890s creating a fine Victorian house with a stabling block and a driveway planted with trees. The garden was landscaped and a tennis court built adjacent to Long Lane. Charles Bond bought Breve House in 1883 and owned it until his death in 1909 and was thus responsible, not only for its extensions, but also for the development of Oaklands and of the Wiverton site. These properties on his death were left to his daughter, Mrs Ada Davey and his son, George Bond. Charles Bond also played a prominent role in overseeing the financial arrangements for building the church extensions of 1880-1886.

An early photograph of The Pines (plot 22) about 1885 before extensions

Oakhill, although outside the original O'Connorville settlement, was purchased in 1883 by the Gill family from the Grosvenor Estate. Oakhill was built in the 1730s by Robert Grosvenor. The Gills were for many years associated with a high class gentleman's clothier business in Watford and it was grandfather Gill, who, having purchased Oakhill built the Red House, now called White Lodge, in the 1890s at the northern end of Oakhill grounds adjacent to Long Lane; he also built Flint Cottage (opposite Oakhill) on the other side of Long Lane as a gardener's cottage. When the cottage was constructed, a cross to remember the Quaker faith was built into the wall adjacent to the back door. Did the Gills have Quaker connections? Or was it the gardener who was a Quaker? Maybe the builders were Quakers? Since that time many locals have even spoken of Heronsgate being a Quaker settlement and indeed families with Quaker connections have lived in Heronsgate.

The land to the north of Oakhill and the land bordering the northern end of O'Connorville was for the most part owned by Mrs L. Akerman; before selling what is now known as Long Lane House to F.C. Blyth in 1911, she built three properties: Hillside, Athelstan and Fernhill. The Long Lane houses reflected the new affluence of Heronsgate and were magnificent monuments to the period.

The inner areas of Heronsgate were also making their own progress. Laburnums and the Hop Garden (plots 18 and 19) are almost certainly the site of the original Herringsgate Farm which was demolished when O'Connor bought the Estate in 1846. A pre-Chartist map shows a lane (probably now Stockport Road) leading to four buildings including what was the farmhouse. Evidence of

Oakhill about 1890

outbuildings on the Hop Garden land support this theory. However, in the Chorleywood Library there is an 1805 map which shows Herringsgate Farm; having overlaid the old map on a modern map, it seems possible that The Grange (Heronsgate House) lies on the original site. It was more likely that O'Connor and his builders would have used an existing lane, Stockport Road, and branched the new lanes, Nottingham Road and Halifax Road, off it. Pre-1846 maps show a footpath opposite Stockport Road, running from Long Lane to Hill Farm. This is further evidence that there was a lane which was improved to create Stockport Road; the footpath would have made it possible to continue the journey from the old lane and Herringsgate Farm to the farms to the east of Long Lane and to Chorleywood. Finally I found a plan of Herringsgate Farm dated 1838 which confirms the assumption that Laburnums and The Hop Garden were the original site (see page 22).

Laburnums and Heron Cottage (plot 9) were extended at the turn of the century. At Laburnums the outline of the original two-storey cottage can still be seen and building was done by relatives of the McCullochs; whilst at Heron Cottage the original single-storey cottage remains intact, although the inside has been altered and extensions added to the eastern side. At the time when the internal alterations to the original Chartist cottage were made, the old, sloping slated roof to the outbuildings was removed and was replaced by a higher two-sided steeper roof, which created more spacious living. Heron Cottage had lost part of its original two acres when St John's Church was built in 1865.

At this time the west side of Halifax Road saw its first developments. In the 1890s The Firs, now called High Holly, part of the original Ford plot (Laurel Cottage plot 15), and Lindens at the north end appeared. Bradford Road was to see The Limes built with a separate stable block and the original Chartist cottage at the front destroyed. This work was done by the Ford family who had by then moved from Laurel Cottage, their home since 1847. Further up the road at Hope Lodge and Endlands (plots 20 and 35) the Chartist cottages remained, but considerable extensions were made. In 1904 F.C. Blyth purchased Hope Lodge and he was to exert considerable influence in this northern part of Heronsgate until his death in 1952. Blyth built quite an empire in his time. Having purchased Hope Lodge on the original Chartist acreage, he also acquired Mumfistells (Long Lane House), which he later called Midgham Cottage, where he lived with his wife and with their servant H.G. Denne. Blyth rebuilt the house, formerly the farrier's cottage, in 1922. In the meanwhile he had purchased Endlands and other nearby land.

It appears F.C. Blyth divided his time between Midgham Cottage, Endlands and Hope Lodge. When I spoke to Mrs Babcock (Long Lane House), in 1997, she referred to a mysterious lady as 'the painted lady' who lived in Hope Cottage. Ron Clarkson recalls that his mother used to clean for Hope Cottage before the Second World War and that it was a 'Lillie Langtry' who lived there. The census returns for the years 1902 to 1933 show that a Mrs Lambert lived in Hope Cottage. Could this have been the Lillie Langtry? Lillie Langtry, often known as the Jersey Lillie, is remembered as the greatest actress of her day and a former mistress of the Prince of Wales. Ron Clarkson recalls that when his mother knew Lillie Langtry the actress was a recluse and nervous about opening her front door to visitors. Coincidentally, the ball in the late 1970s held at Ladywalk to raise money for the appeal against the M25 was by chance called the Lillie Langtry Ball because of the TV series about her at the time and it offered the opportunity to wear Edwardian dress. Few of the revellers at the ball suspected that Lillie Langtry was rumoured to have been a resident of Heronsgate from the turn of the century. In fact Lillie Langtry (Lady de Bathe) died on February 12th, 1929, in Monaco aged 75.

F.C. Blyth held an important post in the Bank of England. He was to become a church warden of St John's and a member of the original Heronsgate Association committee. He had acquired much of the land at the northern end of Heronsgate by 1918 including Endlands, Hope Cottage, Long Lane House and Ford's orchard – formerly part of The Limes – and lands to the south, north and west including what are now the allotments in the Swillett. This land had been bought from Lord Rendlesham or Mrs Akerman. Blyth sold the land which is now the allotments to the Chorleywood Council for £1 prior to the First World War. In the grounds of Long Lane House he fanatically planted trees, built ornamental water ponds and placed two cannons acquired from the Bank of England at the front of the house. At this time there was a path from the allotments down the side of Endlands into Bradford Road.

At the southern end of Heronsgate in Nottingham Road there were many changes. A country house was built on plot 24 in 1880 by A. Hawkins, a London businessman, which was to become Beaumont House Preparatory School in 1905. Northwards up Nottingham Road South, the triangle of original Chartist plot numbers 29 (Rosemary Cottage), 2 (Ladywalk Cottage) and 3 (Whitegates) saw considerable activity and new buildings were erected.

The information from the deeds held by the current owners states that Whitegates (Lawrence House) was built in 1904 and Ladywalk Cottage (Nelson House) was built in 1906, but the Ordnance Survey map of 1898 shows that both Whitegates and Ladywalk Cottage had already been built. Whenever it was, the original double cottage on plots 2 and 3 – close to the lane and bisecting the boundaries – was demolished and the new houses were built on new sites. In regard to Rosemary Cottage (plot 29): Edward John Gyles and Francis Ebenezer Gyles (A.F. Bird's father-in-law) bought the four acres and six perches from Thomas Baxter Summerfield subject to the usual fee farm rent £10 5s 6d, payable to the Reverend Prowting Roberts and the annual quit rent of £1 16s 10d payable to the Lord of the Manor in July 1901. In December 1904 the Gyles sold a 99-year lease for Rosemary Cottage to Posseen Hill for an annual rent of £7 and kept a remaining three acres and six perches for themselves. A deed of partition was completed in 1905 between the Gyles and Edward Wagstaffe Chandler, their solicitor, and in 1906 the Gyles had Homeland built in the Edwardian style of the day. It is said the work was supervised by Ebenezer Gyles' son-in-law, Frank Walker, who had a liking for property development.

Nelson House (plot2) looking north. This house was subsequently burned down

Further northwards up the road the Kinghams had lived at Daphnes since 1880. William Kingham was a draper and a prominent member of the community, being, amongst other things, a church warden at St John's. The 1881 census shows that Mrs Kingham was a schoolmistress; she looked after seven children (including her own two), who boarded with her and whose occupations in the census are recorded as scholars. Also living with the Kinghams was a girl, aged 15, who was a domestic servant. The house had been enlarged to cope with its ten occupants of 1881. The Kinghams in the early 1900s built Bowood and Wood Croft, whose occupants respectively are shown in the Kelly's Directory of 1906 to be W. Neatby and W. Smith. By this time Mrs Kingham had begun her smallholding enterprise. Rosecot had been owned as a country cottage by A. F. Bird's father-in-law and in the early 1890s the Birds had begun their family's long association with Heronsgate. In 1910, under the supervision of Bertram Haigh, Rosecot was to see major architectural change.

Two photographs of Laburnums (plot 18) around the turn of the century. Note the later extensions

At the northern end of Nottingham Road, the Dinslage family were particularly active; they were in residence in Myrtle House (plot 10) in 1890 and in the mid 1890s sold part of their two-acre plot to Percy Wheeler who built Lindens in 1898. In 1907 the Dinslages sold Myrtle House to R. Javal-Cremieu and they moved into The Orchard on land purchased in 1898 from the Connorville Post Office (plot 19) three-acre site. They were in residence at The Orchard for over 10 years and thus were associated with Heronsgate for close to 30 years.

It was in the 1890s that Heronsgate houses first began to acquire their names, although this was not common practice until around 1906. Prior to these dates most houses were known by their plot numbers as confirmed in the Winding-up Act after the dissolving of the National Land Company, or by their owner's name. However, the old Chartist schoolhouse had been referred to as Heron's Gate House in 1882 and in the census of 1881 and had previously been called O'Connorville College. Perhaps the most important development during this time on the boundaries of Heronsgate was the construction of the imposing and magnificent Ladywalk and this, although it was built during this period is dealt with in detail in the next chapter.

In 1876 St John's had been incorporated into the joint parish of Mill End and Heronsgate and the Reverend Neild was its vicar between 1875 and 1896. At Christmas 1896 Charles Wallace Neild, the first vicar of the united parishes of Mill End and St John's, died of cancer aged 49 and his wife died within three months. The Reverend Neild had been very concerned about the poor of Mill End (nicknamed 'Tiger Bay') and had done much good work to improve the sanitation and health of the area. He and his wife were buried at Aldenham by the Reverend Kenneth Gibbs. The west window at St John's was built in memory of the work and dedication of its first vicar of the united parish.

Again the Ford family is amongst the subscribers (it is known there were six children). Mrs Hazel was the little old lady who was the cleaner of both St John's and also the Wesleyan chapel (now the village hall and school). She lived in The Swillett and in addition to her ecclesiastical duties she 'sorted' for Heronsgate residents. The Reverend Auriol F. Murray, the grandson of the former Bishop of Rochester, became the new vicar and he was succeeded in 1912 by The Reverend Walter Breffit who came from Norfolk.

To conclude, the years between 1880 and the start of the First World War had seen major changes in Heronsgate. Gone were the years of uncertainty and disappointment at the failure of the O'Connor concept of self-supporting agricultural properties. Although the years 1860 to 1880 had seen most properties change hands, the new owners generally came from rural backgrounds and Heronsgate changed little. But from 1880 onwards the Estate came to be viewed in a new light. It began to attract people with money and families from a different social background. The Prowting Roberts family moved out but still continued to exert an influence, and the Gilliats took a keen interest particularly in St John's Church. People wanted to live in Heronsgate; it was in the country but near London and with the improvements in transport it was accessible. Thus Beaumont House was built; Chartist cottages such as Herons Lodge, Breve House, Heron Cottage, Laburnums, Sherwood, Myrtle House, Pinhaye and Rosecot were expanded and built into large houses. Old Chartist plots were subdivided and substantial houses built at Home Close,

List of Subscribers
To the Late Rev. Charles Wallace & Mrs Neild Memorial Window
St John's Church, Heronsgate
May 5th, 1897

Duff Mr & Mrs	Jones Mr
Corsbie Mr & Mrs	Bird Mr & Mrs
Gill Mr & Mrs	Porter Mrs W
Pattisson Mr	Harvey Mrs
Pattisson Mrs	Wells Mrs
Bond Mr	Hedgecock Mrs
Bond Mrs	King Mr & Mrs
Bond Mr G.H.	Rhodes Mrs
Curtice Mr & Mrs	Cartmel Mrs
Gilliat Mr J.S. M.P.	Chapman Miss
Hawkins Mr & Mrs	Kingham Mrs
Henderson Rev C.K.	Doggett Miss Edith
Holland Mr	Doggett Miss Amy
Kingwell Mr & Mrs	Fenson Mrs
Robinson Mr	Ford Mr & Mrs
Wilks Mr & Mrs	Roe Miss Millie
Bond Miss Eva	Baldwin Mr C
Bond Miss Ada	Hazel Mrs
Corsbie Miss A.M.	Hunt Mr
Curry Mr C.A.	
Ford Mr & Mrs D	

F. Auriol Murray	James Gill
Vicar	Church Warden

List of Subscribers to the Neild Memorial Window

Herons Court, Oaklands, Lindens, Homeland, Ladywalk Cottage, Whitegates and Stanmore Lodge. These developments in many cases involved the building of servants' quarters, often cramped and small, and stables for horses and carriages. James Welch, the blacksmith in The Swillett was kept busy with shoe repairs and mending and repairing harness and tackle, while the horses – with or without carriages – had to watch out for the occasional motorized vehicle or penny-farthing or bicycle. The lanes of Heronsgate and the lanes and roads leading to Chorleywood and Rickmansworth railway stations and the other nearby towns were occupied by all forms of transport including the more common pedestrian.

The wellbeing and prosperity of Heronsgate was also shown in the fact that houses changed hands less frequently and some families stayed for long periods; the Ford family were still here and the Kinghams, Dinslages, Beatsons, Josephs, Marchants, Andersons, Bonds, Felkins, Gills, Giffards, Vereys and Horace Clempson (St Cecilia - plot 23) the music teacher at Beaumont House were to enjoy long associations with Heronsgate.

Flint Cottage 1890s looking north up Long Lane; White Lodge, Fern Hill and Athelstan have not yet been built

Everything seemed to be settling down. Robert Hunt and his wife began a long period of custody as beer retailers of the Land of Liberty which was to last from about 1906 to the 1930s. Mrs Chapman lived at Laburnums prior to 1890 and was still in residence in 1908. In the early 1900s Miss Fanny King came to live with her; Monty McCulloch refers to them as Grandma Chapman and Aunt Lizzy. By 1917 Laburnums was registered as an invalids' home with Miss Fanny King as the proprietor. Kelly's Directory shows that Octavius Langtree lived at The Poplars in the 1900s. Miss Lily Hocker (predecessor of the Miss Richardsons) ran a girls' school at The Firs in 1912. Madam Kirkby-Lunn, the well-known opera singer, bought Heronsgate House in 1913, and Arthur Bird first moved into Rosecot around 1890. Herons Lodge was run as a summer retreat for the Young Women's Christian Association with Miss Fitzgerald acting as superintendent. There were two churches, and although the original O'Connorville school had become a private house, a new school had been founded called Beaumont House. Thus Heronsgate in 1914 was a lively community reflecting the prosperity of late Victorian, Edwardian and early Georgian England. However, the 1914-18 war was to have a dramatic effect on Heronsgate. People expected the war to end quickly in a glorious victory, but it dragged on for five horrendous years. As everywhere else, the community was to be deeply affected by the Great War. Many local residents lost their lives and in 1918 Heronsgate was not such a confident or prosperous community.

 CHAPTER TEN

Ladywalk from the Mists of History

L ADYWALK WAS FORMERLY just outside Heronsgate's borders and the house underwent the most alteration of any residence in Heronsgate for it was completely rebuilt in the 1930s for the Leonard family of Carless, Capel and Leonard, the oil magnates. Hugh Leonard bought Ladywalk in 1931 and constructed the new Ladywalk to face south to gain maximum advantage of the sunlight hours, regardless of cost, on a 67-acre site. It was to consist of 12 bedrooms with four bathrooms, a fine lounge hall and four reception rooms with buildings and accommodation for staff; it had beautiful formal and walled gardens and a petrol pump for the Leonard family's Rolls Royce. It was a superb residence befitting the aspirations of a successful businessman of the post-war years. The new Ladywalk which was finished by 1934 was a marvellous acquisition for Heronsgate and the Leonard family were to play a most influential part in the continuing development of Heronsgate.

But Ladywalk has a fascinating history. Life there in the early 1900s has luckily been well-remembered by Mavis Waller. She spent happy years there before the house was rebuilt. There was an old Ladywalk built in the late 19th century, according to legend on a former convent site, by Thomas Wilks, who was recorded as living in Ladywalk in 1890. Wilks was a member of the family who were the tanners of Mill End. Ladywalk was sold to Professor George Carey Foster BA LLD FRS JP in 1900. He lived there until his death in 1919 when the house was sold to the Montgomery family.

Professor Foster was born at Sabden in Lancashire in 1835. His early education was at private schools until he became a student in Chemistry at University College, London where he graduated with honours. In 1858 he went to study at the universities of Ghent, Paris and Heidelberg. In 1862 he was appointed Professor of Natural Philosophy at Glasgow University. In 1865 he was elected Professor of Physics at University College, London and thus began his long association with the university. He was a distinguished scientist and administrator, much loved and respected by his students and colleagues. However his obituary states 'he was not a good lecturer, he was far from fluent, but if his halting words were taken down they were invariably accurate and sensible'. He wrote a large number of articles on Physics and Chemistry; his report on organic chemistry was a pioneer in its field. He became a fellow of the Royal Society in 1869 and was a vice-president of the society between 1891 and 1893 and 1902 to 1903. Between 1900 and 1904 he was Principal of University College, London. Heronsgate gained a distinguished academic when he moved to

Ladywalk in 1900. His daughter Mary Felkin was by this time living at Heronsgate House. He, like Prowting Roberts and Heyworth Talbot, was associated with the legal world, becoming a J.P. His obituary dated 1920 states that 'in his domestic life Professor Foster was exceptionally happy, his eight children are all living and his wife only predeceased him by 18 months. He died at Rickmansworth on February 9th, 1919, aged 84'.

Mavis Waller (née Parrott) remembers Ladywalk:

'My earliest memories of Ladywalk are rather hazy, being only a small child when we moved into the flat above the garage, stables and harness room. My father had been demobbed from the Royal Garrison Artillery at the cessation of hostilities in 1918. My father was fortunate enough to find the position of head gardener at Ladywalk. He was a Chorleywood man, and well known for his agricultural and horticultural skills. 'We were luckier than most, as there was accommodation; many ex-servicemen did not find jobs and "homes fit for heroes" as was promised. As I developed into childhood I was blissfully unaware of this and took for granted the good life which we enjoyed. The grounds seemed to a small child to be endless – with parklands and the famous wood where the legendary lady walked.'

In 1911 an article written by A. Sainsbury Verey MBOU, a resident of Heronsgate, was published in 'The Watford Observer'. He had written about 'The Ladies' Walk' in somewhat lyrical terms, imagining – with a fair amount of poetic licence – its distant history and its more recent past when there was a Convent:

'Very restful is the "Ladies' Walk." Standing high upon the crest of a steep acclivity at the approach to the locality, which the famous Chartist loved perhaps not wisely but too well; it is a narrow halt of woodland composed of beech trees with graceful larches interspersed. At either end a path leads up to it, the one at the lower end passing by the farmstead, upon the site of which once of old stood the Convent. Through the length of the wood runs a broad walk carpeted with the russet-brown beech-mast of successive harvests, over which, in the winter, those handsome feathered visitants, the brambling finches, make merry and wax fat, finding refuge here from the rigour of the season in their far-away Scandinavian homes.

Looking outward from the wood, a wide expanse of swelling upland and lowly dale greets the eye. In the hollow the hamlet nestles, embowered in the verdure. Behind it, rise the chalk hills mutely revealing the story of the primeaval, while ever onward through the green valley the winding river flows. Peaceful sheepfolds, cattle browsing in the meadows, poppies glowing amidst the gently undulating corn. On the fallows the busy plough is at work, attended by its feahered familiars the rooks and plovers.

Within the wood, over which the spirit of the past seems ever brooding, stretches above, canopy mounting upon canopy, an over-arching screen of daintiest embroidery, as boughs and tender twigs and sprays with pendant, delicate green leaves, gently toyed with by the scarcely moving air, unite in forming a myriad patterns of nature's supreme handiwork. And as the golden shafts of sunlight, glancing past all obscacles, fall upon grey tree trunk, fresh young foliage and ruddy path, the whole scene becomes transformed into a soft and glistening glory.

Here nature holds full court, and at it her subjects delight to disport themselves. In the dells and on the grassy slopes, wild hyacinths assert themselves bravely, their blue flowers and leaves of lustrous green vieing in friendliest rivalry for the palm of beauty. Scattered everywhere about, pale primroses cluster thickly, rising from their leafy beds with gold-tipped moss commingling. Growing here also are to be seen wood-violets, anemones, sturdy campions, golden celendine, wild strawberries, geraniums, meek star-faced stichworts, chaste woodruff with its wheel-like leaves.

A pheasant crows. In a fork of a spreading tree appears a small brown head with ears erect, and two glistening black eyes are gazing down intently – only the squirrel watching, and jealous of intrusion, is eager to know if all is well. A nuthatch trips briskly up the trunk of a tree. From the crown of a lofty beech a wood-pigeon rises awkwardly, impeded by the branches, and flies away. A jay screams harshly, and hastens to betake itself to more secluded haunts. The cry of a woodpecker rings startlingly on the still air. Otherwise so quiet is it that the frightened wood-mouse, springing from underfoot and hurrying away over the dead crisp leaves, makes its passage distinctly heard.

Hither then, in the olden time, came the good sisters of the Convent. At first to plan and lay out the ground, to arrange and plant the trees and then with thoughtful care to watch and tend their growth, quite possibly doing much of the work with their own fair hands. After a while, when the trees had grown sturdy and a retired and cool retreat presented itself, they came again in leisure moments for rest and relaxation. And as they walked and conversed one with another they plucked the flowers by the wayside with beechen trails to fashion them into posies, garlands, or wreaths; culled the herbs also whose medicinal properties they well understood, to dispense them in their charitable labours. Or reclining in the grateful shade, perchance they embroidered banners for the Crusaders to take with them to Palestine, as their supplications ascended to the Lord of All that a blessing might attend the effort and the Holy Land pass at length into the possession of the followers of The Cross. How hope must have sunk low in those gentle breasts, and how weary grown the spirits on that day when the sad tidings came to them that their hero, he of the "Lion Heart", had disappeared, none knew how or where to revive again however, when, after a long interval, they learned that the minstrel Blondel had at last discovered him and brought him ransom. What a pageant of rulers passed them by. Saxon and Norman, Yorkist, Lancastrian, Plantagenet, Tudor, and Stuart, some protecting, favouring, others persecuting them. Wars and rumours of wars came to them many a time and oft – it mattered not to those tranquil lives. William the Norman plants his iron heel upon the soil of Britain, and Harold, fighting manfully, falls and with him the Saxon line; the Wars of the Roses rage, deluging the land with kindred blood; comes the Armada proud in its might, only to be overwhelmed by the great heart of England and shattered against Albion's rock-girdled isle; The Cavalier engages the Roundhead on the field of battle, brother opposed to brother – to culminate in the tragedy of Whitehall. All one to those patient votaries. Not for them the strife and the tumult. So, unperturbed they went their way by quiet paths, occupying themselves with their self-denying ministrations, content only to bring food to the hungry, solace to the sorrowful, help to "him that hath no helper".

Eventide. Hush! It is the vesper-bell - The Last Vesper - calling them. Sic transeunt omnes.

Nameless and forgotten, now they lie where once the old Convent stood. Yet, still the blossoms of spring falling drift lightly on them, and the wind-vexed leaves of autumn cover them about. The summer's sun smiles down upon them, and the winter's snow enwraps them anew in fair, white vestal robes. Yes, they all have passed away – long since, and well the pious sisters sleep. Only the "Ladies' Walk" remains. But in it the sweet voiced bird of night still sings their requiem.'

Heronsgate residents at the turn of the century pause at the style before entering Ladywalk Wood

The site of the convent was in close proximity to Findlay's farm and was abandoned by the early 18th century, but the legend lived on and hence some say Ladywalk was built on the site of a convent. Mavis Waller continues:

'The gardens where my father and his team grew a vast number of vegetables and salad plants; the greenhouse and southfacing walls which were home to a variety of fruits such as peaches, nectarines, grapes and tomatoes were a joy. There were strawberry and asparagus beds and lots of soft fruits. The dairy herd of Friesians gave us all the milk we needed; each morning I would descend the stairs from our flat to cross the courtyard to the dairy, where Mr Butler, the cowman, would fill my white enamel mug with the creamy frothy liquid still warm, TT tested but otherwise untreated –unlike the chalky, tasteless substance we "enjoy" today. When a cow calved we had the third milking, which my mother would bake in the old kitchen range, having added sugar, nutmeg and a little water if the mixture was too rich; this made a delicious custard which we ate with fruits – I wonder what they do with it these days? At the first opportunity I would steal away to the stables, where Mr Masser would be grooming Kate and Queenie. Kate was a fairly large horse, probably about 15 hands, but of course she seemed to me to be about twenty feet tall! Queenie was the pony who pulled the trap, but when the brougham was used it had to be a combined effort!

'I grew to love these gentle creatures, feeling no fear, and would be allowed to ride Queenie around the paddock… Mr Masser, the groom had no family of his own, and so made a great fuss of me. The chauffeur, Mr Usher, would sometimes take my mother and me to the village, named The Swillett because of the abundant natural springs in the area… Mr and Mrs Montgomery, along with their son Herbert (whose pet name was Sonny) lived in the big house, as we called it, and were cared for by Laura, the cook, her daughter Jessie and various cleaning ladies. I think there was a butler, but he was not very friendly. My mother and Laura became good friends as my mother was probably lonely for the company of other ladies… Sir Henry Wood used to practice in the barn before Proms.'

Sir Henry Wood died over 50 years ago, but as his grandson said in 1998, 'My grandfather conducted almost every concert for the first fifty seasons of the Promenade Concerts, affectionately known as The Proms, and created with Henry Newman, the finest musical festival in the world.' Mavis Waller goes on:

'As well as Ladywalk, Mr and Mrs "Monty" as they were affectionately known also owned the Chorleywood Hotel, later renamed The Sportsman. In those days it was an up-market establishment where actors, diplomats and musician friends of Sir Henry Wood (who lived in Appletree Farm on Chorleywood Common opposite the Black Horse) would stay; of course, being handy to the railway station was handy for London. Ladywalk provided most of the produce needed for our house guests and the hotel; the hotel would also take in our overflow when necessary. The car, pony trap and brougham would be used to transport the guests, if they wished, to places of their choice.'

The Chorleywood Hotel was a most popular meeting place for the social and artistic elite of London and for some Heronsgate residents. It offered comfortable accommodation and good food and a lively atmosphere.

'One day I was summoned to the big house to be presented to the Japanese ambassador who had requested that he be introduced to the little girl whose father was responsible for providing the wonderful selection of fruit and vegetables which he had enjoyed each day. He gave me a large box of chocolates, which I grasped excitedly quite forgetting to say "Thank you". I was called back by my mother and given a lecture on good manners – I never forgot to say "Thank you" again! There was a back entrance to Ladywalk which led into the lanes of Heronsgate; this was fitted with an old-fashioned "kissing gate" which was a great source of amusement to me.' (This was the footpath shown in the Ordnance Survey maps of 1898 and 1914 leading from Long Lane to Ladywalk Cottage and into Nottingham Road South).

'Just down the road was Nottingham Road South, where there were a few houses, one belonging to Mr and Mrs Dyer, who ran a small post office and a shop with the help of two of their daughters, Phyllis and Madge. I do not know what Phyllis did for a living otherwise. Madge rode a delivery bike for Mr Jesse Snook, the village butcher who was a very accomplished equestrian performer. Mr Snook was a very kind man, whose shop was beautifully clean. The walls were tiled in white with blue Dutch windmills on every other tile, and there was always fresh sawdust on the floor… One day while playing in the grounds I noticed my mother and father looking skywards: I saw an enormous cigar shaped, silver object in the sky over the rooftops. This, I was told, was the R100 airship on its way back to Cardington for mooring.

'When I was about seven the estate was sold and the new owners brought staff with them so we had to leave. It broke my heart, but perhaps it was for the best as the house was pulled down and was later rebuilt facing the other way round. It is still impressive, but not my Ladywalk; that has gone forever but the memory of it will remain with me always.'

Entrance to Ladywalk Wood from Nottingham Road South

Miss Montague was recorded as the new owner in 1922 and Archibald Wilson was the owner when Ladywalk was sold to the Leonards in 1931. The Leonard family lived there happily for over three decades. Peggy Walthall, eldest daughter of Hugh Leonard and sister of David and Audrey, now living near Cirencester in Gloucestershire remembers her days at Ladywalk:

'My father bought Ladywalk in 1931 and it took 3 years to pull down the old house and build the present one on exactly the same foundations. We moved in in 1934. In those days we had a large staff both in and out: three gardeners, chauffeur/handyman, groom for three horses and a pony, cook, kitchen maid (always Welsh because my mother came from Wales) two housemaids, butler, nurse and a daily help. We had a very happy childhood. There were lots of outdoor sports, riding, walking, tennis parties etc. Ladywalk has a flat roof and on nurse's day off, I loved to sneak up and climb out on to the roof and over the edge and down on to the gutter. I was seen one day by the cook and had the whole household staff trying to persuade me to come down! They were all standing round outside the house.

My father used to leave the house at eight o'clock every morning to drive to work in Hackney Wick, always getting there by nine o'clock. He never missed even all through the Second World War, though he quite often had to stop and get under the car during an air raid. He was the commandant of the Home Guard and they always met at Ladywalk every Sunday evening and then played snooker. All the bits of wrought iron were removed during the war to go towards the war effort - notably the lovely gates at the top of the steps by the front drive. Ladywalk was often burgled - one day they stole so much they had to use the Rolls Royce to cart it all away!'

David Leonard recalls that Alfred and Ivy Willis lived at Ladywalk Cottage after the Second World War and during the 1950s. Alfred Willis was the farm manager for Hugh Leonard's small-holding enterprise; he was also the joint owner of the Guernsey herd, which three years in succession won the small farm award for best Guernsey herd cream and milk in Hertfordshire

Lillian Carpenter of Selwyn Avenue, Richmond, Surrey and nanny to Michael Bowler (Herons Lodge - plot 13) during the war, told the following story to the Watford Observer in March 1997:

'I have, alas, no exact date except to say it was during the war and I was returning late at night to Rickmansworth after seeing my fiancé, who was then a curate in London. The walk from Rickmansworth Station to Long Lane, where I was then living was a considerable one. I doubt whether many young people would undertake it on their own these days. On this particular night there was, strangely, no gunfire. I was about 200 yards from where I was living when I heard a nearby church chiming midnight. A bright, full moon shone, lighting up the lane, when suddenly a headless, draped figure appeared about 50 yards in front of me, and moved steadily towards me. Before reaching me the apparition suddenly turned into a very thick hedge and disappeared. Though petrified, I glanced to the place in the hedge where it had disappeared as I quickly passed, but there was no visible break suggesting a gate or opening.

I ran the rest of the way home, passing a property called Lady Walk and entering a gate next door which led to the house where I was then living. Exhausted, as the drive to our house was a long one, I thought I would never reach familiar surroundings. Next morning I told my employer, who hastily declared: "For heaven's sake, don't tell the maid, or she'll be leaving us"!

The story was that the lady, as in the aforementioned Lady Walk, was murdered in the last century, and that at certain times her apparition appeared. So I assumed, I must have been in the lane at one of those spe-cial times. You can imagine I avoided a late night in the lane again! I am afraid my family did not take the story seriously, and would joke and say "Mum, what about your ghost story about the lady with her head tucked under her arms?" Alas, I have never been able to find out any more of the history of the unfortunate lady.'

Beaumont House boys, Michael Gibbins remembers, were frightened to go down to Ladywalk woods after dark for fear of coming across the headless lady. Was she one of the nuns from the con-vent near Findlay's farm?

In 1968, Ian and Barbara Steers with their four children, Austen, Nicola, Nigel and Jeremy moved from Home Close to Ladywalk. Hugh Leonard had lost his wife, Dora many years before and the children had married and settled in their own homes, but he lived on at the great house quietly and unobtrusively. The fine Ladywalk house, whilst maintaining its structural excellence, had become somewhat lonely and when Hugh died Ladywalk was sold. Its new owner, Ian Steers, was the ideal purchaser. He restored Ladywalk to its former glories and offered a warm welcome to his many friends and the residents of Heronsgate. He provided courteous and considered advice on many matters affecting the lives of residents, including the controversial problem of the M25 motorway and plans to make Heronsgate a conservation area. For nearly 30 years the Steers enjoyed beautiful Ladywalk – the house certainly attracted long-standing residents. But in 1997 the Steers' occupancy was to come to an end and the house was sold to a family from Saudi Arabia.

 CHAPTER ELEVEN

The Years of Consolidation 1918-1939

The war was over; it had left its dreadful toll. In remembrance of Heronsgate and nearby residents who had lost their lives, a war memorial was erected outside the church adjacent to Stockport Road. The memorial was designed by Bertram Haigh and was placed on its present site in 1921. It is a memorial to those who were killed in action. It remembers:

Private Fauntleroy Copland, The Nook, Heronsgate (Wiverton). No. 2005 London Scottish Regt. Died 14 June 1915 aged 18. Buried in France, Cambrian Churchyard Extension, Row E, Grave 33

Lieut. George L'Estrance Cramer, Woodside Cottage, Shepherds Lane, Chorleywood. 2nd Bttn., Royal Munster Fusiliers. Died 16 July 1915, aged 18. Buried in Bethune Town Cemetery, Plot 2, Row J, Grave 8.

Capt. George Finch, Royal Army Medical Corps. Died 8 October, 1918. Buried in Iraq, in Basra War Cemetery, Plot 1, Row O, Grave 21.

2nd Lt. Claude Pendarvis Goodman, 4th Bttn., The King's Liverpool Regt. Died 16 August, 1916. Buried in Caterpillar Valley Cemetery, Langueval, France, Plot 14, Row B, Grave 7.

Capt. Robert Thomas Patey, MC, 1st Bttn., The King's Liverpool Regt. Died 20 May, 1917. Buried in France in Heninel Croisilles, Road Cemetery, Plot 2, Row B, Grave 7.

Beaumont House boys who died in the First and Second World Wars are mentioned in the Beaumont House chapter 16.

People looked back on the prewar years as a golden age, an age of stability and prosperity, an era in which a great British Empire had been established and a civilization created which should be restored, but what kind of future lay ahead for Heronsgate and the surrounding areas? The surrounding villages, towns and farms played their role in Heronsgate's postwar life, offering work, shopping facilities, banking and social amenities. By the early 1920s The Swillett was still a small but expanding settlement. Jesse A. Snook was not only a fine equestrian performer, but he had also established a butcher's shop in the property next door to what is now an etchings studio; Blackett's Stores (now called Hadley) was at the northern end on the far side of the main road as it bends towards another set of shops already in business at the northeast end of The Swillett. Almost all The Swillett cottages and houses, as we see them today, had been built. There were three pubs, The Stag, The Dove and The Land of Liberty; some say The Swillett was aptly named. However the real origin of this village name lies in that it was built on a 'swill', which is an old term for a deep bowl within gravel. This 'swill' has never been known to run dry. Chorleywood,

Groceries are delivered in the 1930s at the corner of Stockport Road and Nottingham Road by Mr Fred Fuller

according to the census of 1921, had 2,444 people amongst whom were counted the residents of The Swillett and Heronsgate. Heronsgate's population had risen to over 300 accounted for by the new houses, the large families of those days, and the number of living-in servants.

Chorleywood had doubled its population since 1901, but still in 1921 had comparatively few shops. There was Young's, the ironmongers, and Ryders opposite on the corner of Berks Hill and Lower Road. C.F. Pain, the chemist, was situated on the corner of Lower Road and Shire Lane. Tracy's Stores had opened just by the railway bridge in 1904 on the present site of the insurance brokers, but had moved – some believe – to nos 2 and 3 Colleyland in 1910. It was a general store, butcher and post office in the 1920s. When I owned no 1 Colleyland in the 1980s, its former function could be seen in the scullery where there was a large beam used for hanging the grain which would be used to bake the bread. For this cottage had been the bakery (possibly Wilsons), established in the 1910s. Lower Road and Chorleywood West may have contained comparatively few shops, but Colleyland and The Swillett had their range of shops.

When The Sportsman Hotel, then called The Chorleywood Hotel, was built in the 1890s, it attracted a number of temporary shops which stayed. These included Achille Serre, Edlins, The A1 Boot depot, Coutts Bank – the first bank in Chorleywood, Swannell and Sly – the estate agents, and Darvell's coal merchant's office. The Chorleywood Hotel in the 1920s under the Montgomerys was to be particularly popular with the artistic and musical fraternity as recounted in Mavis Waller's memories in chapter 10. The roads of Chorleywood were not surfaced until 1914, and even in the 1920s presented hazards for pedestrians, horse traffic and the motor vehicle. The Memorial Hall, to commemorate those who had lost their lives in the First World War, was erected in 1922.

The iron shed – once the navvies' canteen for the railway builders, then Rose's tea room – was by this time the clubhouse for Chorleywood Golf Club, which had an interesting 18 hole golf course running mainly around the perimeter of the 180-acre common land opposite. The course was reduced in 1922 to nine holes due to an economic crisis within the club, falling membership and difficulties with the locals. The committee did not encourage the locals to join. It wished the club to remain primarily for members of both Houses of Parliament, Harrow schoolmasters and members of the Guards Club. Membership started to fall when the railway authorities withdrew the rights of the golfers to concessionary travel tickets. There was a major disruption when 150 live grenades were discovered on the common due to the activities of the Bomb Squad in the war. The golf club also fell out with the locals over the question of grazing rights: the golfers did not like the sheep and the grazers did not like the fairways being mown, and went so far as to protest by lying down in front of the golfers as they were about to hit their shots. The locals were also angered by the fact that there was no protection for them against injuries by flying golf balls.

John Gilliat, the president of the club, had died in 1912, and John Henly James Batty, the new Lord of the Manor of Rickmansworth, became president of the club in 1918; but he was unable to calm the locals whose antipathy to the club had been furthered by the fact that they were only regarded as potential groundsmen or caddies. There had been earlier mini problems, including the question of Sunday play. There was the time when the vicar of Chorleywood church had been asked to remove a notice which he had placed in the middle of the 12th green; the time the golf club roller ran out of control demolishing the right hand end of the kennel complex of the Berkeley Hunt near Darvell's pond. And there was a clash with the cricket club when they found the golfers crossing the cricket pitch on the way to the 12th green, but this was solved amicably by the golfers playing the first hole twice. However, another major crisis arose when the locals asked the golf club to sell the orchard on the south side of the clubhouse for the erection of the Memorial Hall. This greatly angered many of the golfers who regarded the orchard as their short cut from the station. The situation worsened when the Montgomery family, who were landlords of the Sportsman and lived at Ladywalk, threatened to close part of a footpath crossing their land to the golfers. However, relationships were to change for the better when an artisans' section was opened in 1924. I was unable to trace anybody from Heronsgate as having been a member of the golf club prior to 1924: they, too were barred from being members.

Soon after the war, transport services expanded. From about 1900-1920 the Old Berkeley Hunt and later Bertram Mills (the circus owners) had provided a twice-weekly horse drawn carriage service from Rickmansworth to Wendover starting at The Swan Inn and stopping at the White Horse (near Chorleywood church), and the Bedford Arms, Chenies where horses might be changed. The Bedford Arms was owned by the Duke of Bedford of the Russell family until 1954. Passengers completed the journey at Wendover having stopped at other coaching inns on the way. The earlier stagecoaches had not passed through Chenies. To complete the journey to Heronsgate, The Gate Inn, not far from the White Horse, would provide a horse or horse and trap for hire. On one such journey home in 1921 a Heronsgate resident might have seen Michael Collins, the Irish leader and freedom fighter entering a cottage near the Black Horse whilst negotiating terms for the partition of Ireland. These horse drawn carriages were a much valued form of transport. The railways had helped the situation for Heronsgate residents. However public transport was vastly improved in the area in 1921 when route 336 Leyland double-decker buses and 336a AEC half-cab buses started on a route from Rickmansworth to Chesham via Chenies taking the high road through Chorleywood. They went four times there and four times back on a daily basis. The buses were a much-welcomed addition; but still most people travelled only on essential occasions and horse transport was common until 1945.

Flaunden with a population of 175 and Sarratt with a population of 628 were seldom visited by Heronsgate residents; but Rickmansworth was a popular attraction: it was the nearest large town, and with its rural surrounds boasted a population of 8,657, growing from just over 7,000 at the beginning of the century. It was to see considerable residential development in the early 1920s, particularly at Grove Road and Springwell Avenue. It was a thriving town offering a complete range of shops, services, pubs and hotels. The old coaching inn, The Swan is first mentioned in 1656 and the railway hotel, The Victoria was opened in 1887. Heronsgate residents would walk or go by horse or rail to Rickmansworth not only to work or shop but also for their social activities. A cinema in the old town hall, opposite The Swan Inn, opened in 1912; a swimming pool in Ebury Road opened in 1909. Wright's garage, built in 1920, made the automobile available to the few who could afford it. Further away to the east and north were other large towns such as Berkhamsted (7,292 people), Hertford (10,702), Hemel Hempstead (13,826), the city of St Albans (25,593) and Watford - together with its rural surrounds – a settlement of over 50,000. And, of course, to the south: London.

Thus by 1921, the areas surrounding Heronsgate were expanding rapidly not only in population numbers, but also in new buildings and the facilities offered. The main drains had been laid out and

High Street, Rickmansworth looking east towards Church Street. The Swan Inn is on the left

a sewerage system developed in Chorleywood. Heronsgate had its own drains but the sewerage was stored in cess tanks collected by the Wearing brothers under contract. Gas was the main source of power. The first electricity cables were not laid in the area until 1926. Heronsgate's lanes had altered little since O'Connor's days, but they were busier. No longer was it a rural backwater. Some people might pass Heronsgate by; but the workers from Dodds Mill in Chenies, from Wilks Tannery in Uxbridge Road in Mill End, the gravel diggers from Rickmansworth, and the watercress-beds workers in West Hyde used to visit the Land of Liberty or The Dove or The Stag pubs.

But still farming was the main activity of the area and there were a number of large farms close to Heronsgate. The Wearing family have been farming in the area for three generations and had established themselves when the first settlers moved into Heronsgate in the late 1840s. At one time they farmed Clements, Hubbards, Blacketts (now Dove Park), Bullsland and Hill Farm. By the 1920s the six Wearing brothers were farming Bullsland, Blacketts and Hill Farms. They had about 800 acres of mixed farm land, of which 100 acres were devoted to pasture land for their milking herd of 50 cows. Farming was all organic in those days – hence the low stocking rate per acre. The milking was done twice a day by hand by a team of four milkers sitting on their stools and it took two to three hours to complete the task. The milk was then put into churns and taken by horse and trap to the neighbouring communities, such as Heronsgate. Here each household had its measuring cans, usually one pint.

Wearings were not the only farmers who delivered milk to Heronsgate. Sammy Clark in his pony and trap was a regular sight in the Heronsgate lanes and he worked for Poulters (Shepherd's Farm, Mill End). In addition to the milking herd, the Wearing brothers carried on the typical mixed farming activities of the day: cattle were reared for their beef, sheep for their wool, pigs for their pork, poultry for their eggs and meat, and all to produce their young to keep the stock numbers at the required level. There were also the arable crops, particularly wheat and potatoes. The wheat harvest was cut, threshed and stored in the granary. Later the grain was placed in two and a quarter hundredweight sacks hired from the railway authorities at Chorleywood. It took two men to lift these sacks on to the lorries which would take the wheat to the purchasing merchants, for instance, at St Albans. The potato crop would be dug out, picked up by hand, put on the horse drawn farm trucks and placed in 18-inch deep holes. Then the holes were covered with straw and soil and clamped with a cover to prevent damage and rotting by the weather.

At peak times there would be over 20 workers employed by the Wearing brothers: milkers, general farm labourers and casuals. There were characters amongst the workers, such as 'Uxbridge Emma' and 'Jessy' who lived in a hut in the woods to the east of Heronsgate. Jessy was the supreme hoer of the area. He could do one acre per day, while Emma sat and brewed the tea and made the refreshments to keep Jessy content. (He was found dead of a heart attack in his hut in the 1950s). Then there were 'Jack' and 'Noddle'. Jack was a general farm worker and he and his wife used to keep the workers happy on a summer's night, while Noddle played the accordion and Jack sang as they boiled or fried their evening meal. Often the local gravellers used to come and talk and the air was full of country chat. There was 'Ginger Billy' who worked for the Wearing brothers and 'Welsh Tommy', who had a poor chest as a result of being gassed in the First World War. Alfred

Miles was the champion milker and ace post splitter. He had a great reputation amongst his fellow workers. They were good men who worked hard by day and loved their beer by night. On most nights the Wearing workers could be seen at the Dove pub, opposite the present post office, together with the gravellers and millers. The gravellers were usually men who had been forced to leave their homes to live a wandering life. Although evenings at The Dove were boisterous, there was never any harm done and strangers were always welcome. Willy Webb, the butcher, who in the 1950s was to build a bungalow in Heronsgate, was mine host from the 1930s to the 1950s at The Dove, having taken it over from his parents-in-law who ran it in the 1920s.

Other important characters were the horses, not usually the English shire horses, but rather the French equivalent – which were clean-haired and did not gather the mud after a day in the fields. They did the heavy work, the ploughing and carting.

Findlays, similar to the Wearings, was a mixed farm. It supplied milk to Mill End, West Hyde and Maple Cross. These farms were at their peak in the 1920s. They were an important source of food and also a cultural influence on Heronsgate. The 1930s and the years of depression were to be a warning to farming, but Wearings and Findlays survived and are still enthusiastically farmed by their successors today.

Heronsgate was much influenced by this mix of urban expansion and successful farming. As a result of its still rural situation, it maintained its own agricultural character as seen particularly in a number of smallholding enterprises, but it also was to continue its own special development.

The two schools Beaumont House and The Firs – both established before the First World War, and the YWCA, provided the link with the past. The Misses Richardson ran The Firs as a girls' school with some boys throughout the 1920s before it moved to Heronsfield in Old Shire Lane. Later the Miss Richardsons moved into Waterfield next to the Land of Liberty where they lived until after the Second World War. Amongst pupils who attended The Firs were Dorothy Haigh (Bertram Haigh's daughter) and Michael Bird of Rosecot. Beaumont House continued to offer an excellent education for boys of preparatory school age until the 1970s.

Herons Lodge was used by the Young Women's Christian Association until 1930. At first the lease was held from Baron Kinnaird by Miss C Watson and after her, by C.W. Groudace and finally by I.M. Pitt. The estate of Baron Kinnaird (he died in 1927) sold Herons Lodge as a free-hold property in 1930. Baron Kinnaird, whose family seat was at Rossie Priory, Perthshire in Scotland was the 11th Baron. Kinnaird House is now a hotel, famous for its food and giant salmon. Baron Kinnaird had been a director of Barclays Bank, Treasurer of the YWCA, President of the YMCA, President of the Football Association (he played for England) and although the YWCA no longer had its hostel in Heronsgate, Baron Kinnaird's successors still continued to support and take a keen interest in the YWCA. A.L. Mulholland was the new freehold owner and in 1933 it was bought by Mrs E.M. Bowler. She had a three-roomed cottage built to house their gardener, Mr Clarkson who had moved with Mrs Bowler and her son from their home in London; the Clarksons would later move to Wood Croft. Thus began the Bowler family's long association with Herons Lodge which survives to the present and it is now lived in by its third and fourth generation of Bowlers.

Laurel Mount (plot 16) at the turn of the century with extensions at back

Peacetime brought back the money and ability to develop Heronsgate's houses. The first rumblings of building activity began immediately the war was over. In 1918 Heronsgate House, the site of the original Chartist school was to change its name to The Grange and its owner Gordon Richards was to carry on the structural changes begun by William Hutchison. Alterations were made until 1930, leaving this fine house much as we see it today.

The 1920s and 1930s saw much development elsewhere too. Between 1928 and 1929, Major Aston, the owner of Craven Cottage, opened up Cherry Tree Lane and built Westfield Lodge, Newells Cottage, Virginia, Berry Cottage and Tighe-an-Bias (now called The End House) each with one third of an acre on the original four-acre Craven Cottage site. They were built in the neo-Georgian style; Charters was a further addition in the 1930s. The Cherry Tree Lane houses were the first and only multi-house developments in Heronsgate and became known, rather disparagingly, as 'Aston Villas'. In 1933 Dr Ross purchased an acre of land from the Daphnes plot to add to her property – Tighe-an-Bias – and thus increased the acreage of the Cherry Tree Lane houses.

The 1930s saw more development. Penny Firs built in 1937-8 by Mrs Davidson (Betty Bird's aunt) on a half-acre plot of land formerly part of Rosecot was a new addition to Halifax Road. Mrs Davidson returned to Heronsgate on the death of her husband. She had her house architecturally designed similar to her former home in Sussex; it was built internally of oak and pine with windows of a ship's design. Improvements to Chartist cottages went on, for instance, at Rosecot and Craven Cottage, often under the supervision of Bertram Haigh, the architect. The Chartist cottages – with few alterations, and new smaller cottages were by now often occupied by gardeners, handymen or women in service at the big houses. This was particularly the case in Nottingham Road, where Pixie House was built in 1934, and a new gardener's cottage was built at Bramble Close in 1936.

Both these new additions were on the Daphnes plot 31, owned by Mrs Kingham until her death in 1929, and then by the Topleys.

By the end of 1936 all the main services were available to Heronsgate residents; some chose not to take advantage of these facilities. The first electricity cables were laid in Chorleywood in 1926 and reached Heronsgate shortly afterwards. Gas had been available since 1907, when the Rickmansworth Council laid the mains to Chorleywood. Running water had been pumped into Heronsgate in the late 19th century since the Rickmansworth and Uxbridge Valley Water Company was formed in 1884. The water was obtained from boreholes in the chalk, often only 15 feet deep. It was then brought up to the surface via a number of pumping stations which fed into a common system. Additional pipes and stations were added as required – for instance, a pumping station was built at North Hill, Chorleywood in 1939.

The telephone was slow to come to Heronsgate; the post offices prior to 1912 had turned down offers to become a telephone exchange. Chorleywood West sub post office, at the bottom of Shire Lane, had opened a telephone office in 1905, and it would have been possible for Heronsgate households to acquire a line via Chorleywood, but expensive. By 1936 some houses in Heronsgate were on the phone, connected to the manual exchange in Lower Road near to the downside railway exit. Walnut Tree Cottage acquired its own underground telegraphic line in July 1925.

The sewerage system was laid during 1936 causing much disruption in the lanes as the pipes ran down the middle, but soon this was forgotten and the lanes were restored to their O'Connor-like appearance. Some houses still had their outside toilets but Heronsgate was mainly keeping pace with the conveniences of the early mid-20th century.

Between the wars many Heronsgate residents were earning their livings in the surrounding areas and in London but the O'Connor smallholding tradition was carried on by the likes of Mrs Kingham at Daphnes, Don Warman at Homeland and the Misses Kidner, who ran a boarding kennels, at The Orchard.

Mrs Kingham was a widow. She died in 1929, aged 75. She had given up her small school, previously mentioned and farmed

The main drains are laid outside Craven Cottage and Rosemary Cottage (plots 29 and 30) in April 1936. Sam Clark (Roy Clark's uncle) is unconcerned and delivers milk to the residents

her four acres with great enthusiasm and skill. A visitor to Mrs Kingham's property in the 1920s described the day in the following terms:

'It is with great pleasure that I accepted Mrs Kingham's kind invitation to go to her farm. It is a nice, compact little farm of about four acres stocked with well fed healthy rabbits, black calves and poultry. My hostess proved to be one of these sensible, thoroughly level headed women. She is self-reliant enough to depend upon herself for the superintendence and management of her farm. She likes to visit her whole premise once a day at least, so that repairs may be attended to and errors recti-fied. She is an absolutely practical lady farmer and she employs only one man. Mrs Kingham orders her own corn and meal, her bill for these averaging £2 a week; but even this sum is liable to fluctuations, as she makes a rule of having two merchants on her supplying list, and she naturally patronizes the more moder-ate. She rarely purchases a rabbit hutch, but converts wooden cases instead. These are painted black, properly divided inside, and judging by the contented appearance of the inmates they answer the purpose just as well as the latest development in rabbit accommoda-tion. One very neat little house is a combined one for pigeons and rabbits. Mrs Kingham keeps a neat house, bakes her own bread and is just as praiseworthy in her housework as in her farm work.'

Mrs Kingham packing hampers

Frank Warman bought Homeland in March 1920 from Alice Greig who had purchased the property from E.F. Gyles in 1916. The property also included Rosemary Cottage (the original Chartist cottage) which was leased by Posseen Hill. By an agreement between Posseen Hill and John Henry Hortin and Frank Warman the leasehold was sold in November 1920 to Doctor John Wilkins for £700. In February 1928 Doctor Wilkins bought the Rosemary Cottage freehold from Frank Warman, but he, Frank Warman was to buy back Rosemary Cottage in April 1938 and unite Homeland and Rosemary Cottage again. When Frank Warman bought Homeland and the leasehold of Rosemary Cottage in 1920 he also bought out his fee farm rent for £400. On payment of £1 16s as a quit rent Frank Warman acquired certain rights over Chorleywood Common. Frank Warman was a butcher at Smithfield, and it was Don aged seven at the time of the purchase of Homeland and the youngest of seven children, who, when the time came to go to work in the family business at Smithfield, decided he would prefer to run a smallholding. Don started by growing mushrooms using shell cases to build a shed, and rearing free-range hens. But the war came and Don was sent to Wales as a radar controller.

Not a few residents earned their livelihood in service. Just before and during the war, Mrs Libby, formerly Miss Spence was in service for the Van Duzers at The Firs (High Holly). This involved being up at five thirty in the morning to bring tea or coffee to Mr and Mrs Van Duzer. This was followed by boiling the water on the Aga and bringing a hot jug of water to Mr Van Duzer so that he could shave; then it was time to clear the fireplaces and help with breakfast. Next, the breakfast things had to be sorted and the house cleaned and dusted and polished and the bed linen changed and the beds made up. Lunch was normally just after midday and, with luck, there were two hours free in the afternoons - enough time to walk the dogs or cycle to Chorleywood. Dinner was at seven o'clock, by which time Mr Van Duzer, who was a director of Johnson and Johnson, the well-known American company, had returned from the office. By nine-thirty Miss Spence was ready for bed, tired but satisfied. Getting one day off per week was nice, but having every third Sunday free was the real highlight. 10s per week was the pay, but Miss Spence had her own bedroom and she could use the kitchen and was supplied with a blue uniform. She would change for meals into a black dress with a little white hat and white apron. She was expected to wash her own clothes, but the linen and sheets went to the laundry at Mill End. It was a disciplined life, and her father was strict. He, for instance, made sure she did not go into The Land of Liberty pub or The Swan at Rickmansworth. The Van Duzers also had a cook (Florence), Miss Spence's mother, a gardener and chauffeur. The other big houses – Ladywalk and Sherwood also had their teams of people in service.

Alfred Mansfield bought Croft House in the early 1930s, and in his book 'I was in Kitchener's Army,' he writes about life in Heronsgate at that time:

'The original O'Conner cottages of five rooms were blessed with one tap on main water supply, no provision was made for any type of installation for heating the water. Facing south on the cottage I proposed to occupy, a large glass verandah had been added. Our first move was to convert one of the upstairs rooms into a bathroom and separate toilet. Downstairs one room became a second bedroom pro tempore. The other two rooms served as kitchen and living-dining room. The glass verandah proved of great value, providing a considerable amount of badly needed space for furniture which we now had. My sister-in-law decided to purchase from me the second cottage (Glenthorne) to which, after temporary alterations, she added three additional bedrooms and a large lounge.

My wife, whilst still in favour of country life, looked with great disfavour on the primitive sanitary arrangements and the lack of gas, electricity and hot water. We thought over the matter very carefully and decided that my financial position had considerably improved, job-wise, and, having arranged the sale of the second cottage, ought to remodel the whole building and install the missing facilities. With a great deal of trepidation I approached a building society for a loan. This was readily forthcoming after inspection of the property and consideration of the plan we had for modernisation. Quite soon we were surrounded by workmen knocking holes in walls and adding a new section facing south, overlooking the garden.

Gas and electricity lines were brought in and eventually a modern dwelling emerged having four bed-rooms, three of good size, the fourth the original cottage bedroom, kitchen, sewing room, dining room, a large lounge and, for good measure, a long entrance hall with covered porch entrance. Part of the original cottage was still visible displaying a sign probably taken from O'Conner's crest. All the cottages carried this ornamental design. Next, my thoughts turned to improving the garage, formerly a cart shed, and converting some ancient pig styes into stables. Most of this latter work was done without professional assistance and proved a very satisfying experience.'

So the years 1918 to 1939 saw great contrast in the lives of the residents of Heronsgate. Some were able to lead very pleasant leisurely lives: the husbands worked hard and played hard, the wives ran the home and the children went to the best private schools. They had their servants; they could entertain their friends with lavish meals, spend their time writing letters, playing bridge and tennis and billiards and croquet. They could visit the smart London restaurants and theatres. Ascot racecourse, Lords cricket ground and Henley were close; they could dress in fashionable clothes. But many were happy with a far simpler lifestyle. Life was more difficult, but they could still enjoy some of the pleasures of the more wealthy. Others were not so privileged; they worked long hours for low wages, but they respected their employers and enjoyed a disciplined life in a rural environment.

CHAPTER TWELVE

Post Offices 1890s-1950

ROWING CONFIDENCE IN THE PERMANENCE of the Heronsgate Estate was seen in the buildings and extensions of the 1890s and early 20th century and the optimism was confirmed by the establishment of a post office. Many residents speak of there having been three post offices and research supports this, although the dates found to be accurate for the three post offices are at variance with previous conclusions. Findings are based on photographs, the Ordnance Survey maps of 1891, 1898, 1918, other maps, visits to the Post Office archive centre, Kelly's Directories and deeds of some of the houses.

Laburnums and Connorville (plots 18 and 19) in the 1890s

The 1891 Ordnance Survey map shows no post office, whilst the 1898 shows a post office at Connorville (plot 19, The Hop Garden). The Swannell & Sly 'For Sale' notice for 1898 mentions it as a shop and post office, so we can conclude it became a post office between 1891 and 1898. The post office archives first mention it as a post office in 1895 when W.M. Fuller was appointed sub-postmaster. Kelly's Directory for the same years lists Thomas Chambers as owning the post office; he also combined the post office with a grocer's shop. Previously in 1890 William Chambers, a relative of Thomas Chambers had run it as a grocery (and before that in 1882 Thomas Baldry is named as the shopkeeper). In 1898 the grocer's shop-cum-post office was up for sale and the following For Sale notice appeared in a local newspaper:

'Heronsgate near Rickmansworth. Mr W.H. Swannell has been favoured with instructions from the owner to sell by auction at the Swan Hotel, Rickmansworth on Wednesday November 30th, 1898 at 7 o'clock precisely the whole of the valuable Freehold Shop property situated in Nottingham Road, Heronsgate comprising grocer's shop and Post Office with two sitting rooms (one with bay window), kitchen, scullery, paved yard, large timber built shed and stabling, together with half an acre of garden, well planted with fruit trees, and two and a half acres of valuable pastureland. Subject to a rent charge of £8 12s 6d. Let at the annual rent of £32 4s and a nominal rent of 5s per annum from the Wesleyan Chapel.'

The fee farm rent of £8 12s 6d was payable to the Prowting Roberts family. Clearly when the Wesleyan chapel was built in 1884, the land had been bought from plot 19 and the sale notice refers to that property; subsequently, the shop and post office were not sold and continued to be run as a shop and post office but some of the adjoining land was sold to J. Dinslage.

The first Heronsgate Post Office at Connorville (plot 19) with Miss King and Mr Saunders

In 1898 the postmaster's salary was raised and in 1899 a telephone office was offered by the central Post Office under guarantee, but the offer was not taken up. In 1900 Thomas Chambers received a warning about being irregular in accounts, and in 1901 there were unsatisfactory comments about arrangements for serving the public.

In 1902 H. Saunders, having formerly been the cab proprietor, took over the shop and Miss Fanny King became the sub-postmistress. In the photograph of the Heronsgate Post Office – at times known as the Connorville post office – which was taken about 1902, the two people shown are Mr Saunders and, I am reliably informed, Miss King who is accompanied by her spaniel dog. Miss King was also to have trouble with the authorities and in 1905 she was cautioned for irregularities in the accounts; in 1906 she received a severe warning for incivility. It was in this year that the Connorville post office closed at this site. In 1907 the Dinslages moved into The Orchard on land purchased from the Connorville three-acre site. Harry Wallbank became the sub-postmaster and shopkeeper on a new site at Glenthorne (plot 34, now part of Croft House). In 1908 Harry Wallbank's allowances were increased on account of his evening duties and in 1909 a boy messenger was employed. All was going well and in 1911 a telephone office was offered again under guarantee, but again the offer was not accepted; then in 1912 trouble came. A minute in the post office records says that there was a deficiency in the accounts. Mrs C. Wallbank, the assistant sub-postmistress was guilty of embezzlement, and the sub-postmaster Harry Wallbank had resigned.

There is no further mention of Heronsgate post offices in the post office archives except to record that in 1912 Henry Dyer became the sub-postmaster in a new post office established at Laurel Cottage (plot 5) leased from Lawrence Josephine Richards, who was the wife of a former

The second Heronsgate Post Office at Glenthorne (plot 34)

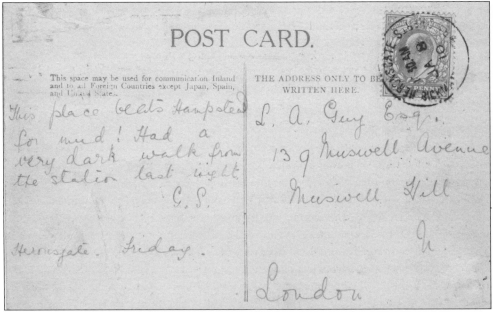

A post card stamped at the Heronsgate Post Office on 8th January 1910. Note the message!

postmaster in Paddington. The Dyers were, in fact sub-lessees, as the Richards had acquired the lease of the property from Sydney Walker in January 1906. Sydney Walker was a Londoner. The Richards leased Laurel Cottage for 99 years for the sum of £240, and for a yearly rent of £4 to be paid quarterly. Laurel Cottage was also subject to the three annuities payable to the Putnam family, the fee farm rent payable to the Prowting Roberts family and the £1 16s quit rent payable to Thomas Ayres, Lord of the Manor at Rickmansworth. Laurel Cottage post office was to have the longest history of the Heronsgate post offices.

From 1912-1948 the Laurel Cottage post office-cum-general stores was run by the Dyer family, first as lessees of the Richards, then in 1921 Henry Dyer who used to be Harold Aston's gardener at Craven Cottage (plot 30), bought the Laurel Cottage lease from Lawrence Josephine Richards for £300. He arranged to borrow £200 from Mrs Richards at six percent. He had the extra responsibility in that their eldest daughter, Kathleen, was blind and deaf; in 1921, aged 16, she was boarded, lodged and taught at the East London Home and School for Blind Children in Upper Clapton, Middlesex. Henry Dyer had to contribute three shillings per week for Kathleen's education and this had to be paid every Tuesday at the Rickmansworth Council offices.

In August 1924 Sydney Walker, the owner of Laurel Cottage had paid off his fee farm rent by paying the Reverend Prowting Roberts £128 and earlier in September 1921, Walker had paid off his duty to pay the quit rent by paying Chorleywood Council £1. Sydney Walker described as a 'gentleman' never lived in Heronsgate but he had bought Laurel Cottage from George Antill in 1899 and it was George Antill who had bought the land from Philip Ford, the original Chartist in 1895 and it was Antill in his brief ownership who built Rowandene between 1895 and 1898.

Post Office work and gardening were satisfying. The general stores were very popular. Here the children could buy their sweets and adults purchase their goods and meet and chat. Mavis Waller remembers:

> 'Just down the road was Nottingham Road South, where there were a few houses, one belonging to a Mr and Mrs Dyer, who lived there – also running a small post office and a shop selling all kinds of wonderful things – a real Aladdin's cave! They were ably assisted by two of their daughters, namely Madge and Phyllis – the third daughter, whose name I did not know, was blind and away at school a great deal.'

In 1935 Henry Dyer died; he left his wife his estate and she ran the post office; his daughters Kathleen, Madge and Phyllis eventually inherited the estate. Emily Dyer died intestate in January 1940 and her daughters carried on running the post office during the war years. Amongst Emily Dyer's documents were found a fire policy for an annual fee of 12s 9d and documents for her funeral and burial in the parish churchyard of Rickmansworth for 9s 6d payable to James Peddle, the funeral director and descendant of the census officer, previously mentioned. But there was no will. The Laurel Cottage post office and shop continued to be run by the Dyer sisters until October 1946 when His Majesty's High Court of Justice confirmed Kathleen Dyer, spinster and Phyllis Longhust (née Dyer), the wife of George Longhurst, the groom at Ladywalk and former jockey, to be the rightful inheritors of the estate; they sold the post office to Miss Troup and moved to The Beehive (plot 1). Miss Troup ran the post office for more than three years and then sold it to the Robertsons, who had boarded at Laburnums during the war. It was closed in 1950, and no longer was Heronsgate to have its own post office although the post box remains.

In 1950, the nearest post office was to be found in the parade in The Swillett. It remained there until the 1960s when it moved to Heronsgate Road; it has now also closed.

CHAPTER THIRTEEN

The Second World War 1939-1945

BRITAIN IN THE YEARS 1918 TO 1939 did not see the expected return to former glories. There had been little attempt to modernise the staple industries such as coal, textiles, shipbuilding; the morals, manners and fashions of the 1920s provoked some outrage. The depression of the years 1929 to 1932 led to unemployment, a lessening in world trade and a fall in prices. The attitude of the ruling classes was to let things sort themselves out. A feeling of helplessness and drift appeared in the people of Britain. There emerged a desire to 'get away from it all' and this showed itself in the popularity of rambling, hiking, youth hostels, the Green Line coach trip and the Butlin's holiday camps.

Heronsgate was largely immune to this deepening domestic and economic crisis, those in employment were well-off and Heronsgate residents were prominent in commerce, the professions and the armed forces; they were able to offer work to domestic servants, gardeners and handymen. So when the war started, Heronsgate reflected the prevalent social divisions but not the economic problems of other areas particularly as seen in the North of England; moreover it was a prosperous, happy and creative community. The war was to unite Britain in a common goal – to defeat Nazi Germany and to remove the threat of German dominance of Europe.

Sunday September the 3rd 1939 was a hot sunny day, an idyllic day, but it is remembered as the day Britain and France declared war on Germany and the beginning of the long campaign to keep Europe free from Nazi tyranny. What did the war mean to Heronsgate? The war dominated, dictated and threatened the lives of people in the locality, not least from the skies, as the bombs fell. The local workforce was decimated as recruitment for the armed forces took hold. Those left behind suffered the privations of rationing, the blackout and the blitz. Although Heronsgate was never hit and nobody injured, there were some near misses: 105 high explosive bombs, 57 incendiary bombs, six parachute mines and one V1 flying bomb fell, and eight people were killed, 11 seriously injured and 45 slightly injured in the Chorleywood/Rickmansworth area. On the nights the 21st and the 22nd October 1940 thirteen high explosive bombs fell in a line from Mill End to Rickmansworth. Dog fights in the sky over the area became commonplace. Heronsgate residents watched them with apprehension.

In the war effort Heronsgate played its part; many of its menfolk were involved in active service, and their numbers included the following families: Arnell, Bird, Clark, Goldsmith, Davidson,

The Auxiliary Fire Service practising at Beaumont House in 1941

Evans (Oaklands), Evans (Field Cottage), Mansfield, Morris, Ross and Simeon. Those who remained behind formed themselves into units of the Air Raid Precautions, Auxiliary Fire Service and Home Guard. The Home Guard used Chorleywood Common for bayonet practice. Here trenches had been dug, areas ploughed up for allotments and mobile Bofors guns brought in. Heronsgate witnessed its own defensive construction in the form of anti-tank concrete blocks placed in the field opposite Ladywalk Cottage (plot 2), but these were never used; some residents built air raid shelters. The population of the county grew by 150,000 mainly through evacuees and troop billeting. The ladies played their part too. They knew 'wasted food costs ships'; they saved scrap paper, aluminium and iron. Mrs Birdwood and her Sherwood ladies, for instance, sorted screws, wrought iron and similar items for munitions for our forces; avoided careless talk because it 'costs lives', made sure to 'make do and mend', were careful to 'put that light out', helped 'dig for victory' and did whatever was necessary to further the war effort including driving ambulances or helping in the canteens at Chorleywood House, where many serving men were lodging.

The Second World War halted development in Heronsgate, but life went on. Air Raid Precautions Group 1 (Heronsgate) of the Chorleywood Division was formed, together with a Home Guard and an Auxiliary Fire Service. In connection with these, the Land of Liberty public house was the headquarters and Beaumont House is listed as 'Main Post 1' with The Firs and Oaklands being 'sub-posts'. Mr Leonard was the officer in charge; Mr Birdwood was an officer, Mr Bowler the sergeant, while Don Warman and others served. Amongst these was Clement Attlee's daughter who was found one morning asleep in the kitchen of The Firs after a hard night with the ARP. Van Duzer was the head warden.

During the war Clement Attlee, Churchill's deputy, lived at Berry Cottage with his aide-de-camp Captain Willis. Before catching the train from Chorleywood to London, Attlee and Willis had their breakfast of boiled fresh eggs collected from the Clark's hens! Miss King still ran her home – now for epileptics – at Laburnums and Mr Topley fitted them with gas masks to the consternation of the local residents, as the epileptics used to delight in hiding in the hedges at night and jumping out with their arms in the air at passers-by. Laburnums was also used as lodgings for officers, who lived in the attic. One family, the Robertsons, was to stay and establish a connection with Heronsgate which lives on today. Opposite was Heron Cottage, which Guy and Jane Gardiner bought in the winter of 1941 / 2 to get away from the bombs in London and for Guy to be closer to his work at Hatfield in the aircraft industry. Guy Gardiner worked for De Havillands where he became a director. First he was involved with the technical school, then he worked on Mosquitoes. Later he was in charge of propellers and, finally, he was involved with the Blue Streak rocket and missiles.

Mrs Libby (née Spence) remembers during the war the Home Guard siren by the post office in The Swillett, which used to howl its warning when the German planes flew over. One day in 1940, Mrs Libby recalls, the air was hot with bullets and a German bomber came down in the woods; another day there was rumour of a signaller acting for the German planes and of parachutists landing. That night when Mrs Libby was out she heard quiet rustling in the hedge; she was petrified, but calmed down when the dim figure went 'Baa-baa'. Mrs Libby said you could see the barrage balloons above Harrow and that a gun called 'Big Bertha' used to move up and down the railway line outside Chorleywood station, so that no one knew its exact whereabouts. It was manned by the Home Guard. Another day there was a huge whistling sound and soon after a bomb

Fire fighters dressed for action. (Don Warman centre; Frank Warman second from left)

landed in Maple Cross splitting a house in half. Nobody knew what it was, but it was probably a 'doodlebug'. Mrs Libby remembers the Sherwood ladies working hard to collect their boxes of sweepings and iron for munitions.

The land girls were billeted at The Swillett and one worked at The Firs, tending the fruit trees and digging the vegetable patch. Don Warman had returned to Heronsgate due to ill health and in February 1940 married Marjorie Brown. They had met when Don used to deliver eggs to Ladywalk and when there was a shoot. Marjorie was a Norland nurse and had come to Ladywalk with the family in 1934 to look after Peggy and Audrey Leonard. Now that Don was home it was one of his tasks to make sure the land girls were well cared for. Mrs Libby also had a wartime romance – she met her husband-to-be at Chorleywood House where he was lodging whilst serving in the forces, and they married in 1945.

Geoffrey Leake was a small boy of three at the beginning of the war. He lived at Rowandene during the war years and he recalls:

> 'My earliest memories can be pinpointed to a time close to the outbreak of World War Two. I can just remember playing on the wooden patio whose boards were taken up to line the "Anderson" shelter which gave us some protection from possible random bombing during the early days of the war. Our first evacuees, some time in 1940, were two brothers. Their sisters stayed with Miss Anderson at Daphnes. But none of us could cope with their ways, and they remained in Heronsgate for only a short time. Then, there was Joan Hughes, a child of my own age; but after a few months she was taken away by her elder sisters. In October 1941, Harold Davis came down from Brixton. He stayed for some months and came and went over the next few years. We got on very well together!'

Other Heronsgate residents had their evacuees too; the Clarks recall that evacuees were either government or privately sponsored and that they, themselves, arranged for 'Verci' to live with them during the war; she had been living in London with her parents, who were anxious about the bombing raids. When the war was over she emigrated to Australia. Verci is now married with two children and she and her family keep in touch with the Clarks.

Geoffrey Leake continues:

> 'In the early days of the war, two German planes (at least, I think I was told they were German) came down in the field below Ladywalk Wood. The craters remained unfilled for a long time. I think there may have been another crater somewhere behind what is now The Dell, but it was not left unfilled for long.'

Roy Clark says that to the best of his knowledge two aeroplanes landed in the Heronsgate area: one was a Spitfire which crash-landed in the field behind Walnut Tree Cottage and the other was a Westland Lysander which came down in the fields below Ladywalk Wood.

Geoffrey Leake again:

> 'The story goes that a man with a foreign accent and carrying a map was seen near the Post Office asking for directions … I wish I knew more! (Was he a spy?). Dr Arnell's son (Pinhaye) used to do low runs over his parents' and his neighbours' parents' houses from time to time in a Spitfire. There was a siren, not in Heronsgate, but certainly an audible part of the wartime scene, and it was situated on the edge of

Chorleywood Common, opposite the Memorial Hall. In 1943, one of the first V-1 flying bombs to hit England came down in the open space between "the stiles" and the closest houses on the Mill End estate. No one was killed, but one man was severely injured and crippled for life.

I remember being warned that if ever I heard a "wheelbarrow" coming (we recognised the V-1 by the noise it made) and the sound suddenly stopped, I should dive under the nearest hedge. I never had to do that, but I remember standing at the garden with my mother and father one Sunday morning, and watching a V-1 come across. I thought it might hit the tall trees in the front garden, but my parents were not concerned. That one landed in Chesham.

When food was rationed, anyone who kept more than a certain number of chickens was expected to supply others on a regular basis. If you could find a poultry keeper to register with, you were assured of a supply of fresh eggs. Mother and father decided this was a good way to help the war effort and, at the same time, to provide that little bit extra for family and friends. Shop eggs were never very fresh! Once mother got into the swing of it, we must have had at least a dozen hens, and twice a day there would be a saucepan of scraps – potato peelings, and so on – boiling away for them. From about 1942, we had several local customers. Our air raid shelter was made of corrugated iron around four, six foot hoops in the shape of an inverted U buried to a depth of about four feet and covered with earth. It would have been eight feet long. In 1945 it was carefully dug up by Fritz Finkenhofer, a man in his thirties with a wife and son; he was one of many German prisoners of war held at a camp near Chorleywood Common. While awaiting repatriation, these men were allowed out to work for a small wage. If my memory serves me right, the minimum pay was a shilling a day – this may be compared to the £2 12s 6d a week earned by a bus conductor at about this time. Fritz was an exceptional man, who would keep his fellow prisoners waiting while he made sure we had enough firewood for the night.

As can be imagined, some of the young men with him were very disillusioned. What a wonderful Christmas dinner we had that year! We started with about four guests. By late afternoon, when others were returning from work (yes, on Christmas Day), there must have been over a dozen crowding into the dining room. By nightfall, the cupboard was bare.'

Geoffrey's father was too old for military service but he used to travel daily by train from Chorleywood to his office in Moorgate and his memories of his staff at the office include the following:

'A junior clerk, Miss Betty Hughes aged 17, had her home wrecked. Crawling out of the debris, she helped to rescue her little sister aged five, and her grandmother. Remembering a lodger's baby upstairs, she clambered up; the banisters were torn away, and she put her leg through a gaping hole, but succeeded in bringing the baby down safely. This was all done in the dark with water from broken pipes squirting all over the place and the smell of escaping gas. Strike a match and you go where the bomb was intended to send you! Then, too, there was the smell of fire from burning homes close by.

Betty lost everything, but with the help of a married sister who lived nearby she was at work early next morning, clad in a borrowed dress, dressing gown and slippers. After spending a few days at Rowandene to recover from the shock, she was given a better job at our head office, whilst her young sister, Joan, stayed at my home as a refugee. They had neither father nor mother, both of whom had died some years before'

Richard Leake also remembers how his office which overlooked Moorgate station was partly wrecked after the station received a direct hit. One evening it took him five hours to reach home by foot, then bus, then train, on foot again, bus again, train, bus, and so on. During the blitz he never knew when he would be home, but he never missed a day at the office. Other residents had similar memories to those mentioned; the war dominated the lives of all.

St John's continued its association with St Peter's, Mill End and in 1940 it was joined by St Thomas's, West Hyde to form the Parish of Mill End and Heronsgate with West Hyde. Walter Breffitt had been the vicar until 1925, when the Reverend Irvin Frost Smith came from Watford. From 1934 to 1947, the Reverend William George Eeles was the vicar of Mill End and Heronsgate and after 1940 also of West Hyde. The Reverend Eeles is fondly remembered both for his work in the parish and for wearing his Home Guard uniform with pride. By the end of 1945 St John's was the spiritual centre of the community having been served by a succession of conscientious vicars; but the Wesleyan chapel was declining in popularity and marred by falling numbers. Beaumont House continued to offer an excellent education and Peter Vezey had begun his reign as headmaster. The war in Europe was over and a new era was about to begin.

List of Colour Plates

Linen sampler by Ann Dawson 1847. Courtesy of Angela Grezo (née Killick). This sampler was found by Angela in an antique shop in the Portobello Road, London in 1981. Fortunately, Angela recognised the O'Connorville school house.

'Rosedene' Photograph courtesy of Zoe Long, Dodford.

'Crowthorne' A pen and ink drawing by Dorothy Haigh. Courtesy of Linda Fernandez.

'Map of the O'Connorville Estate in the Parish of Rickmansworth in the County of Herts'. September 1853 by Edward Burnell Surveyor 32 Bedford Row. Courtesy of Michael Bowler.

'A Topographical Description or an Exact Plan of a Freehold Estate called Woodwick situate in the Manor of Rickmersworth in the County of Hertford done the 30th April 1760 on an actual Survey Extended to the Extream Bounds therof by Ja Backer'. Courtesy of Hertfordshire Archives and Local Studies.

Photographic collage showing the exterior and interior of St John's Church, the Neild stained glass window in St John's and The Wesleyan Chapel (The Hall).

Ann Dawson 1847

Britannia's the land where fell slavery's chain
Had bound fast its victims in hunger and pain
Where no eye would pity when no hand would save
Then came forth to break it o connor the brave
A band of brave fellows whose hearts caught
The sound arose from their slumbers and
Rallied around resolved in defiance of fool
And of knave for freedom to fight with
O connor the brave for
The charter
And no
Sorender

bible and hankor

The chartist school at o connorville near London

"Crowthorns", Chartist Cottage

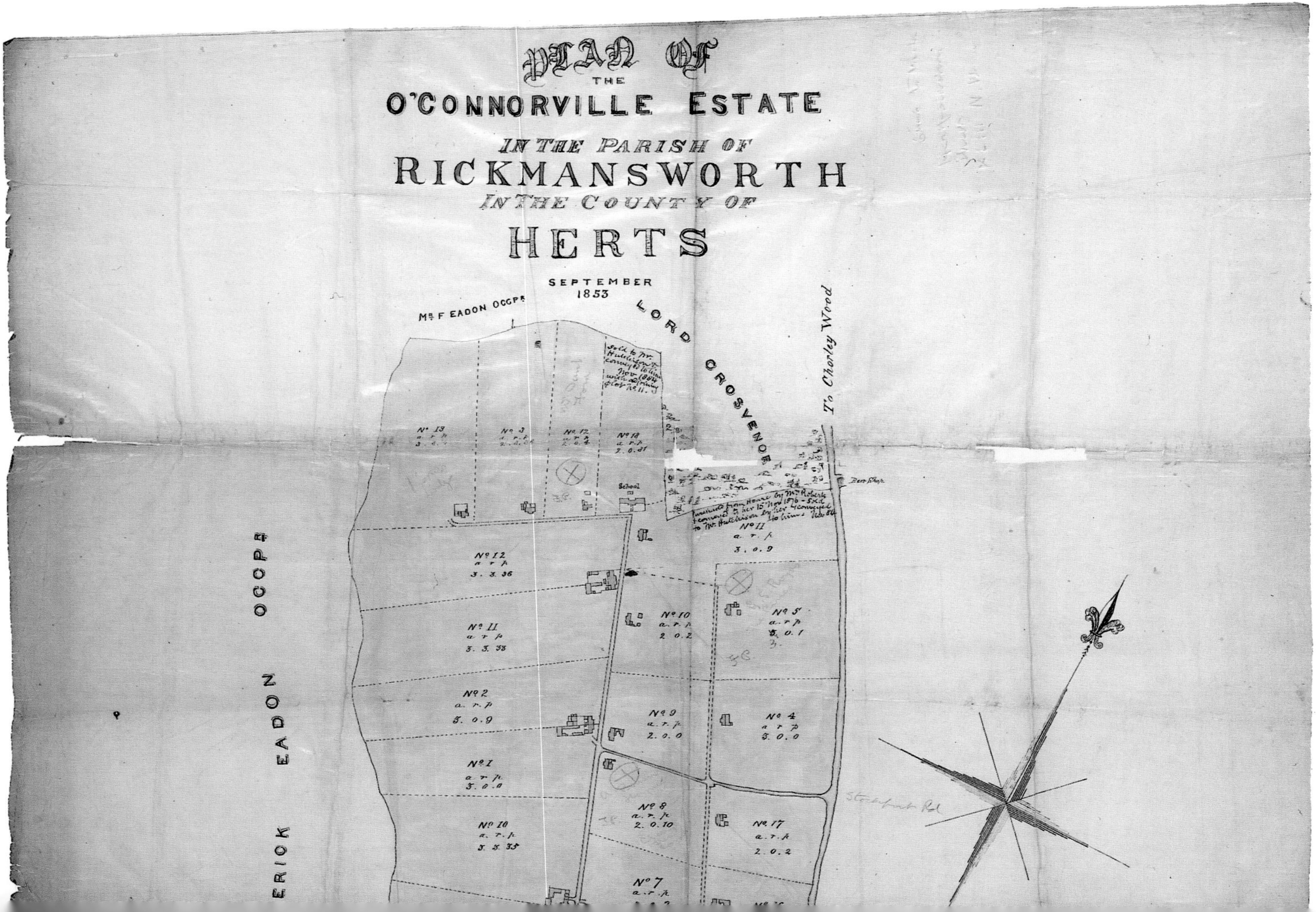

PLAN OF
THE
O'CONNORVILLE ESTATE
IN THE PARISH OF
RICKMANSWORTH
IN THE COUNTY OF
HERTS
SEPTEMBER
1853
M^r F EADON OCCP^R
LORD GROSVENOR
To Chorley Wood
School
Nº 13
Nº 3
Nº 12
Nº 18
Nº 11
a. r. p
3. 0. 9
Nº 12
a. r. p
3. 3. 36
Nº 10
a. r. p
2. 0. 2
Nº 5
a. r. p
3. 0. 1
Nº 11
a. r. p
3. 3. 33
Nº 2
a. r. p
3. 0. 9
Nº 9
a. r. p
2. 0. 0
Nº 4
a. r. p
3. 0. 0
Nº 1
a. r. p
3. 0. 0
Nº 8
a. r. p
2. 0. 10
Nº 10
a. r. p
3. 3. 35
Nº 17
a. r. p
2. 0. 2
Nº 7
ERICK EADON OCCP^R

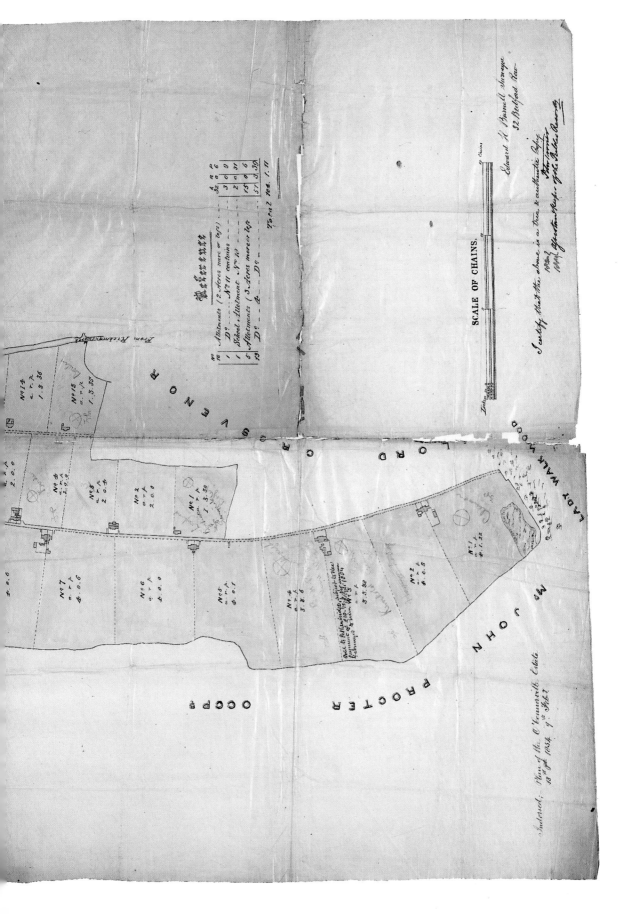

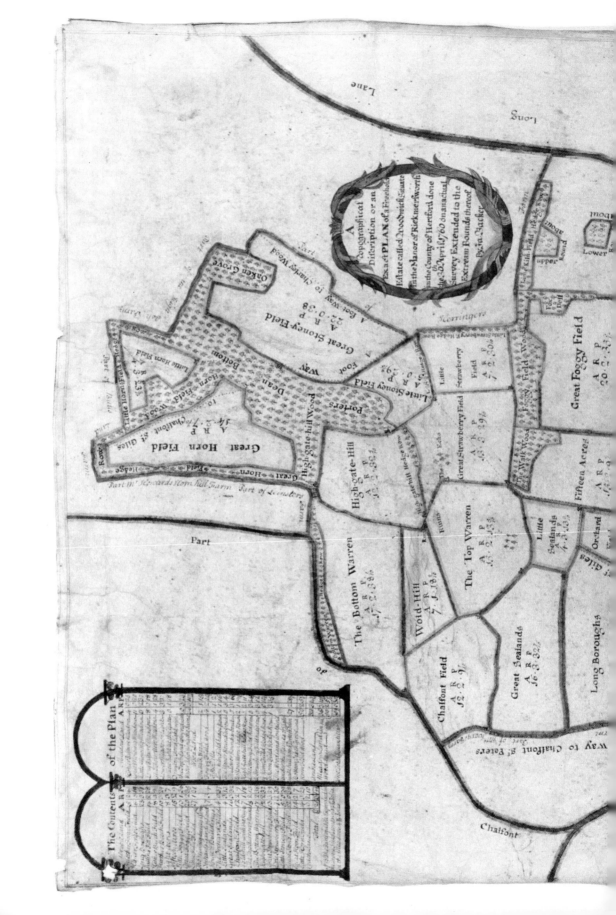

The Turkinpike and Roads from the
sferal parts of Uxbridge and adjoining as Descended from the Town of Uxbridge
with the Branches of Uxbridge and that
which divided between the Parish and
Verge to the County of Rickmansworth

E

Part

Part

Road

Mill End
Mill Cut

Rickmansworth
Ux Bridge

Shire Ditch

The Miter

Colne

The Way to Ravensora

Of

Drayton Road

MIDDLESEX

RIVER

Further
Beech-Field
A. R. P.
10. 3. 29½

Mill-Cut

Hither
Beech-Field
A. R. P.
8. 3. 9½

Puttina-Pit-Field
A. R. P.
12. 0. 28¼

A Scale of Poles

Mill-End

PART   OF

THE

Coach Lane
A. R. P.
6. 0.

A foot Way to Harefield

The Road to the Meadows

Cross

ple
Road

Uxbridge

Hither Pasture
Meadow
A. R. P.
4. 0. 28¼

The Great
Mowing

Meadow
A. R. P.
10. 2. 20

OF

Little Mowing
Meadow
A. R. P.
4. 2. 2½

Long Pasture Meadow
A. R. P.
8. 3. 18¾

Four Acre
Meadow
A. R. P.
4. 1. 4

Lower
Meadow
A. R. P.
3. 2. 12

Part   of

PART

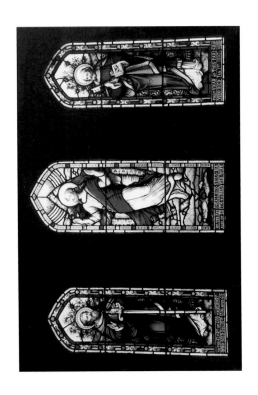

CHAPTER FOURTEEN

The Church Since the War

The church under its vicar, Canon Alan Horsley, is stronger than ever before but changes and improvements have taken place. St John's has been well served by its vicars since the war. Geoffrey Lewis Edwards BD, AKC, formerly Canon of St Albans, was vicar between 1947 and 1972; he was succeeded by Richard Barrie Swift MA and followed in 1982 by Malcolm Stephen Cherry. Canon Dr Alan Avery Horsley MA, PhD, formerly Canon of Peterborough, became vicar of the parish of Mill End and Heronsgate with West Hyde in 1991. Canon Horsley is much admired and respected for his scholarly sermons and devoted interest in the affairs of the church and the wellbeing of his parishioners. St John's has been splendidly served by a number of residents and its churchwardens including Hubert Birdwood, Harry and Kay Bowler, Michael Hatfield and many others.

In the late 1960s the church offered many interesting features. On the altar could be seen a cross and candlesticks designed by Keith Aitken (Lindens) and given in 1957 by the family of the late Mrs Talbot. In the south wall of the chancel was a credence shelf improved under the supervision of Mr Aitken and a silver wafer box given in 1959 in memory of the Reverend G.N. Ryley. Also in this wall was a memorial tablet to Frederick Felkin, who died on the 30th of July 1903 and his wife Mary Elizabeth Felkin who died on the 21st of August 1928. Here also was the Glastonbury chair donated by Miss Roberts, a prayer desk and the lectern donated by Mrs Roberts. Wrought iron triple candelabra were fixed to the north and south walls, two on either side. In the nave were the new seats installed in 1962 and tapestried hassocks made by Heronsgate residents at various dates; there is one with anemones embroidered by Gill Gibbins in memory of our mother Edna Kathleen Foster. A list of subscribers to the new pews installed in 1962 follows:

Mr & Mrs Aitken	Mr Clark	Mr Leonard	Mr & Mrs Poxon
Mr & Mrs Babcock	Mr & Mrs Davidson	Mr & Mrs McCulloch	Mr & Mrs Sainsbury
Mr & Mrs Bird	Mr & Mrs Evans	Mr & Mrs Nockold	Mr & Mrs Steers
Mr & Mrs Birdwood	Mr & Mrs Greaves	Mrs Parsons	Mr Talbot
Miss Bolam	Mr Hale	Mr & Mrs Phillips	Mr & Mrs Tyrell
Mr & Mrs Bowler	Mr & Mrs Harman	Mrs Petri	Mrs & Miss Venn
Mr & Mrs Browne	Mr & Mrs Hatfield	Wing Com & Mrs Panter	Mr & Mrs Yiend
Mrs Craven	Mr & Mrs Killick	Mr & Mrs Pope	

There was also a memorial pew donated by Beaumont House School students past and present. The total required and subscribed for the new pews was £392 10s.

On the west wall was the Beaumont House war memorial wooden plaque. Above that, the stained glass window in memory of the Reverend Neild and his wife and above this, a small circular window of stained glass; just beneath this, a memorial to the Reverend G.N. Ryley in the form of an oak cross. In the ceiling we would have seen the electric light pendants installed in 1958 under Mr Aitken's supervision and the motifs on the edge of the pendants corresponded with those around the edge of the cups of the candelabra.

In 1952 to the joy of the worshippers, a self-operating electric heating plant was installed. Prior to this, church members took it in turn to stoke the boiler in cold weather to prevent the congregation becoming frozen to their pews and failing to respond in the accepted manner to the dictates of the service!

In the intervening years since the late 1960s a number of interesting events have occurred and the church and its grounds have seen changes. The great storm of 1987 caused anxiety in Heronsgate and concern about the well-being of the church. During the night of the 15th and early morning of the 16th of October 1987, hurricane winds of between 97 mph and 110 mph struck the south of England and, indeed, the whole of the British Isles. (However, it was fortunate the hurricane struck at night or more than 19 lives would have been lost). Michael Fish on TV on the night of the 15th of October had hinted at no such weather phenomenon. Heronsgate residents woke on the morning of the 16th to find that the storm had left its mark mainly in fallen trees:

The Grange lost some of its Corsican pines and the monkey puzzle tree planted by William Hutchison over 100 years before. The gale force winds had also knocked down a tree in the church grounds. Fortunately, no structural damage was done to the church itself and it offered the opportunity for a restful area to be created. This was achieved by the removal and cutting up of the fallen tree by a number of congregation regulars under the guidance of Stuart Campbell-Ritchie. Stuart Campbell-Ritchie has supplied the following information about the St John's Church garden:

'Mr Hubert Birdwood (Sherwood), a church warden, tended the garden on his own for many years. On his retirement from duties, Mr Tommy Killick (Long Meadow) organised a rota of gardeners. (There is also a rota of cleaners and flower arrangers). In 1982 Reverend Malcolm Cherry succeeded Reverend Barrie Swift and I was asked to oversee the rota. Together with Mr Michael Hatfield (church warden) an agenda was drawn up to restructure the garden. £85 was spent on implements etc with the aim of providing a leafy glade with bluebells and Rose of Sharon, amongst other plants.

In 1987 the hurricane blew down one of the beech trees narrowly missing the vestry but devastating the garden surrounds. The other beech tree had to be felled due to infection by honey fungus. In 1991 the rear area was totally cleared by a working party and laid out as a restful garden by planting grass seed, creating a border and regravelling the paths. Mr Brian Chilvers and I made a tool shed of timber supplied by Mr Ian Steers from the storms of 1987 and 1990

Donations received from residents of Heronsgate during my period as the gardener are:

Mrs Kay Bowler (Herons Lodge)	Golden Heart Ivy
Mr and Mrs B. Carver (Bramble Cottage)	Rhododendron
Mr and Mrs W. Gillott (Virginia)	Plants
Mr and Mrs M. Hatfield (Sherwood)	Plants

Mr and Mrs B. Chilvers (The Orchard)	Oak Garden Bench
Mr and Mrs A. McQueenie (Whitegates)	Gravel
Mr and Mrs V. Wojcik (Breve House)	Timber and Sand
Mr and Mrs R. Warman (Silver Birches),	
Mrs L. Fernandez (Crowthorne),	
and Mrs S. Lye	Silver Birch Tree

The ashes of the following are laid to rest in the front garden:
Mr Hubert Birdwood and Mrs Brenda Birdwood (Sherwood & Charters)
Mr Austen Evans and Mrs Sylvia Evans (Field Cottage)
Mr Cyril Pope and Mrs Madeline Pope (The Limes)
The following ashes are laid in the rear garden:
Mrs Brita Rice (The Grey Cottage)
Mr Ted Lewis (Laburnums)
Mr Donald Warman and Mrs Marjorie Warman (Silver Birches)'

Inside the church, there have been a number of alterations and additions. There is a plaque which remembers Mr and Mrs Evans. It is to be found on the side of the memorial bookcase and says: 'Given in Loving Memory of Mary Sylvia Evans (1896 to 1977) and John Reginald Austen Evans (1885 to 1979) of Field Cottage, Heronsgate'. Also Mrs Roberts' lectern donated in the 1880s has been replaced by a carved wood lectern in memory of Brita Rice. And a memorial book wonderfully engraved and produced by Dorothy Haigh is to be found in the memorial bookcase. It remembers the dates of the deaths of Heronsgate residents. Brian Carver drew the illuminations – Birds of Heronsgate – and each month a page of the book is turned to correspond with the current month. A majority of the features mentioned earlier remain to provide a fine, working church.

Repairs to the church fabric are always needed and Michael Hatfield, the church warden, told me about some recent improvements:

'In 1994 St John's Church needed a new roof. The estimated cost of £9,500 was beyond the resources of the small congregation. St John's committee set up an ecumenical fund raising committee. They prepared a brochure and sent it to present and past residents of Heronsgate. The response was overwhelming: £18,000 was raised, a quarter coming from past residents. This enabled St John's to undertake a complete refurbishment of the church: the roof was re-slated, gas-fired central heating was installed, the 30-year-old lighting replaced, decayed sections of flooring renewed, new carpet fitted in the chancel, the vestry completely refurbished and the church redecorated inside and out.'

Most recently, inspired by Pam Hatfield with the encouragement of Canon Horsley, the idea of meetings in a quiet garden has been conceived. These gatherings offer an opportunity for stillness and reflection and for learning about Christian spirituality. They give visitors a chance to come to the peaceful Sherwood garden, to 'come with me by yourselves to a quiet place and get some rest' and contemplate. The days have a theme and are led by experts in their field. Recent themes have been a day of meditation inspired by the poems of R. S. Thomas, Welsh priest and poet; God in the garden, following the popular footsteps of clergymen, botanists and naturalists; Chartres Cathedral, letting this ancient monument of faith lead people into contemplation. The quiet garden days illustrate how the Church works beyond its normal boundaries and shows its importance to many within and outside Heronsgate.

Sunday and Wednesday services are attended by a strong group of regular worshippers; and at Easter time and at other dates in the Christian calendar special services are held, but it is at Christmas time that the church is most full. The church is also used for weddings, christenings and funerals; St John's is indeed a focal centre of the community.

CHAPTER FIFTEEN

Houses and Gardens 1945-1970s

It took some time for the British Isles to recover from the Second World War. Petrol rationing, coupons for food and clothes, and Britain's declining position in the world left their mark. By the end of the Second World War, Rickmansworth and Chorleywood had become well-established residential townships, whilst The Swillett had grown into a sizeable settlement with cottages and houses on either side of the road. The Swillett had two pubs, The Stag, and The Dove which was opposite the present post office; at that time it was not a post office but was run by a newsagent - John Birkett. Opposite was the path leading to Quickley Lane and on the left was a small workshop which was used by Ernest Brooks, the boot repairer. Back on the road and to the right was Metro Motors Garage. Mr Quick ran the local general store until P.C. Ball took over; Snook, the butcher, had a shop opposite, Albert Welch had his cycle repair business next door to Snook. The Welch family had given up running the forge. Around the corner and towards Chorleywood was the parade, where W. Webb, the butcher could be found along with Mrs L. Stembridge – the greengrocer, Mrs Elsie Sharp – the haberdasher, and a post office store. This had become a post office when the Heronsgate post office closed in 1950 and was to remain the local post office until the 1960s when it moved to its present site. Thus The Swillett was more or less self-supporting except for a bank; the nearest ones were in Rickmansworth and Chorleywood where there was a Coutts Bank by The Sportsman. But the area had seen little development since the mid 1930s.

Heronsgate mirrored this general malaise, but soon optimism returned. This was reflected in the construction of a number of new houses, extensions to old houses, the arrival of new residents and the desire to create a better Britain. This chapter seeks to explore the further development of Heronsgate and to point out that during these years 1945-1970s, when the British Isles underwent social change, Heronsgate reflected this development too. Victorian values, by which only few were privileged – reflected in previous chapters – gradually disappeared. Heronsgate was to adapt in its own way to the changing social environment. It can be noted here that the Fitzsimmons family – one of the few remaining original Chartist settlers – finally moved out of Heronsgate in 1946 (Kelly's Directory showed them still to be residence at The Beehive in 1942)

Miss Calder, the actress, was the first to build a new house; it was built before the war ended. She owned Woodene and its four acres, but she wanted a house with a view over the fields at the bottom end of the property. There was, however, a problem with the services and the considerable expense of their installation. She also refused to go on to the mains and therefore a septic tank system had to be positioned near the lane. Thus Farfield was built on its present site; a Jacobean garden was laid out over the septic system and a large hole for a pond was excavated by German prisoners of war, which they were later told to fill in.

In 1953 Donald Bruce and his wife bought the plot, on which they built Pinecroft, from Cherry Tree Corner. Thus another Chartist plot was subdivided. The house was not completed until 1956, when the family moved in; it was their home until 1979. Donald Bruce had the house built by his own building company to a Japanese pattern with all eight major rooms on the south side, and hall and landing corridors on the north side. The roof was made of cedar shingles.

Donald Bruce was educated at Donnington Grammar School, Lincolnshire; he had been a major in the Royal Corps of Signals on Eisenhower's staff during the invasion of Normandy and had been mentioned in dispatches. Before moving to Heronsgate he had been Labour member of Parliament for North Portsmouth in Clement Attlee's post Second World War government, during the years 1945 to 1950. He had been given the post of Parliamentary private secretary to the Minister of Health, Aneurin Bevan, the charismatic left wing socialist. and was to help Bevan to steer the National Health Service Bill through Parliament. This created a free health service for all and was in place by 1948. Donald Bruce was also to serve on a select committee for public accounts during the years 1948 to 1950, and by the time he lived in Heronsgate he was working as managing director of Myton Builders, and also writing on economic matters. He was a qualified chartered accountant. In 1974 he was made a life peer and took the name Lord Bruce of Donnington, Baron of Rickmansworth. Between 1975 and 1979 he became a member of the European Parliament and in the House of Lords he has been a Labour spokesman on treasury, economic and industrial questions. The family sold Pinecroft in 1979; Lord Bruce's first wife and children still live in the area.

In a recent letter dated the 7th of May, 1998 to 'The Times', Lord Bruce of Donnington expressed his concern about the Maastricht Treaty and the power of Brussels in the future of Europe. In this case he wrote about Mr Duisenberg's appointment to share its presidency of the European Central Bank:

> 'Indeed many may feel that this whole sordid episode once again demonstrates the power of a Brussels bureaucracy over events and choices foisted on the people of Europe, and unfortunately their governments, to do exactly as it wants without being accountable to anybody.'

It was nice to see a 'Heronsgate person' taking an influential role in British and international affairs.

Fred Babcock bought Midgham Cottage in 1953. It consisted of much of the land formerly belonging to Hope Cottage (the house had been sold in 1941), Ford's orchard, formerly part of The Limes, and lands to the south, north and west. In all there were about 14 acres and the property was renamed Long Lane House. The house was extended in 1985, shortly before Fred Babcock's death. He is survived by his second wife, Peta, who still runs the property as a smallholding.

In the early 1950s the Philbys lived at Little Aymers. In 1955 the house was sold to the Chings. The Philby's two sons attended Beaumont House. Kim Philby went to Westminster School, moving on to Trinity College, Cambridge in the late 1920s; here he became friendly with Guy Burgess, Donald MacLean and Anthony Blunt. In 1944 he joined MI6 and was head of the anti-communist counterespionage department. He, himself, was already a secret communist, having joined the communist party in 1933, when on a visit to Vienna; in that same year he became a Soviet agent. In 1949, Kim Philby became first secretary to the British Embassy in Washington. It was his job to act as liaison officer between MI6 and the CIA. In March 1954, Burgess and MacLean, Philby's diplomatic colleagues, went missing. They were about to be investigated by the police for being Soviet spies. Who had tipped them off? The feeling was that there was a 'third man', a senior diplomat and suspicion was aimed at Kim Philby. He was recalled from Washington to appear in London for interrogation by MI6.

One day in early April in 1954, police cars appeared in Heronsgate to block all the exits but Philby was not there. Later Philby was interrogated by MI6 and in November 1955 he was able to force Colonel Lipton, a Labour MP, to retract his allegations that Philby was the 'third man' involved in the disappearance of Burgess and MacLean. At a press conference Philby denied he had ever been a communist. In the House of Commons, Harold Macmillan, then foreign secretary, supported Philby and the case against him as being 'the third man' was dropped. However, in the same year, Philby resigned from his position in MI6, sold his house in Heronsgate and moved to Beirut where he worked as foreign correspondent for 'The Observer' and 'The Economist'. He obtained this post with the help of the British Foreign Office. During his time in Beirut, he passed information to both British and Soviet intelligence. Philby's association with Heronsgate had ended, but Heronsgate residents' interests were roused when in 1963 he disappeared to Russia and became a Russian citizen. In July 1963 the Government admitted Philby had tipped off Burgess and MacLean and that he had been a double agent. When questioned in 1964, Donald Bruce said he did not know that Philby had lived opposite him.

Kim Philby died in Moscow, but later his body was returned to England and he was buried in the cemetary at Penn church, not far from his home in Heronsgate. Another name associated with British intelligence was RJ Hollis who was captain of Denham Golf Club in 1956 and head of MI5. Was Hollis responsible for the police activity in Heronsgate in 1954?

Cecil Goldsmith, who had started his Esperanto School at Esperanto House (Lindens) in the late 1930s, was still running the school in the 1950s. I remember when my family moved into Heronsgate, a sign near the church on the corner of Stockport Road and Halifax Road which marked the presence of the school. Geoffrey Leake remembers Esperanto House: 'As being divided in two, but who lived in the second part was a bit of a mystery. Cecil Goldsmith was a little man with a deep scar on his face, who impressed a small boy by his secrecy. To further the mystery, his visitors were Europeans of every nationality who spoke this strange Esperanto.'

Who was this mystery man? Cecil Goldsmith was born on the 16th November 1889 at Gloucester and was educated in Birmingham. During the First World War he served as an officer and was wounded in action in France. In the 1920s he began his lifelong interest in the Esperanto language and became a leading figure in the attempt to establish Esperanto as the '1st second-language' of the peoples of the world. The vocabulary used in Esperanto is based on European sources:

60% Latin and French origins and 30% Germanic origins.

The London Esperanto Club was founded in 1902 and the British Esperanto Club in 1903. Cecil Goldsmith became the secretary of the Esperanto group in Birmingham in 1920 and later was secretary of the British Esperanto and of the International Esperanto Associations. He was secretary of the international conferences held at Birmingham (1920), Leamington (1923), Canterbury (1929), Birmingham (1931) and was general secretary of the 23rd International Conference held at Oxford in 1930. He was also a director and secretary of the Esperanto International Publishing Company. By 1937, Cecil Goldsmith was living in Heronsgate, firstly at Lindens, then called Esperanto House and in the late 1950s he moved to One Hundred (Fernhill) where he resided in the 1960s. He was married with two children and carried out his work at Esperanto House and his printing office at The Forge in the Swillett (next to the Stag public house). This involved correspondence with other Esperanto enthusiasts, setting and marking examination papers in Esperanto, administering courses, dealing with accounts, organising official functions and arranging worldwide travel for representatives. The printing office 'Esperanto Printers' under the guidance of Goldsmith's daughter and her husband, Mr and Mrs Oliver, published and printed journals and books in the Esperanto language.

Heronsgate was an important centre for the Esperanto movement and indeed its headquarters from before and until just after the Second World War when the Esperanto Centre was established in London. Cecil Goldsmith died in the 1960s and shortly afterwards, the Olivers took the printing business to western Australia where they continued to operate until 1989 when the publishing rights were sold. The Esperanto movement continues to flourish and is particularly popular in Japan, China and Iran. It is a planned language easy to speak; in 1998 3,200 people from 70 countries attended a conference in the south of France. Cecil Goldsmith of Heronsgate is remembered as a leading figure in the history of the movement.

In 1954 Monty McCulloch's father-in-law had Rusper built. Monty's great-great-grandfather, Mr King, (O'Connor's overseer), had purchased Laburnums from the Chartist James Short. Rusper was built in part of the original Laburnums site and became the home of Colin and Monty McCulloch. Colin became a well-known legal figure and drafter of parliamentary bills.

In 1956, Warbie Knight the owner of Pinhaye, sold two half-acre plots which had been an orchard, from his original two-acre Chartist holding; planning permission had been obtained by the previous owner, James Jones. Firstly Hunters Moon (The Birches) was built for John and Audrey Herring. It consisted of three bedrooms, a kitchen and two living rooms with a single integral garage. The second plot, St Joseph's, named after the patron saint of homes and families was built for Harry and Christine Poxon. It was the last example of a subdivision of a Chartist plot. Both houses since 1956 have seen their improvements and additions; Christine Poxon still lives at St Joseph's.

The central part of Heronsgate near the church may have seen the most exciting events of the 1950s, but things were happening elsewhere too. The 1950s also saw the arrival of new residents – some like Tommy and Dora Killick were attracted by the prospect of running a smallholding. When Tommy Killick bought Long Meadow he found that his predecessors Roger and Kay Barker had built pigsties and a milking parlour and used a naval pump to liquidize manure over their holding.

Roger Barker was a solicitor, but his love of the land turned him to greater ambitions and he left Heronsgate for New Zealand where he became a sharemilker. The Killicks – full of enthusiasm on their arrival in 1953 – bought a cow from the Leonards, and a sow with piglets from their predecessors. The Killicks had one acre of their own land and rented about three acres from Miss Calder (Farfield) for one pint of milk per day and responsibility for fixing the fences. Soon Dora was producing cream and butter and skimmed milk for the piglets, but they were not allowed to sell milk and in 1963 the Killicks ceased their smallholding activities. They had, however, been following the original traditions set up by O'Connor and carried on by people such as Don Warman, Mrs Kingham, J. Reynvaan (a poultry farmer at Croft House between 1906 and 1917), F. Ball (a poultry farmer at Glenthorne in the 1920s) and Kay Bowler.

Tommy and Dora Killick describe Heronsgate in the 1950s as being 'a walking crossroads from Mill End and Rickmansworth to the Chalfonts and Chorleywood'. The Misses Lawrence, who were laundry maids at Beaumont House sold cherries from St Cecilia to the passers-by. One of the sisters was later Horace Clempson's housekeeper, the other married and lived at The Beeches. Mr Bird walked in the opposite direction to get to Watford Grammar School and Angela Killick bicycled to the Uxbridge Road and left her bicycle in a barn (on Findlay's farm) before catching a bus to school. The bicycle was always there when she returned and Tom and Dora had no worries about her safety. At the party to belatedly celebrate the centenary of the founding of Heronsgate held at the Hall in 1958, Tommy provided a cake made with the Chartist emblem on it; he was working at the Bakery Research (Chorleywood Road) at the time.

Some were attracted by the smaller houses. In 1953, my mother, who was ill with cancer, wanted to have a little house near the shops and railway station; instead she fell in love with Heronsgate and only achieved her intention of acquiring a smaller home in Rosemary Cottage. Others such as the Greaves liked the rural atmosphere.

In 1953 Daniel Ford, descendant of the original Chartist, sold The Limes to the Popes. The Ford family had had over 100 years' residence in Heronsgate. Geoffrey Leake's mother was friendly with the Fords and she remembers them as a charming couple who often spoke of the family having once owned the land on which Rowandene stands; they were responsible for building a new house and coach house on the The Limes two-acre section and demolishing the old Chartist cottage in the 1890s.

Meanwhile Don Warman was continuing with his smallholding enterprise. Grandpa Warman died in 1948, but Marjorie had been able to increase the Warman tribe by producing Sheila in 1941, Linda in 1945 and Richard in 1951. They lived in Homeland Cottage until 1947 when Homeland was sold to the MacPhails and the Warman family moved into Rosemary Cottage. By 1950 Silver Birches had been built and Rosemary Cottage sold to the Stephens as a third of an acre plot. Marjorie's mother (Mrs Brown) later moved into Rosemary Cottage Annexe and lived there until 1964. Don was working hard at his smallholding, using the land at the back of Homeland and the land belonging to Silver Birches. At its peak the Warman smallholding had 5,000 hens housed in small sheds and was run on a free-range basis. Don was one of the largest egg producers in Hertfordshire. Feed was bought from Silcox of Rickmansworth (later Bartons) and the eggs cleaned, graded and placed in

Part of Don Warman's smallholding in 1937 with Stanmore Lodge and Long Meadow in the distance

trays for 48 eggs with five trays to a case before they were sent to a packing station. Don also reared pigs and often had five sows in the pigsties at the back of Silver Birches. The piglets, sometimes as many as 60, were kept warm by special lamps and were protected by bars from being crushed by the sow. After being whelped they were fed on meal, but not pig swill, and sold at six months. Another part of the smallholding enterprise was the growing of vegetables and soft fruit. Potatoes, peas, raspberries, strawberries, red and blackcurrants and other crops were produced. Marjorie made jams and bottled the vegetables and fruit. Eggs were sold to Heronsgate residents and other outlets such as P.C. Ball's shop. However, P.C. Ball used to love to bargain and he would not pay the proper price. Chickens were sold to the locals, generally as a special request, and particularly at Christmas time. Don and Marjorie loved the work, but the mid 1950s proved difficult times for the smallholder; in 1958 Don became ill and he was forced to give up the smallholding. Later Don developed Parkinsons and in 1993 died of the disease. Feargus O'Connor would have been pleased with Don and Marjorie Warman.

In the Bradford Road part of Heronsgate only Endlands retained most of its original Chartist acreage; Hope Cottage and The Limes had lost some of their acreage to F.C. Blyth. The original enlarged cottage and barn at Endlands had been burnt down and a new post Second World War style house had been built in 1950. Alfred Mansfield wrote: 'Endland had not been occupied by the people to whom it was left and stood empty after Miss May Beatson's death. Arriving home one afternoon, (in 1941), I found two fire engines, one in my drive, the other further up the lane – they, too, knew it was unwise to proceed further up the lane on account of the cul-de-sac. Hoses had been run out across the meadow to Endland which was well alight; nothing could save it. Soon only a few walls remained standing until the war's end when the gentleman who had so long wanted the property was able to purchase it. The house was then demolished providing bricks sufficient for several houses. A very nice house was later built for the new owner's daughter. The stand of lovely trees escaped all damage from the fire and the odd bombs dropped nearby by the Germans.'

Mr and Mrs Yiend remember:

'When in 1956 we moved into The End House circumstances were very different from today. No speeding vehicles in the lanes, for example, for the simple reason that apart from Stockport Road they were as rough, and rougher sometimes, than Cherry Tree Lane is today and with hollows to collect the rain! Yet never was there any hesitation by tradesmen to make deliveries. The baker called three times a week, the greengrocer twice and the fish man once, with two milk deliveries per day; the butcher and the grocer brought instant service on receipt of a telephone call.

Nor did the lane surfaces worry the Beaumont House boys either. On school days every morning, a succession of small boys wearing purple caps and purple blazers wobbled along on their bicycles, punctiliously raising their caps to all they met – even if they fell off in the doing of it! Every Sunday, boarders from this excellent school (fees £36 per term for day boys) attended St John's and once a month was compulsory attendance for the entire school with the senior boys reading the lessons.

We were a mixed community with the well to do living not many doors away from the gardeners, agricultural labourers, the company directors and the banking and civil service fraternity. Seven residents (by no means all impecunious) kept pigs and some had their chickens too. So all, regardless of their station in life were subjected to the same difficulties of rough roads, large gardens, no street lights or pavements; after all, come to think of it, this was why they had all come to live here anyway. The atmosphere of individuality and of character was everywhere to be found leading to a warmth of a generous community spirit and cooperation.

The Hall had no car park then but by the kindness of the then owners of "The Orchard" the ground alongside the Hall was given to the Heronsgate Association, and the committee and helpers bent their backs to clear the area and lay a rough base. The question then arose what to do with the old and decrepit upright piano that had been used in the Hall since time immemorial. The answer was obvious: bury it under the car park! And there it remains to this day.

Meanwhile a generous gift of a baby grand came from a resident in Long Lane so this also was transported with the assistance of a borrowed tractor and the brawn of residents down Long Lane one Saturday afternoon where the procession became mixed up with the local hunt dressed in all its finery. The Lanes Committee was first created in 1957, as far as memory serves, the emphasis being to muster a team of residents with picks and shovels on a Saturday morning once a fortnight, or was it once a month, for the purpose of filling pot holes with a barrel or two of macadam. Believe it or not a considerable amount of good work was done in this way and with a cheerfulness and fun that emphasized the nature of a friendly but independent community.

One is hesitant to name names now of some of the great characters who lived here then; some have died but not all, but they will never be forgotten for the originality and personality of their interest and approach. All were devoted first and foremost to the upkeep of Heronsgate in the independence and freedom loving traditions of its Chartist history. It is difficult to imagine that we shall see their like again here particularly now that the lanes have been built like motorways to suit surburbia.'

The 1960s heralded another period of change. Ian and Moreli McDougall bought Herons Court in 1962 from R.J. Parsons free from the incumbrances of the perpetual yearly rent charge of £6 8s. It has already been noted that in 1920 R.J. Parsons purchased the fee farm rent from the Reverend W.P. Roberts and F.A.Toynbee, but the Venns at Wiverton were still expected to pay the rent charge of £1 12s to the McDougalls. So after the annual combined cutting of the back hedge and when the McDougalls and Venns were enjoying a gin and tonic after their labours, Mr Venn used to slip £1 12s into Ian's pocket. The Hagyards used to pay the fee farm rent for a while too.

Francis and Isobel O'Loughlin purchased Penny Firs in 1963. Mrs Davidson had died and her son, Ian, had moved to Canada; he had rented it out for a while, but now it was empty and up for sale. The O'Loughlins were pleased to buy and settled in quickly with their family to live in Heronsgate. In 1984 they purchased additional land of just under half an acre from Arthur Bird (Rosecot).

Meanwhile at the Grange, Heyworth Talbot, a legal man like Prowting Roberts, was in residence from 1940-1969. He was a Quaker and chairman of the board of governors at Leighton Park School for many years. Amongst his many talents was his ability as a lay preacher; he was also devoted to his gardens and home. He improved the gardens by planting heathers and bulbs, building an ornamental water garden, erecting walls, tool sheds and creating a grass tennis court which gave much pleasure to many Heronsgate residents. Heyworth Talbot was succeeded at The Grange by Sally and Antony McMurtrie. They too kept their five acres in immaculate order with the help of the Miles family who lived in The Lodge. The McMurtries have followed the traditions of the Heyworth Talbots by being sympathetic and kindly supporters of St John's church.

Time was moving on. Only Ladywalk kept its team of workers: a live-in housekeeper, gardener-cum-chauffeur, and daily helps; but the other large houses had given up their in-service element and the gardeners – Bunce, White and Clarkson had long gone. Their gardeners' cottages were to be occupied by families such as the Carvers (Bramble Close) who were themselves devoted gardeners; they created an idyllic garden of rhododendrons, camellias, azaleas, interesting trees (two from New Zealand) and rare plants (most of which have disappeared down to Somerset). Wood Croft became the home of the builder Clive Morgan, and Linda Fernandez (née Warman) moved to Crowthorne on the death of Mrs White.

Crowthorne offers us the best example of an original Chartist cottage and is a Grade II listed building. The old well is still there, as also are the ones at Laurel Cottage, Chartist Cottage and Rosemary Cottage. They are marvellous memorials to O'Connor and his builders, being expertly constructed with brick; circular at the bottom and a narrow neck at the top. Each year in March the boys and girls of Highgate Wood School (London) are given a guided tour of Crowthorne as part of their study of the Chartists for their A-level examinations.

Pam Hatfield (Sherwood) speaks with pride and enthusiasm about the open garden days in the early 1970s, open to all from two in the afternoon until six o'clock for 25p, children and pensioners tenpence. Children under ten were admitted free and accompanied children were allowed to use the two swimming pools. All the money raised went to The Red Cross Fund. Tea and biscuits were available and there were produce stalls. These were indeed happy days and the gardens presented a marvellous picture; sadly a spate of burglaries in 1977 put a stop to this very popular event. Four gardens were open for the event.

Sheila Sills of the Watford Observer visited Heronsgate in the summer of 1974 and started her tour of the four gardens at Herons Court, the home of Mr and Mrs I.D. McDougall. She spoke about the main garden as being large and formal with a spacious lawn bordered by high holly hedges. She admired Ian McDougall's industry, for there was a mile of hedges, all of which Ian cut by hand. There were roses, herbaceous borders and an extensive kitchen garden from which the McDougall family produced all their own vegetables. They had four hungry sons to feed. The greenhouses were interesting: one was hanging with luscious bunches of grapes, while the other housed a most exotic plant – grown from a leaf brought back from Singapore. The plant is a member of the epiphyllum family and blooms beautifully only once a year for about three hours. This was, of course, an event not to be missed, and it did cause Ian and Moreli to be late for more than one dinner party. There were also some enviable streptocarpus – lovely blue flowering house-plants in the greenhouse.

Down the lane is Sherwood, the home of the Hatfield family. This garden, Sheila Sills said, pleased both the children and the adults. Here was a magnificent Atlantic Cedar with unusual and beautiful cones. There was a rope ladder which enabled the children to climb this magnificent tree. Another large tree supported a swing, and the children's enjoyment was increased with a tennis court and swimming pool. Sherwood has a fascinating garden, full of contrasts. The main part is a large Victorian family garden, but hidden away is another garden with the swimming pool screened from the house – the whole area was professionally landscaped in 1973. Another feature is a secret garden. I wonder how much influence the Carvers at Bramble Close had on this feature? A huge mulberry tree graced the garden.

It is time to leave Sherwood and go to Herons Lodge, the home of Mrs Kay Bowler, and to see her lovely garden. Not so lovely as it should be, according to its owner! The drought had made even the heather dry, the phlox hadn't opened properly and the roses weren't as good as usual and so on. However, the garden still looked good to Sheila Sills and, with its wide lawns and background of great trees, it made a peaceful spot in which to walk or sit. Mrs Bowler was another supporter of cutting hedges by hand. She believed hedge trimmers sliced leaves in half and left a lot of dead ones.

The last and largest of the four gardens was Ladywalk, the home of Mr and Mrs I. Steers. This is a beautiful park-like garden which it was a pleasure to wander round, with its lovely trees, yew hedge-lined walk and courtyard gardens (one with a graceful oil jar filled with flowers). There were roses, heather beds, a beautiful old brick wall round the kitchen garden, another mulberry tree and a quince. There was also a perfect swimming pool. Barbara and Ian Steers served tea behind the house where there is a lovely green vista down the long lawn and over the ha-ha to the countryside beyond. The trees at Ladywalk were planted to represent the battle formation at Trafalgar. Sadly over the years, many – like ships – have been lost in storms. For many years Peter Meakin tended the grounds of Ladywalk with loving and enthusiastic care and, indeed, supplied plants from his greenhouses to the residents of Heronsgate.

In conjunction with the open garden days, Dorothy Haigh used to run a small exhibition in the Hall. She put on a small exhibition of her wood engravings as well as old maps, papers and documents connected with the history of Heronsgate.

Today Heronsgate is just as proud of its gardens. Peter Meakin has retired from Ladywalk, but the gardens are still well cared for and recently a rhododendron walk was built at Sherwood. Open days are over but the garden tradition lives on and the best spring garden competition emphasises this. Clearly the residents of Heronsgate enjoy the challenge.

CHAPTER SIXTEEN

Beaumont House School

The Beaumont House Crest
'Truth with Wisdom'

BEAUMONT HOUSE was built in 1880 by A. Hawkins, a Londoner, to be used as his country house. It was a typical huge square-fronted Victorian house built on the original Chartist plot 24. In 1905 it became a preparatory school for boys aged seven to 14 with Walter J.F. Giffard MA as the founder. In the years after 1905 the school acquired more land from Chartist Cottage (plot 25) for playing fields and its grounds expanded to about eight acres. Walter Giffard had been Fell Scholar of Christ Church and a member of the Harrow XI. In 1907 extensions were added to the left of the original building by Mr Darvell the Chorleywood builder; this is now the house formerly occupied by John and Pat Jackson. In 1921 Walter Giffard acquired from Edward Reid (at one time owner of Rosemary Cottage), Chartist Cottage and this was incorporated into the Beaumont House grounds until Walter Giffard died in 1932 and the land was subdivided. Chartist Cottage (previously known as Holly Lodge) was leased by the solicitors of the estate to Major F.A.S. Hinton, and on the death of F.E. Giffard, it was sold to George Bagley of Whitegates as a freehold property consisting of one rod and 20 perches, but with rights to a cesspool on Beaumont House lands.

John Harvey Keating (Glenalmond and Caius College, Cambridge) became headmaster in 1933 and he set up a joint partnership for a while with Teddy Ilott before he was joined in 1939 by Peter Vezey. Mr Keating retired in 1941 but Peter Vezey was to remain headmaster until the school's closure in the 1970s.

Walter Giffard: the founder of Beaumont House School

In Walter Giffard's reign as headmaster the number of pupils rose quite rapidly. By 1907 there were 15 boarders and 12 dayboys. In most subsequent years there were well over 40 boys but the best year was 1919 when there were 52 boys. By the time J.H. Keating became headmaster over 300 boys had passed through Beaumont House. The pupils came from all over the British Isles: some even came from overseas. Many came from the nearby towns of Chorleywood, Rickmansworth and Watford, but only a comparative few from Heronsgate. Their numbers included Warman F.W., Warman D., Warman K., Haigh S.J.N., Parsons J.R., Reid T.E.B. and in 1929 Topley R. was registered as a new boy. Walter Giffard was enthusiastically supported by his wife, who took a very active role in the life of the school. He taught mathematics and his other loves were cricket and music – shades of Neville Cardus.

144

In the early days cricket fixtures were played against Miss Gilbert Smith's XI, The Stragglers, which included some old boys, Mr Miles XI, Miss Matheson's XI, Mr Henry's XI, The Paters XI, Gayhurst (Gerrards Cross), Chartridge Hill, Shirley House (Watford) and UCS (London) – whose team was coached by Mrs Felkin's son. As school numbers increased the list grew: Dirleton House (St Albans), Orley Farm, The King's Choir School, (Cambridge), The Briary, Swanbourne House, Sunbury House, Shortenills, Durston House, Westfield (Orpington) and the staff all became part of the regular fixture list. In 1929, 19 matches were played – 14 won and only five lost. A. Bywaters created a school record by scoring 628 runs at an average of 31.8 and he scored 114 against Gayhurst. In the staff match of that year, when they beat the boys, D. Warman scored 11 and was out – caught Hall, bowled Bywaters.

Horace Clempson, who was to make his home at St Cecilia (plot 23) next door to Beaumont House, joined the staff in 1905 and he and Walter Giffard made enormous contributions to the music at Beaumont House, as did others such as Mrs M.F. Sears, Helen Frankland (née Greaves) and Sue Treanor in later years. Horace Clempson was still at the school in Peter Vezey's time, although his main contribution by then was as the organist at St John's Church. In the early days he and Walter Giffard entertained the parents, friends and boys with their concerts, theatrical and musical productions.

In 1915, for instance, Miss D. Clarke contributed a violin solo, playing an effective 'morceau' from the facile pen of Mr Giffard, who also sang a patriotic song. But it was the boys who contributed to the greater part of the programme. The production of 'Chevalier du Guet' in 1919 given in French was regarded as 'one of the best theatrical efforts Beaumont House had ever made'. In 1929 'Le Tresor de Carnac', a Breton play with songs and dances and music specially composed by W.J.F. Giffard, was produced in the Chorleywood Memorial Hall.

Walter Giffard was Beaumont House's first headmaster and its longest serving. Other names associated with the school in this era were Sir Henry Giffard, who regularly presented the academic and sporting prizes on sports days. John Wentworth Luther was Walter Giffard's partner during part of the First World War years until the early 1920s. He also taught mathematics and he was the editor of the Beaumont House magazine. The teaching staff generally consisted of eight or nine members and in 1907 the school list shows it to be W.J.F. Giffard Esq, R.A. Hodgson, Esq, E.J.P. Askew Esq, H.E. Clempson (music), Mrs Giffard, Miss Leach, Miss Shutler and Sergeant F.R. Gwynne (late of the 21st Hussars). Amongst other staff in Mr Giffard's time were H. Lupton who was at Beaumont House for just over 11 years (1911-1922), the Reverend W. Breffitt, who was vicar at St John's Church 1912-1925 and Mr J.M. Pennycook who as well as his teaching duties took a keen interest in the boxing. The school was founded on sound values with a good balance between academic, sporting and cultural involvement.

Walter Giffard's successors, John Harvey Keating and Teddy Ilott, carried on the traditions established. His Majesty's Government Inspectors commented favourably on the academic standards and the music. Both headmasters were keen cricketers; and other sports, particularly boxing, shooting and golf were encouraged. The Beaumont House magazine took on a more literary appearance with some first class articles by the boys, and the Old Boys news section became most informative. Teddy Penn writes about the years 1935 to 1940 (it was his son, Charles, who read the lesson at Mrs Vezey's funeral):

'For some strange reason Teddy Ilot/Ilott or Illott played golf with my grandfather on St Augustin's Golf Course in Ramsgate. We were introduced at my grandfather's house when I was taken there on holiday. Neither of us was very impressed, but presumably Ilott, as the joint headmaster of Beaumont House, needed more pupils and my grandfather thought that I needed correction.

When I joined in 1935 (possibly 1936) the headmastership was a joint venture of Teddy Ilott, completely bald thirty-fiveish, I suppose, and very fierce, and Mr Keating, a bit older, less fierce, broad, a bit bald, with reddish hair and complexion. I then lived at Croxley Green and travelled daily to Beaumont House on the school bus, which I probably had to meet in Rickmansworth. I seem to recollect that this ancient vehicle (no doubt War Office disposals ex WW1) was painted in the school colours (purple!!) and could not therefore easily be confused with Green Line or anything else. I would guess that this monstrous vehicle cruised, when serviceable, round Chorleywood and Rickmansworth collecting boys who couldn't find any more desirable mode of transport.

As a sickly child I spent little time at school, but became a boarder during the winter months. I recall only one other member of staff, a matron (I only remember her because she caught me peeing in my weekly bath and was not amused) and my concern at her unnatural behaviour when she married Teddy Ilott – as they were both obviously far too old.

My peers included Raymond Borer (son of a Rickmansworth solicitor), Ryman (he of the stationery family), Southern (a much better entomologist than me, who offended me by calling our house a box) and Brown (tall, sandy-haired, whose arm I broke in a bicycle accident – prelude to a long life of exciting driving). The regime was more or less benevolent and beatings not too fierce. I recall two. One for sliding on ice in the goalmouth – not during a game – and one for peeing through the lavatory window (inside to outside) – a competition I was proud to win. Sad that the Head was outside listening to our conversation. I was not beaten, however, when, taken short, I entered the "Staff Only" loo and forgot to lock the door and was promptly sat on by the new girly teacher, also taken short. It was thought I had been punished enough.

In 1939 we moved to Nightingale Road, Rickmansworth and at that time, or perhaps before, Peter Vezey became Headmaster. I believe that Mr Keating went off to Truro Cathedral School and Ilott I know not whither. Journeys to school were by bicycle from then on, usually via Mill End with my blazer and cap hidden so as to avoid the presentation of such a good aiming mark to those who were generally considered "rather rough".

Sometime in 1940 I took time out from breaking Brown's arm to observe a high performance and most secret aircraft landing in the field below Bottom Wood. It was there for some time and no-one showed any interest. I can now reveal that it was probably a 2-seater Taylorcraft from an Army Co-operation Squadron.

At some time during my career there I remember a cross country run in miserable weather - as I stumbled over some knotty roots I grabbed at something nearby to prevent a fall – it happened to be Mr Vezey's cardigan. To my absolute dismay it sort of unravelled and disintegrated in my hands until seriously unpicked and several inches shorter – no longer a decent fit for the man. Many years later I was able to redress this demeanour by getting my son to present him with a new cardigan on his last day as a pupil

146

at the school. Shortly afterwards the M25 cut a swathe through the countryside close to Heronsgate and the poor old school reached its sell-by date.

I left Beaumont House in 1940. On my first return visit 25 years later I found Peter Vezey in the garden, in great voice, in Latin instructing small boys to weed a flower bed. He recognised me at once and recalled my name immediately without prompting, as did Mrs Vezey a few moments later when she looked out from an upstairs window – and I had thought Mr Vezey had never noticed me during my schooldays!'

Another, who remembers Beaumont House was Harry R.F. Keating, the crime writer who was at Trinity College, Dublin, before me; he was interviewed by Carole Rosen and the following article about his years at Beaumont House appeared in 'The Telegraph Magazine' in 1991.

'He divides the world into those who have happy memories of their childhood and those who don't. The crime writer puts himself regretfully in the second category, and had mixed feelings about making a return visit to Beaumont House, the preparatory school near Rickmansworth in Hertfordshire, where his father was headmaster from 1933 to 1941.

"Coming back after 40 years, I still have butterflies in my stomach. I remember pushing a car that had broken down along this narrow lane with my father's co-headmaster, Peter Vezey. My father contrived to pick partners with whom he didn't get on. They were always having rows, and if Vezey ticked me off, father tended to think he had been unjust. On this occasion, I must have said something that annoyed him and he shouted, 'Keating, take a black mark for being pert'. I didn't know what pert meant and I didn't dare ask."

'Much to his surprise, the solidly built Victorian mansion seemed to have changed little since his school days. The grass tennis court was still outside the front door. "I can remember endlessly trying to hit the ball over the net, and that huge hut with the corrugated-iron roof was the gymnasium. We used to have assembly in there. When the weather was very stormy, we were allowed to sing Eternal Father, strong to save. We had a terrier called Sam, who always used to howl if he heard that hymn. So, it was always, 'Please, Sir, is it stormy enough for Eternal Father?' and Sam had to be taken out. My father knew what boys liked."

'Malcolm and John Jackson, the present joint owners of Beaumont House, were also pupils at the school. But, unlike Harry Keating, they had such blissfully happy memories of their time there, that when Peter Vezey retired in 1970, they bought the school and turned it into two family houses. They have retained relics of its past life, however. The honours board is still in place in the hall, school magazines and photos are piled on the dining room table. Malcolm even produced a school cap – complete with the school motto Cum sapientia veritas – for Keating to wear.

Upstairs, the names of the dormitories are still over the bedroom doors. Keating and Malcolm Jackson swapped memories of Matron's room, the nightly temperature-taking and ministrations of Virol. Next door was the Sick Room. "My mother painted it purple when it was fumigated after an outbreak of measles. She was the ideal headmaster's wife, always comforting any little boy who felt homesick. I slept in the senior dormitory. No heating, of course. We used to slide between freezing sheets at night, and in the morning there would be ice on the wash-bowl."

For a boy brought up surrounded by other boys, Keating's life sounds surprisingly solitary: "I was the only pupil here for one year at the beginning of the war, when my prep school at Bexhill was evacuated".

'During the holidays he would run around the huge playing fields telling himself stories. "very good for a would-be author. My father gave me the middle name Reymond, and someone asked him why he had given me this misspelt name. My father answered, 'It's to look good on the spines of his books'. Unfortunately, he died before my first book came out in 1959, but if he's up there, he'll know. I was originally destined to carry on this school after him, but in 1941 he had a blazing row with Vezey and, in an impulsive gesture, sold out his share for much less than he should. He took a teaching job at a minor public school, Sutton Valence. He couldn't afford to send me to university, so I left school at 16 and worked as an engineer for the BBC. He died of a heart attack when he was 56. It was quite a bad moment when I passed that age and became older than my father had been when he died. I thought I should have done the decent thing and died too.

"At the bottom of his desk I discovered three short stories, including one called Swat M'Charda, about a boy who had worked much harder than his contemporaries. I remembered his reading it to me when I was 11, when I thought it was marvellous. At 20, I was devastated to realise it wasn't any good."

'Had Keating used Beaumont House as a setting for any of his crime stories? "I based 'Caught in the Meshes' on the tug of divided loyalties caused by the problems of seeing my father as a headmaster. 'A rush on the Ultimate' also has a prep school setting and a headmaster who runs a croquet tournament for his friends in the holidays. But he's based on the head of my first prep school, not my father. I decided at Trinity College, Dublin, after my Army Service, that I didn't want to teach. My wife persuaded me to write detective stories. We met when she was in rep in Swindon and I was a trainee journalist on the Wiltshire Herald.

I've just published my 30th book, another Inspector Ghote mystery called 'The Iciest Sin'. That was how Rebecca West described blackmail in the Vassall case, when I was a sub-editor on The Daily Telegraph, I've never forgotten it."'

Under Peter Vezey's headmastership the school went from strength to strength. At its peak Beaumont House had over 60 pupils; all boys, and half of the total were boarders. Pupils continued to come from all over the British Isles and overseas and often were sons of parents with a services background. Heronsgate boys increased their numbers too. There where five dormitories, each offering homes for six boys. These dormitories were named after the bays in the Channel Islands – one being called Bray. There were six forms of ten boys (seven years to 14 years). Quotes from a prospectus of the late 1960s are interesting; it begins by stating that Beaumont House was regarded as efficient by the Board of Education and that P.H. Vezey M.A. (Haileybury and Worcester College, Oxford, sometime Inspector of Schools, Education Department, S. Nigeria) was Headmaster:

'Scholarships, Exhibitions, and Naval Cadetships have regularly been won. Preparation is for no particular Public School and among these to which boys have passed on, in addition to The Royal Naval College, Dartmouth, are: Aldenham; Bradfield; King's School Canterbury; Charterhouse; Cheltenham; Clifton; Cranbrook; Denstone; Dover; Eton; Gresham's, Holt; Haileybury; Harrow; Malvern; Marlborough; Merchant Taylors; Mill Hill; Oundle; Radley; Repton; Rugby; St. Edward's (Oxford); Shrewsbury; Stowe; Sutton Valence; Tonbridge; Uppingham; Wellington; Westminster, and Winchester.

The grounds of about eight acres in extent, contain the schoolhouse, two cottages and bungalow, a large gymnasium, an open-air swimming bath, rifle range and cricket pavilion. There are about four acres of playing fields (including a nine hole miniature golf course and a tennis court), and a flourishing orchard which keeps the school supplied with fresh fruit.

The school is intended to be for members of the Church of England or of other Protestant denominations. Prayers are said daily before morning school and all boarders attend a service on Sundays. Day-boys have to attend on Ascension Day and on the first and last Sundays of term, when boys read the Lessons.

Instruction is given in all subjects required for the Scholarships Examinations and the Common Entrance Examination for the Public Schools by a well-qualified staff, and singing and boxing form part of the ordinary curriculum. Boys are given lantern lectures, write contributions for the magazine, and have gardens. Interest in natural history, for which splendid scope exists, is also encouraged.

It has always been the Headmaster's endeavour so to train a boy that he may develop a spirit of initiative and independence but at the same time a readiness to be helpful. It is also his firm conviction that a preparatory school should be a large edition of a family and the number of boys in the school continues therefore, despite economic pressure, to be restricted.

Football (both association and, for older boys in the Spring Term, rugby) cricket, swimming, boxing, gymnastics, golf, and tennis are carried on under proper supervision, and the boys are out of doors as much as possible. Physical Training is given all the year round. No boy is excused without a doctor's certificate.

As well as all the more ordinary equipment there are such things as a cinematograph projector, and an episcope, which the boys are encouraged to learn to manipulate themselves.

Extreme care is exercised in the matter of health. There is a resident matron, and the school medical officer, who lives within easy reach, visits the school regularly. Boys are weighed at fixed intervals and temperatures are taken nightly.

Mrs Vezey (Diploma in Domestic Science, Reading University) and a housekeeper attend to the diet and try to make it conform as nearly as possible to modern scientific ideas. Fresh fruit is supplied regularly and generally at least once each day from the school grounds, and the milk (pasteurised) is of excellent quality. There is a breakfast of two courses, in addition to bread, butter and marmalade; "elevenses"; dinner (2 courses); tea, and supper. The dormitories are bright and airy and the Headmaster personally supervises the dormitory discipline.

Fees are payable not later than the first day of the term, and a full term's notice in writing is required before the removal of a boy, otherwise the next term's fees will be payable in lieu of notice. The Headmaster reserves the right to require the removal of any boy whose conduct or work he considers unsatisfactory and no claim shall arise for the return or remission of any portion of the payment made or due for the term in which the pupil is removed. A reduction of 10 per cent is made for the second of two brothers while they are together in the school. Fees may need to be adjusted. At present they are as follows:

Boarders (under 10)... ... ...   62 guineas a term

Boarders (over 10)... ... ...   66 guineas a term

There is a Termly charge of £2 15s for laundry

Day Boarders (under 10)... ... ...   33 guineas a term

Day Boarders (over 10)... ... ...   37 guineas a term

Fees for Day Boarders, whose number is strictly limited, include "elevenses", mid-day dinner, and tea.

Entrance Fee: There is an Entrance Fee of two guineas for Boarders and one guinea for Day Boarders, payable when the entry form is returned after a boy has been accepted for admission.

Swimming, a guinea a term, Summer only, is compulsory unless a doctor's certificate is produced, but Shooting on the school's miniature range, a guinea a term, and Piano, three and a half guineas a term, are optional and can be taken by those boys whose parents desire them so to do.

There is a School Fees Insurance Scheme in operation so no allowance will be made for absence. A boy's entry is only accepted subject to his parent's or guardian's agreement to the above rules and conditions.'

The staff generally consisted of six or seven full-time masters or mistresses and a matron and cook. John Jackson (old boy from the 1940s) remembers Beaumont House as a happy well-balanced school, offering a sound academic base with plenty of sport, including rugby, soccer, cricket, athletics, boxing, shooting, swimming and an old-fashioned discipline. Mr Vezey used to ensure boys were well up with current affairs. Beaumont House boys are remembered fondly by many of today's residents for their ability to doff the purple cap at all and sundry, and for pumping the church pumps to keep the organ going at morning matins.

I personally like the war time story of preparations for Sports Day when a shortage of petrol and a moribund lawnmower forced Mr Vezey to order the playing fields to be cut by hand by staff and boys – evidently it took a month!

The school was forced to close in the early 1970s, probably due to a number of factors including the death of the supportive and wise Mrs Vezey, the isolation of the area and the consequent difficulty of finding good reliable staff – particularly kitchen staff. Mr Vezey in immediate post war years is rumoured to have directed kitchen staff in terms such as 'Come here Spanish', and 'Come here Italian'. Beaumont House was a great prep school and contributed both on a national and local scale to the lives of many.

Shortly before Remembrance Day Sunday in 1961 a war memorial pew was placed in St John's church; later in 1962 a memorial board was placed at the west end of the church to remember the Beaumont House boys who had lost their lives during wartime. In the two World Wars of the 20th century a large number of Beaumont House boys were killed, but many more served and fought and survived in those terribly destructive wars. The following boys from Beaumont House are remembered on the commemorative plaque and pew:

> MCMXIV MCMXVIII BEAUMONT HOUSE MCMXXXIX MCMXLV
> E. SCHOLA NOSTRA EXIERUNT ET PROCUL HINC PRO PATRIA PERIERUNT
>
> L.G.CARLYON J.C.CRAWFORD J.J.DAWE A.P.DONNELL
> D.G.R.GEDDES B.G.H.KEYMER P.H.NIXON J.Q.F.WALKER
> A.WHALE E.E.C.BRITTON A.J.CAPPS R.J.CARTER
> R.E.COLTART V.L.DARBYSHIRE J.L.GRAHAM
> A.E.A.HOLDEN C.MACVEAN J.F.MARMONT B.J.SMEETON
> R.D.TREBLE
>
> At the going down of the sun and in the morning we will remember them.

The War Graves Commission supplied the following information:

'L.G. Carlyon. 2nd Lt 9th Bn The Cameronians (Scot Rifles)
Died 3rd May 1917. Browns Copse Cemetery, Roeux, France Plot 5, Row 8, Grave 15.

J.C. Crawford. No Trace. There are 75 J and 4 J.C. Crawford.

James Jeffery Dawe. Pte 24th Sqdn RAF.
Died 7th June 1918. Age 19 Rosieres Communal Cemetery Ext. France. Plot 2. Row A. Grave 7.
Son of Sydney & Emily Annie Dawe of 'Ashlyns', Nightingale Road, Rickmansworth, Herts

Arthur Patrick Donnell. Lt Northumberland Fusiliers & Royal Flying Corps.
Died 5th Dec 1916. Age 18. Narborough (All Saints) Churchyard. Son of the Rev C.E. & Pauline C. Donnell of Stamfordham Vicarage, Northumberland.

David Geddes. Lce Cpl No 12653 6th Bn Kings Own Scottish Borderers.
Died 25th Sept 1915. Age 24. Buried The Loos Memorial, France MR19 Part 5. Panel 53 to 56. Son of David & Margaret Geddes of 6, Alpine Terrace, Dalbeattie. Husband of Sophia McBurney Geddes of Woodside Cottages.

Basil Graham Homfray Keymer. Capt DFC & Bar. RAF/ Croce Di Guerra (Italy)
Died 24th Oct 1919. Age 20. Buried Krasnodar Cemetery. Black Sea. Row 1. Grave 6. Son of The Rev Basil Nathanial Keymer, BATD of Gosbeck Rectory, Ipswich & the late Ethel Keymer.

Philip Henry Nixon. 2nd Lt 2nd Btn Gloucestershire Regt.
Died 18th Dec 1916 Age 25. Buried Salonika Lembet Road Military Cemetery. Greece. G.7 Row 0 Grave 27. Son of Eleanor Cartwright (formerly Nixon) & The late Robert Allwood Nixon.

John Quinten Frederick Walker. Lt 57th Sqdn Royal Flying Corps.
Died 31st March 1918. Age 18. The Arras Memorial at Faubourg. D'Amiens Cemetery, Arras, France. Part 23 MR20. Son of Mr & Mrs J.F. Walker of Aspley Guise, Beds.

Arthur Whale. Lce Cpl No 10262 1st Btn Wiltshire Regt.
Died 16th June 1915. Buried Ypres (Menin Gate) Memorial, Belgium. Part 35. MR29. Panel 53

Eric Edward Chester Britton. Lt No 235377 The Duke of Cornwalls Light Inf Attd 36th Btn Kings African Rifles.
Died 15th Oct 1944. Age 22. Taukkyan War Cemetery, Rangood Burma. Bur 3. Plot 15A. Row F. Grave 12. Son of The Rev John Britton BA & Anne Britton, of Tunbridge Wells, Kent

Austin Jack Capps. 2nd Lt No 105273 4th Btn The Green Howards (Yorkshire Regt).
Died 22nd May 1940. Athies Communal Cemetery Ext. France. FR 199. Plot 2 Row B. Grave 18

Richard Jeffery Carter. Pilot Officer No 78881 RAF 904 Balloon Sqdn.
Died 16th July 1940. Age 38. Rickmansworth Cemetery, Hertfordshire UK 3385 Sec. FF Row 3 Grave 2C. Son of Charles & Catherine Carter. Husband of Kathleen Carter of Watford. ARIBA.

Richard Evelyn Coltart. Lt DSC RN HM Submarine H 49.
Died 27th Oct 1940. Age 23. Portsmouth Naval Memorial. Portsmouth Panel 36 Column 3. Son of Dr Guy H. Coltart & Mary Beatrice Coltart of Fulham, London.

Ronald Derbyshire. Ldg Sea. No P/JX 125355 RN HMS Royal Oak.
Died 14th Oct 1939. Age 29. Portsmouth Naval Memorial. Portsmouth, Panel 33. Col 2. Son of William & Lilian Derbyshire. Husband of Edna Margaret Derbyshire of Southsea, Hampshire. (N.B. V.L. Derbyshire on commemorative plaque)

John Luke Graham. Sgt No 778832. RAF (UR) 35 Sqdn.

Died 26th July 1943. The Runnymede Memorial, Surrey. Panel 84.

Alfred Eric Ancel Holden. Sgt Pilot No 1334010 RAF (UR) 15 Sqdrn.

Died 28th July 1943. Age 19. Hamburg Cemetery Ohlsdorf, Germany GER II Coll Grave 9A B. 10-13. Son of John Ancel Holden & Edith Mabel Holden of Moor Park, Northwood, Mddlx.

Colin Alexander Macvean. Flt Sgt Pilot No 999002 RAF (UR) 80 Sqdn.

Died 9th Dec 1941. Age 23. Halfaya Sollum War Cemetery, Egypt EY21. Plot 5. Row D. Grave 10. Son of Patrick William & Phyllis Macvean of Burley-in-Wharfdale, Yorkshire.

John Filmer Marmont. Lt RN HMS Glorious.

Died 9th June 1940. Age 28. Lee-on-the-Solent. Bay 1. Panel 2. Son of Percy & Elsie Marmont. Husband of Joan Marmont.

Bryon John Smeeton. Lt RN HMS Sparrowhawk.

Died 10th April 1940. Lee-on-the-Solent. Bay 1. Panel 2.

R.G. Treble. No trace - there is no R or R.G. Treble listed in the overall index.' (N.B. R.D. Treble on commemorative plaque)

Beaumont House boys are buried in graves in France, Northumberland, The Black Sea, Greece, Belgium, Burma, Rickmansworth, Portsmouth, Surrey, Germany, Egypt, Hampshire, and other areas. They served in all branches of the armed forces having lived in a diverse number of areas in the United Kingdom.

Information about some old boys and staff killed in action follows. All are equally remembered and missed by their families and friends. J.C. Crawford of whom, according to the War Graves Commission there was no trace, was at Beaumont House from 1907-1910 and gained an entrance exhibition to Cheltenham College where he became head boy. He was to serve as a 2nd lieutenant in the Royal Horse Artillery and was killed on August 31st 1916.

Three Beaumont House masters died in the World Wars. P.H. Nixon, who left King's School Canterbury in 1910 came to Beaumont House aged 19, taught languages for two terms in 1910 and did much to improve the learning of French. He left Beaumont House to complete his exams. P.H. Nixon died on the 18th of December 1916. Arthur Whale, who taught in the years 1914 and 1915 and was much admired in the classroom and in the games field, fell in action on 3rd August 1916; The War Graves Commission has his death as 16th June 1915. E.E.C. Britton was a casualty of the Second World War. It is pleasing to record that Mr Luther, Walter Giffard's partner, left in 1916 to take a commission as a sublieutenant in the RNVR and survived and returned to Beaumont House to continue his career in schoolmastering.

One may note the careers of some of the boys who lost their lives in the First World War: D.G.R. Geddes, Beaumont House 1906-1910, was a fine all-round athlete and in the cricket XI at Aldenham. L.G. Carlyon was another fine cricketer and in 1907 he scored 119 runs against Shirley House and 122 against The Briary. B.G.H. Keymer left Haileybury College in April 1916 to take a commission in the Royal Flying Corps. He had been captain of shooting at Haileybury and whilst at Beaumont House in 1910 aged 11 held the National Rifle Skilled shots certificate; he had been a courtier in the school's production of Cinderella. He died aged 20 with the DFC and Bar in October 1919. His grave is at the Krasnodar Cemetery, The Black Sea. 'Oh the futility of war to cut short a life in its prime'.

The Beaumont House magazine of 1919 says this about Basil Graham Homfrey Keymer, Acting Major, RAF:

'We have to chronicle the loss of yet another of our Old Boys in the person of the above gallant young officer who was killed in an air raid on the Bolshevist lines in South Russia on October 24th last. He was in the School from December, 1908, to December, 1912, when he proceeded to Haileybury College. In April, 1917, he became a probationary flight officer, RNAS, and in August of the same year received his commission as flight sublieut, RNAS. Proceeding to Italy in November 1917, he became lieut, RAF, in April 1918. In the following August he was promoted acting captain, and a year later was given a permanent commission in the RAF. He was awarded the DFC for good work in long-distance bombing raids over the Adriatic, and was described in the Gazette as "a very gallant flight leader of exceptional ability and determination." He was also awarded the Croc di Guerra by the Italian Government for cooperation with the Italian forces near Durazzo and Cattaro. It is hard indeed that such a promising career should have been cut short in a side issue, after surviving safely and with so much distinction the perils of the great European War.'

Soon after the Second World War, Gerda and Jo Craven joined the staff of Beaumont House; Gerda, the widow of Jo Craven, remembers her years at Beaumont House with mixed feelings. She first met Jo when he was serving in Germany as an intelligence agent. Since she is German they were unable to marry unless he transferred to the cultural relations service, which he did, but at the end of 1952 the department was made redundant and Jo found himself in England seeking a job. This led the Cravens into the educational world and, more particularly, to Beaumont House where they stayed from 1953 to its closure in the 1970s.

Jo Craven had all the credentials to be an excellent schoolmaster. He was born in Yorkshire, went to public school at Sedbergh and then read modern languages at Cambridge University. Jo was given the job as French master and was expected to teach some Geography, but no German was taught – to Jo's disappointment.

Gerda remembers living in the little school cottage (Bircham Cottage) which was very primitive. She felt very isolated and disconsolate at the remote southern end of Heronsgate. However, it was not long before in 1954 Gerda and Jo moved to the more cheerful Shire Lane, and, interestingly, it was Norry Aston, the school secretary of long-standing and Major Aston's daughter-in-law who found them their house.

Gerda speaks of the Beaumont House staff with great respect. Peter Vezey, the headmaster, could be terrifying but was greatly respected and had the school's interest at heart. He set the highest standards – he was a strong disciplinarian; but, if he had a weakness, it was that he found it difficult to delegate. As the numbers dwindled and Mr Vezey became older, the hard working and most supportive Mrs Vezey died. This became a problem. Mrs Vezey had acted as house-keeper and general factotum. She lived a spartan life but her presence and contribution to the school was immense.

Mr Birds, the Latin master of the 1950s-70s, was a great character, a bachelor and a dedicated schoolmaster. He used to be somewhat eccentrically dressed with his long trousers and often he could be heard clanking his way home after a sojourn at The Stag Pub. Mr Birds was known for the excellence of his teaching and showing off the hole in the chest earned at the Battle of the Somme. He retired to Bognor Regis where he died. Jo and Gerda Craven had stayed at The Swan Inn, Rickmansworth on their interview night and venturing out to find Beaumont House had got lost; they had met Mr Birds wandering in the lanes and he had guided them to their destination.

The Battys were another stalwart pair. Mrs Batty taught handicraft, while Mr Batty, a Methodist, who came from Sheffield, taught English in an earnest and conscientious manner. As in all preparatory schools there was a series of young teachers, often pre-university or just out of university, who taught a variety of subjects, took on the menial duties, helped with the games and offered a valuable service to the school. One such was Peter Moore, a Beaumont House old boy and a resident of Loudwater. The music mistress for some time was Helen Greaves, daughter of Connie (Daphnes), who succeeded Mary Sears; in the 1960s Sue Treanor taught music and gave piano lessons at her home. Purple-blazered boys with cap in hand used to appear at Craven Cottage and, before entering the pristine Treanor abode, would take their shoes off and leave them neatly outside the front door.

Sundays were always interesting. The boarders attended St John's Church every Sunday and the dayboys at least twice a term. The congregation looked forward to the sermons of Heyworth Talbot (the QC and lay preacher): he was a great orator and made the boys feel part of the service. The Philby boys and Gardiner boys would have been amongst the congregation.

Gerda thinks back to the warm summer's day when a robin flew into the church and the sermon was adapted around this robin. Jo used to bring some boys back for afternoon tea and then the Cravens, plus dog, used to walk them back to school.

The Yiends of Heronsgate who had two sons at Beaumont House (David and Simon) remember:

'A feature of Heronsgate during the 50s and 60s (and for many years before that) was Beaumont House School. As a former inspector of schools in Africa headmaster Peter Vezey obviously had very definite ideas as to how a preparatory school should be run: Christian principles, strict discipline and a family atmosphere were prerequisites. The buildings might be in need of refurbishment; icicles might hang from the fifth year's form ceiling; the dormitories might be freezing cold, but a somewhat Victorian tradition of endeavour prevailed! Numbers were kept low deliberately – 30 day boys and 30 boarders, he told us, were his maximum. They were taught by himself, three other permanent masters (all of whom were characters in themselves), a temporary trainee master and visiting staff for music and handcraft. Stars were rewards and stripes were punishments. The latter had to be redeemed by unpopular tasks such as sorting the apples harvested and kept in the apple store. These were cut up and distributed at break together with the daily milk quota but were not regarded with favour.

Mr Vezey certainly believed in making use of all available labour. When at the beginning of the summer term the unheated outdoor swimming pool was required to be made fit for use, it was scrubbed and cleaned by posses of boys shivering in swimming trunks. Pumping out and filling were done by the local fire brigade. Swimming was a must and all experienced parents made sure their sons had learned to swim before their first summer term; otherwise they faced being put in harness and pulled through the pool until in sheer desperation they swam.

Beaumont House School: a classroom

Beaumont House School: the dining room

The culmination of the summer term was the swimming sports. These so frequently seemed to take place on a cold, grey evening where the spectators – wrapped in rugs – shivered on the side lines while the boys, blue with cold, leaped bravely in and out of the icy water. Highlight of the evening was "The Big Dive", in which every boy in the school took part, diving in successive waves until all were in the water together.

Sports day took place earlier in the term and the preparations were indeed thorough. Apart from rehearsals the field had to be prepared and marked out. This provided practical geometry lessons with the boys implementing various theorems including that of Pythagoras to create the necessary angles, curves and distances. At this time of the year, instead of the day boys returning home at 6 pm, it was often after 8 pm when they appeared, even more ravenous than usual.

None of this appeared to have any ill effects, certainly not on our two boys. In spite of these somewhat spartan conditions a loyalty was forged between boys and masters and a pride which brought rich rewards in their competitions with other schools. Their sporting as well as their academic prowess was widely recognised.

The winter term meant Saturday evening films. Before the purchase of a colour projector (which Mr Vezey said he didn't understand, leaving its operation to senior boys) the films, which were black and white, frequently broke during their showing depositing large heaps of film on the floor of the gym. November 5th involved standing with icy feet on the games field while Mr Vezey (and a favoured few) let off an apparently endless supply of fireworks, one by one. The only illumination was torchlight but woe betide any unfortunate who helped himself to more than the permitted one chocolate biscuit. Somehow Mr Vezey always knew and the culprit was always detected.

The last day of the autumn term meant the Christmas carol service in St John's. The boys – no strangers to the church with Beaumont House Sunday being a regular monthly occasion for all pupils – brought in extra benches. Parents overflowed into the nave and sat on the Chancel steps while the boys sang the old carols, always finishing with "God be in my head". Then it began to seem like Christmas.

Perhaps the main claim to national fame was the inclusion of Beaumont House into a television documentary on schools. Contemporary parents watched their sons boxing, playing rugby, learning Latin etc. and to do the television crew justice the programme seemed to reflect the unique atmosphere of what was an old-fashioned school, run by an old-fashioned man with old-fashioned values.'

It might not have suited everyone, but the objective was to provide a high standard of education, an understanding of the value of discipline and the development of character. From the response by scores of old pupils from across the world at a subsequent reunion, Mr Vezey would appear to have succeeded. He certainly couldn't have made his fortune – a term's fees for a day-boy in 1968 were £55 13s.

Simon Scott and Austen Steers who were at Beaumont House from the mid-1960s until 1970 talked and wrote to me respectively about their years there. Their memories are for the most part very happy ones. Perhaps the first year at prep school was a bit daunting, but, as they settled in and made friends, the school provided them with a great start to their education. Austen wishes he could send his children to a school like Beaumont House. They both speak of Mr Vezey being hard but fair, and although the school might have been somewhat spartan and the facilities not great, the dedication of the staff and the spirit of the boys made a Beaumont House pupil a formidable foe on the sports field and prepared them well for their further education and life in general.

Beaumont House School: staff and boys 1967

Teaching staff seated: Helen Greaves, Julian Coward, Jo Craven, Peter Vezey, Joanna Vezey, Stanley Batty, Peter Moore

Simon and Austen speak about the preparation for sports day taking weeks – what with the grass to be cut, the track to be marked and the bunting to be put out. Other tasks included scrubbing the swimming pool by hand, filling it with cold water and then jumping in. A sought-after job was to collect the lead from the rifle range butts. Austen reports 'Mum was often not very pleased', as many a saucepan was ruined. Apples had to be caught at break time and eaten – an unbruised apple tasted better! All food at meal times had to be finished – the alternative was to stay behind until the task was done, but some food seemed to find its way under the dining room floor boards. Mr Vezey always seemed to know who the culprits were, for later he would summon Scott, Gibbins, Steers or McDougall to remove the leftovers which had been hidden.

Rugby shirts hung in the changing rooms all term, getting wetter and smellier but once worn seeming to inspire greater deeds. Highlights in the pupils' lives were numerous. I like their stories about the time when Z Cars was being filmed there: the boys had to have their lunch in the dark and Mr Vezey was shouted at by the director for shouting at the boys. And there was the day when no student teacher was present to drive the bus to St Pauls in London for a rugby match; when they came to get on the tube, the alternative means of transport, half the team was left on the platform. Nobody noticed until the match was about to start.

Sadly the era of Scott, the Gibbins, the Steers and the McDougalls was to see the closure of Beaumont House. The immediate end of this much-loved prep school begins with the illness of Mrs Vezey, but there had been difficulties in the running of the school for some time.

On the last day of January 1969 Mrs Vezey returned home to Beaumont House after nine weeks in hospital and two serious operations. However, she was not well and was forced to spend two weeks in an Eastbourne nursing home. But Beaumont House and the boys were her life; she returned and soon was fully involved in the daily work of running the school. She undertook single-handed the cooking of school lunches and most of the washing up, as well as much of the teatime work and many of the administrative tasks. The school was desperately short-handed. Then, after the end of the summer term, she had a sudden relapse and on the 8th of October, 1969 she died at St Mary's Hospital, Paddington. A service was held at St John's, Heronsgate, on the 13th of October, when the church was packed; flowers covered the floor from the lectern to the altar and were leaning against the walls. The whole school attended. C.E. Penn, the head boy and himself the son of one of the most senior of Mr and Mrs Vezey's old boys, read the lesson quite splendidly, while Frank Heyworth Talbot, excelled even his usual high standard in a magnificent and most moving address. The service was taken by the Reverend J.F. Perry, vicar of St Andrew's, Chorleywood. Letters of tribute and respect poured in from all over the world – Australia, New Zealand, South Africa, Canada, the USA, Switzerland, Germany, Lebanon – some from old boys signed with nicknames by which they have been affectionately known.

Mrs Vezey's death was a tragedy and highlighted the other problems already evident. Mr Vezey had for years been trying to find a suitable man to join him in partnership with a view to succeeding him as headmaster. More recently he had asked four local fathers to come and discuss the situation. He explained that he had considered retiring and would do so if that would make succession easier. But the four fathers would not accept this proposition and said, 'No, you're the attraction, you have got to stay'. The idea of converting the school into a charitable trust was also discussed.

A full parents' meeting was called for the 4th of March 1970 and a committee was formed. It was decided that the solicitors for the Preparatory Schools' Association should visit the school and make a report. The report was extremely favourable and praised the accommodation available and the excellence and size of the playing fields. The academic record of the school was regarded as being very high and the standard of games was good. The solicitors suggested that the decline in numbers was due to Mr Vezey's age and the question of succession. The report recommended that a deputy headmaster should be appointed and Mr Craven agreed to fill this post. It also said some advertising to promote the school should be done; a pre-preparatory department should be opened; and the lanes to the school be improved to make access easier.

Following the report, the parents' committee and Mr Vezey circulated a letter to parents on the 1st of May which explained that discussions were going on with Mr and Mrs Buck of Heronsfield, Old Shire Lane. They were both Cambridge graduates, one a historian and the other a scientist. They would be ideal successors. The Bucks wanted to move Beaumont House to Heronsfield where there was central heating and, being near a bus route, travel would be simplified for day-boys and particularly for domestic staff. Mr Vezey's letter went on to say that he could see no real advantage in moving to Heronsfield where facilities were limited although the transport situation might be improved; Mr Buck could drive a minibus. Recently he had had an offer to improve the science facilities in the school bungalow by connecting water and gas; central heating was only useful as it was labour saving. Also not long ago a considerable sum of money had been spent on maintenance.

Another parents' meeting was held: Mr and Mrs Buck met the parents and answered questions; but, before attending another meeting, they decided not to join Beaumont House. Mr Vezey continued his search for a suitable successor but to no avail. The situation was becoming desperate. The lanes continued to present a problem and financing the school was becoming increasingly difficult. One parent offered to put finance into the school, while others suggested that fees should be increased. Domestic staff were a real worry and matrons did not stay long. One engaged in the summer of 1969 to start in September arrived a day late and then asked if she could have the night off. A week later she walked out. One matron had an uncontrollable temper; another, from a well-known public school, had to go into hospital for a serious operation soon after taking up her post. But all was not lost; the mothers did all they could to help and a rota was organised to fetch and serve the midday meal from the canteen which now supplied the school food; mothers like Mrs Marlow, Mrs Harden and the Heronsgate boys' mothers were a great help in many ways. Finally, when the Christmas term of 1970 started with three full-time masters - J.H.O. Craven, S. Batty, who had been at the school for 17 and 16 years respectively, and J.H. Terry, one part-time master, R. Wallace, all graduates, and of course Mr Vezey, there were only seven boys. It was clear the school would have to close. Earlier in the year, Mr Paul Griffin, headmaster of Aldenham School had told the Watford Observer when the closure of Beaumont House seemed imminent:

'In North London there is a great shortage of good preparatory schools. At Aldenham we have had 21 boys from Beaumont House since 1958 and many have done extremely well, gaining exhibition scholarships to universities including one boy who gained the prime chemistry award to Oxford. Mr Vezey has given great service to the school and it would be a great pity to see him go. He must also be congratulated for his pub-lic spiritedness in not realising for cash the undoubted value of the land on which the school stands'.

The school closed at the end of 1970. Just over a year later, the following report appeared in the local newspaper:

'BEAUMONT HOUSE. The closure of Beaumont House boys' school, Heronsgate, at the end of 1970 marked the end of an era. And for Peter Vezey, its headmaster, who had given more than 30 years to the school, it also marked the end of a lifetime's work. It was a poignant moment for Mr Vezey when, in February 1972, a party and presentation were held in his honour organised by a group of old boys, remembering all that Mr Vezey and Beaumont House had meant to them. Old boys sent donations from all over the world, and in February returned to Beaumont House, where Mr Vezey had arranged the desks, chairs and beds just as they were before the school closed. There they presented him with a silver salver engraved with the school badge and the words "With sincere thanks from his boys". And there was also his portrait – which was shown at the Royal Society of Portrait Painters exhibition. Mr Vezey was also given a summer house for the garden of the cottage at Beaumont House where he now lives, a transistor radio, and a scroll inscribed with the names of the old boys who had contributed. The active life of Beaumont House had come to an end.

As a prep school it naturally prided itself on its successes, and at one time had strong naval links, in days when boys were accepted into the navy at the age of 13. From here boys were prepared for Britain's famous public schools. Among its most famous boys were Air Marshall Sir William Foster-Dickson, Chief of Air Staff and later Commander of the Chiefs of Staff; and Eric Shipton, the explorer and climber of Everest – both at the school during the First World War.

It was always the headmaster's aim "To train a boy that he may develop a spirit of initiative and independence, but at the same time a readiness to be helpful" and he always gave great attention to manners. No more will Beaumont House boys read the lessons at St John's at the beginning and end of each term. The old boys still plan to meet at the school, happily to be bought by two former pupils for use as their homes. The end of an era perhaps, but the school's spirit will survive in the lives of many men for a long time to come.'

CHAPTER SEVENTEEN

Controversies

T HE HERONSGATE ASSOCIATION has had to cope with many problems since its inception. In the last 25 years, there have been two major controversies: one where all acted together; the other where sympathies were not united. The Heronsgate Association was responsible for organising a protest against the route of the M25. £25,000 was raised for the services of a prominent barrister. Petitions were sent to Parliament and A.J.P. Taylor, the historian, wrote to 'The Times' stating that Heronsgate was an area of historic importance and the M25 would do much to spoil its character.

A.J.P. Taylor FBA was an Honorary Fellow of Magdalen College, Oxford. He was asked by the Association to produce a document on the effects of the M25 on Heronsgate. In his historical inquiry published in 1978 he wrote in detail about Chartism, the Chartist Land Company, the Chartist settlement and gave reasons for preserving Heronsgate:

> 'Five Chartist settlements were created: O'Connorville, renamed Heronsgate, Minster Lovell, renamed Charterville; Snigs End, Lowbands and Dodford. They represent the dream of a return from the factory towns to the rural countryside. Though small in themselves, they expressed a widespread feeling. The factory workers who found no escape in the Chartist land settlements took a different route to the same objective by emigrating to the colonies and the United States. The many millions who left England for the New World achieved the vision which O'Connor had first set before them.
>
> Heronsgate is the first and the best preserved of the Chartist settlements. Being an untried experiment it is somewhat smaller than the others. It retains much of its original character: its roads still narrow and quiet, the houses still largely intact and the schoolhouse as the outstanding point at one end. Despite such modern incursions as motor cars, it is still much as the original settlers found it. The Estate was first purchased as Herringsgate Farm in 1846 and consisted of 103 acres on which dwellings were built on an equivalent number of plots of land. The total acreage was divided up into 17 two-acre plots, five three-acre plots and 13 four-acre plots, plus four estate roads laid in the form of an H with a serif at the top of the left hand upright and cross member extended to the right. All the roads were made nine feet wide to permit the passage of an agricultural cart and the total length of the roads was one and a half miles. These roads have not altered in width or structure since 1846 except that the surfacing of some of them has been partially improved in recent years and they are still known by the names given to them originally.

The original 35 cottages built on the Estate with the exception of one were of two-storey construction. Their interior design varied in some degree and they are thought to have been advanced compared to other cottages of the period found elsewhere. They had windows which opened, kitchens with tiled floors and included an iron grate with oven and boiler for hot water. All were made of brick and were slate roofed. Reports of them by observers at the time expressed surprise and amazement at their advanced design.

The Estate as purchased by O'Connor for his Land Company extended to the boundary of Ladywalk Wood. The wood itself remained in private hands but there was no sharp division between it and the settlement. The cottagers had access to the wood and a right of way leads through it so that it ranks as an amenity of the Estate. The early settlers seem to have gathered wood there for kindling though there is no legal arrangement for them to do so. The settlers merely took the wood for granted. Since the Winding-Up Act passed in Parliament in 1851 and the sale of the Estate, little has changed in its character and layout.

All the original cottages remain with the exception of three burned down many years ago and one other of which no trace apparently exists. The various two, three and four-acre plots have in some cases had their boundaries rearranged but the original boundary of the Estate as a whole is clearly identifiable. Lowbands, Gloucestershire also preserves many of the original houses though the schoolhouse is almost unrecognizable because of later improvements. The overall plan is also difficult to follow except by patient exploration with an estate map. I found it the least interesting of the Chartists settlements in its present form.

Charterville, Oxfordshire, was intact until recently and made a fine display of a Chartist settlement with the schoolhouse on the main road. The general layout was clear despite a modern road running down the centre. Almost the entire settlement has now been destroyed in favour of a modern housing estate, leaving the schoolhouse in solitary glory. This vandalism should never be repeated. At Snigs End, Gloucestershire, most of the original cottages survive and the schoolhouse has become a public house, The Prince of Wales. Nothing, however, has been changed in it. But, the essential character of the settlement has been largely lost. There is a busy main road through the centre. There are filling stations and workshops so that it is difficult to recapture the atmosphere of the original settlement.

Dodford, Worcestershire, was the last of the settlements and not completed before O'Connor's bankruptcy. Hence the projected plan cannot be grasped without knowledge of the other settlements. Dodford has however one point of historical interest. When Jesse Collings was preparing the proposal of "three acres and a cow" for Joseph Chamberlain in 1884, he took Dodford as his model. From all this it follows that Heronsgate is an incomparable model of the Chartist dreams a century and more ago. Reasons for preserving Heronsgate are that there are features that distinguish Heronsgate from the other settlements. It is the only one with some two-storey, semidetached dwellings. All the others have only bungalow cottages, an indication that O'Connor was becoming less ambitious as the work went on. The so-called roads with their evocative names – Stockport Road, Nottingham Road, Halifax Road, Bradford Road – remain unmetalled apart from Stockport Road and with their original nine foot width, exactly as the Chartist settlers found them.

Heronsgate is the only settlement secure from through traffic and even the cars of the inhabitants move cautiously. Some of the houses have been extended and their internal arrangements have been greatly improved. Nevertheless, Heronsgate is the only Chartist settlement which the original lottery winners would recognise at once. Certainly at the present time Ladywalk Wood has become an essential part of Heronsgate. By closing access from the east it preserves the rural character which distinguishes Heronsgate so remarkably.

It may also be remarked that Heronsgate was an early example of what came to be known as garden suburbs or garden cities. When this movement started towards the end of the nineteenth century its pioneers often referred to the Chartist land settlements as their forerunners and on this ground also the settlements merit full protection as monuments to the early enlightenment of our ancestors. In my opinion, Heronsgate and other settlements are as much part of our historic heritage as are the cathedrals and great country houses on which so much money and care are lavished.

Heronsgate is an outstanding memorial to Chartism and its leader Feargus O'Connor. Until recently preservationists have not concerned themselves much with 19th century remains. Now industrial archaeology is a growing field for their activity. Early mills and factories are being preserved with their original machinery. O'Connorville should rank just as high. The effect of the Department of Transport's route for the M25 would be to deprive Heronsgate of its shield against the impact of modern times and forever to destroy its unique atmosphere and character. It is not just the land taken or the noise or the visual effect. It would be the inability of the settlement to evoke the spirit of the past. The alternative route put forward by the Heronsgate residents would in my opinion enable the unique character of the settlement to remain as it is, behind the ridge and Ladywalk Wood. Thus for historical and cultural reasons, the present proposed line of the motorway should be modified, particularly as there is an acceptable and satisfactory alternative'.

Grelle White of the Watford Observer visited Heronsgate and talked to many residents and on Friday October the 27th 1978 wrote an article which started with the headline: 'Heronsgate will fight Route G', and then went on to say:

'The threat of a motorway cutting straight through a local beauty spot and threatening the environment of a small historical village has united the people living there in preparing for a tough fight with the Department of Transport. The proposed route for the M25 extension past Maple Cross goes right through Ladywalk Wood on the edge of Heronsgate, demolishes two houses in its path, and, claim residents, will ruin their rural environment. That is Route G, the preferred route. Route H leaves Ladywalk Wood to form a screen between motorway and village and residents are preparing to battle – to the last legal point – to persuade the Minister to "save Heronsgate and Ladywalk Wood" by making H the motorway.

Amidst battle cries from Maple Cross to get the motorway built quickly, Heronsgate folk have kept quiet, accepting that their neighbours on the A412 must have motorway relief, but getting increasingly concerned that the preferred route G will also be the one announced by the Minister. Maple Cross favour Route G. "But they are half a mile away and the difference to them is negligible," said a committee member, when the Watford Observer attended a Saturday morning meeting of the Heronsgate (North Orbital Road) Committee.

Leading the campaign are father-and-son solicitors, Messrs Colin and Ian McCulloch – who have consulted professionals to establish that geographically, technically and financially Route H is feasible.

"If not we would have dropped it," said Colin McCulloch. They have also retained counsel to represent them at the public inquiry, which is expected in the spring of 1979. At Saturday's meeting, members were discussing publicity material, posters, pamphlets and car stickers which will come hot off the presses the moment their worst fears are confirmed. "Route G is not yet official," said Ian McCulloch, who is secretary for the committee, "but it is 99 per cent certain that that will be the route announced by the Minister, probably in November. All the same we must wait until it is official and go about the whole thing in a sensible, professional matter." The meeting took place at the heart of the former Chartist village.

Further down the lane, on the edge of Ladywalk Wood, people are finding it a little harder to remain cool and professional. Mick Flinn and his wife, Donna, bought their listed Chartist cottage two years ago and restored it with loving care — and faced a lot of concern from local planners lest they should upset its historical value. Now they are surrounded by motorway blight. "The other half of the semidetached cottages has already been bought by the Department of the Environment and the house behind us is likely to be bought by them as well, as it cannot be sold on the open market," said Mr Flinn.

When Donna and Mick moved to Heronsgate two years ago it seemed likely that Route H— on the other side of the wood – would be chosen. "It would have been the sensible choice. It is crazy to put the road this side – but they do not seem to care about things like history and environment," said Mick, adding: "The homes of our neighbours are considered uninhabitable if the road is built here, yet we have been assured that ours will be all right – with a sliproad 60ft from our front door!" The Flinns recently asked someone from the Department of the Environment to pay a visit. "The fellow seemed to think that as soon as the road was built they would be able to sell the cottage next to us – of course some people do not mind noise and fumes!", he added. "But most people who have chosen Heronsgate as their home do."

Malcolm and John Jackson bought their old school – Beaumont House – several years ago and split it into homes for their families. Malcolm's wife, Jane, is in charge of raising funds for the legal battle. "We came here because we like large gardens, animals and nature. We do not want to be fobbed off with double glazing", said Jane, as we walked through Ladywalk Wood, which, she said, could even be saved by making a slight curve in the G-route. Well-trodden paths seemed to indicate that this wood is used by others than the 250 residents in Heronsgate. "Lots of people use this wood on foot and horseback – people from Rickmansworth, Chorleywood and Maple Cross," she said. Concerned that their cause might seem selfish, Jane admitted that, yes, they were fighting for their own environment – but she also feels that Heronsgate forms an important part of the local environment and an extremely interesting chapter in local history. It was the first Chartist village, built in 1835 and named O'Connorville after Feargus O'Connor, leader of that short-lived movement to free the industrial slaves of the north by resettling them in small communities. The movement failed, but the original cottages – now listed and the layout and road names in Heronsgate remain a monument to this historic event.

And to attract local interest –and raise funds – Jane Jackson is planning a village market with everyone in costumes selling home-made goods across the garden gates, with geese and ducks and goats and lots of atmosphere … in the hope that local support can be enrolled to help save the village. There will be an art exhibition in the former gymnasium at Beaumont House and a dance in the Memorial Hall, Chorleywood. Looking across the field from Ladywalk Wood, Mrs Jackson describes how in a fighting spirit she and others put posters in the wood warning people that it was doomed. But the posters were pulled down. "The farmer who owns the wood would obviously rather lose a wood than agricultural land," she admits, but although sympathetic she and her fellow campaigners feel that one man's bit of land does not compare with the future of the whole of the community...

Turning back into Heronsgate, we have stopped in front of two houses, nestling on the edge of the wood and right in the path of the proposed six-lane motorway. One is already empty and owned by the Government. The other has been the home for 43 years, of Annie and David Gilbey. "Where will we go?" said Mr Gilbey, leaning on the gate to his neatly attended garden which could be swallowed up by tarmac in a few years' time. Even so, Mr Gilbey says that he has no feelings for himself, but it saddens him to think of the future in store for the people in Heronsgate. "They say that the loss of the wood is not going to make any difference to the noise in Heronsgate. Of course it will. We notice the difference in the noise from farm machinery between summer and winter when the trees have lost their leaves." said Mr Gilbey ...'

(It should be pointed out there are some minor historical errors in details and dates in these articles).

The case was lost. Rumour contends it was due to some administrative foul up, but the action had almost 100 percent support of the residents. However, it was not the end of the matter. Compensation was given by the Department of the Environment and Transport amounting to thousands of pounds to residents in the south end of Heronsgate; other residents, particularly those in Nottingham Road North and Bradford Road felt aggrieved as they received nothing for the noise and pollution caused by the volume of traffic on the new M25. Some residents took legal action and the matter was resolved with the payment of compensation.

On the M25 question, the Heronsgate residents acted together but the issue of conservation was to split the community. The Heronsgate Gazette of February 1991 speaks about the proposal to make Heronsgate a conservation area:

'Last year, Three Rivers District Council asked for our views on the proposed designation of Heronsgate as a conservation area. During September, all residents over the age of 18, within the area covered by the proposal, were asked to express their views by way of a vote.

The result was as follows:

AGREED IN PRINCIPLE	63
DISAGREED	70

Although the majority of residents voted against the proposal, Three Rivers are of the view that Heronsgate should be designated. Initially they decided to proceed forthwith, contrary to the undertaking given by Councillor Ann Shaw that residents would have an opportunity to comment on any proposed designation when the district plan was published. Derrick Mead, the chairman of the Residents' Association had a number of telephone conversations with the planning department and Mrs Shaw also expressed concern that the decision was contrary to her undertaking. The designated area has been extended: it now appears to include Ladywalk, Oakhill, White Lodge, Long Lane House and The Land of Liberty'

The Council won the day on the grounds that Heronsgate satisfied the criteria for designation as a conservation area, in that Heronsgate did have architectural and historic interest.

It was one of the 19th century Chartist Land Company settlements. The importance of Chartism in British 19th century history is well known.

- The area retains much of the planned form of the original Chartist settlement. The original narrow lanes remain.
- There are five listed Chartist buildings in the area.(Bircham Cottage, Chartist Cottage and Wood Weye, Woodene and Long Meadow, Laurel Cottage and Crowthorne, and Sunnyside). Other buildings are not listed but at least 12 are recognisable as being of Chartist origins.
- The construction of the M25 motorway did affect the southern end of Heronsgate but only marginally and it did not affect the major part of the settlement.
- Rule 4 about painting and minor alterations in a conservation area was not to be applied, but new building would be very difficult, apart from the allowable percentage extension on existing buildings. The council have listed Crowthorne and Laurel Cottage on the statutory list of important buildings and Rosemary and Craven Cottage have been decreed of local interest.

Heronsgate residents have adapted to life with the M25; for some the noise of the traffic is a problem, but for most, the noise is a minor irritant. Conservation and new building however, remain a source of division and argument.

CHAPTER EIGHTEEN

The Dream Fulfilled – 1970s to the Millennium

THE YEARS FOLLOWING 1970 were to see Heronsgate change gradually but radically in its social attitudes and ordered physical appearance. At times it was difficult to detect the changes but the closure of Beaumont House in 1970 marked a watershed in Heronsgate's history. Heronsgate at that time was regarded by local estate agents as an isolated backwater, dark and overgrown with trees and with uncut hedges which made movement along the pot-holed lanes even more difficult. This particularly applied to Nottingham Road. The days of the doffed cap by the Beaumont House boys and the smallholding enterprises were gone and a new Heronsgate was emerging. The only remaining school was the nursery school now run by Mrs C.E. Jeskins at the Hall. Nowadays it caters for boys and girls in the age range from two to five and is open from 9.00 am to 12 noon. Mrs Jeskins is supported by a team of experienced staff who teach a curriculum according to the Schools Learning Outcomes and prepare their students to start the National Curriculum Key Stage One. Children are encouraged to investigate and make informed choices; specific skills taught include reading skills, writing and number development. Physical development is encouraged by the use of indoor and outdoor apparatus. Other activities include regular outings, listening to guest speakers on appropriate topics, cooking, music sessions and nature walks.

The school had opened in 1940 as Walmer House School at Green Street, Chorleywood originally run as a joint venture by Mr Wright and Mrs M. Vanstone. Shortly after the war, Mr Wright transferred the school to Heronsgate Hall where he carried on single-handed. The newly formed Heronsgate Association wanted to find a continued use and source of income for the old Wesleyan chapel.

Mr and Mrs Yiend talk about Walmer House School with affection:

'Sorting through a box of old papers recently we found a receipted bill for £5 8s 9d (including extras of 3s 9d). The year was 1956 and represented the fee for a term's tuition at Walmer House School, Heronsgate, for our son David aged 5.

We remembered then "old Mr. Wright" who, whatever the weather, travelled every day from Ealing to Heronsgate Hall where he somehow, singlehandedly, managed to instill the principles of the three R's into some 15 to 20 reluctant five to seven year olds.

David tells us he had a uniform, "grey cap and a tie with some light blue", and school was 9 am to 12 noon, home to lunch and then 2 pm to 3.30 every afternoon except Wednesday which was a half day.

Friday afternoon was reserved for charades. The children (boys and girls) were taught in groups according to age.

There was none of the "learning through play" that seems to be the norm for this age group today. The children sat on benches at long tables (and very dusty they were too). The floor was rough with plenty of splinters if you fell over; in all, the Hall was a shabby place with indifferent lighting. But Mr. Wright was a kindly man (although he did possess a cane which could be used if necessary!).

He appears to have had few problems with discipline, apart from one memorable occasion which reads more like today at a deprived inner city school. Living locally in rented accommodation was an American Army Sergeant and his Filipino wife. They had numerous children, two of whom occasionally attended Walmer House and were, to say the least of it, somewhat disruptive. One morning the elder boy arrived armed with some rather large knives and threatened Mr. Wright who promptly called the other boys to his aid. With great delight they rushed into the fray and at least two of them, David and he thinks Richard Warman, sat on the offender who was promptly disarmed. Unfortunately, David cannot remember what happened next, he does remember however that the same child arrived one afternoon smothered in sticky goo and on being questioned replied "Mum threw a pot of jam at me"!

However basic Walmer House in retrospect may seem there is no doubt that Mr Wright taught his pupils well. Mr Vezey (headmaster of Beaumont House School), when presenting the prizes at the Walmer House Speech Day at the Florence Brown Hall, spoke very highly of his abilities. He took several pupils from there. Mr Vezey expected a seven year old child to read coherently from the Old Testament (King James version at that) which is some reflection of the standard achieved.'

Mr Wright ran the school successfully and with enthusiasm until his retirement in the late 1950s. The Watford Observer said on his retirement that it was the deep snow drifts of the late 1950s that forced Mr Wright to decide to retire. At the school prizegiving in the Florence Brown Hall, Chorleywood, on a summer's day in 1959, a presentation was made to Mr Wright on behalf of the parents by Mr Peter Vezey, the headmaster of Beaumont House, who received many of Mr Wright's pupils. Mr Wright was given a cheque and a book entitled 'Rider on a Grey Horse' (a biography of Indian Mutiny days) written by Barry Joynson Cork whom Mr Wright had taught and who lived in Shire Lane. Mr Vezey said that Mr Wright would be remembered for his patience.

Heronsgate has seen much development since the 1970s. Chorheron (formerly The Bungalow) on Long Lane, reconstructed over approximately ten years by Charles Dinsdale, the Haberdasher Aske schoolmaster, emerged beyond all recognition from its Chartist origins and bungalow days. During the building programme a shoe clog dating back to O'Connor days was discovered. Other houses along Long Lane, Stockport Road and Bradford Road have all had their extensions and improvements.

Perhaps Nottingham Road has seen the most significant changes. In 1970, Roy Clark built his admirable new home (Walnut Tree Cottage) some distance away from the old Chartist cottage, which is now his garage; he is justifiably proud of his creation. A fine new large house called Briar Wood was planned and constructed by the Wiseman family in 1976, whilst the small bungalow known as Briar Patch built in 1953 on part of the Clark land and lived in for many years by Webb, the butcher, became incorporated into the new building. Farfield under the Grives and Mawhoods underwent major surgery in the 70s, whilst Amberwood appeared from the skeleton of the ramshackle Beehive. The Beehive had a proud history: it had been built by the Fitzsimmons family at the turn of the century – constructed by a chapel builder to a chapel design with a wooden base and corrugated iron walls and roof. When the Longhursts moved there they found a bible belonging to Iris Fitzsimmons dated 1904. Field Cottage witnessed its major renovations in the 1980s under the guidance of Christine Ross who moved from Whitegates. Christine now lives in Rickmansworth, but is often seen at St John's where her organ playing gives pleasure to those attending church services.

In the 1980s Ron Skilton sold the derelict remains of his Chartist cottage to the Redheads, who began their own renovations of the now combined double Chartist cottage to make Croft House a very desirable property; this was completed by the early 1990s. Ron Skilton built his own house Glenthorne on a new site: it was started in 1965, and completed by Mick and Donna Flinn in the 1990s.

The Greasleys constructed a modern house La Casita in the 1950s to replace the old Jennifer Cottage to the north west side of the Hall. In the 1990s it continues to offer a fine example of architectural enterprise. The Orchard has retained much of its original structure of the 1910s, as has Myrtle House whose main extensions were done in the 1890s.

The original Chartist cottages, Rosemary Cottage, Craven Cottage, Crowthorne and Laurel Cottage have all had their improvements and extensions but the pattern of the original construction can still be seen. Crowthorne has seen the least alteration since 1847. Cherry Tree Lane houses have also been improved and extended. Thus, today the whole Estate presents a picture of well-cared for houses, each with its own character and attractiveness.

And just outside the boundaries of the former O'Connorville Estate lies The Land of Liberty, Peace and Plenty public house, now considered part of Heronsgate and no longer out of bounds to Heronsgate residents; it offers a pleasant meeting place for locals and visitors. A wide ranging group of local personalities congregates here. On Sunday lunchtimes the proper locals, often with family connections going back to the previous century, gather to play dominoes and on some occasions listen to Tony Tonks the 'singing window cleaner'.

However, it was the 1970s and 1980s when The Land of Liberty was at its peak. This was the time when Vi Cornhill and Brian, Peter and Shirley Kent, Peter and Sandy Parkin were the landlords. It was Vi, a diminutive little lady with a versatile tongue, who built the pub into a popular watering hole and provider of fine food. She would start at midday, hardly visible behind the bar with a half bottle of champagne and end it with a cursory dismissal of her late drinking customers. In the meantime Vi would have fallen out with Brian (her partner) because he would give away sandwiches or would price every round at exactly £5. At lunch time two sittings would be served and there was much merriment among the eaters and drinkers. Charlie Chaplin and other well known actors, actresses, producers and cameramen including 'Arfur' (Arthur Ibbotson) would visit the pub from Denham Studios nearby to enjoy Vi's hospitality; her cold ham on the bone was a speciality.

Tim Fox, a long-standing friend of the author and great raconteur, recalled that on one visit to the Land of Liberty, Charlie Chaplin ordered his normal 'ham on the bone'; Vi had none that day but said she would cook him anything he wanted. In anger Charlie Chaplin replied 'I would like to make an order for the boot (the sack)'. An old boot was found and was duly cooked and remained in a prominent position on the counter at the back of the bar for many years in memory of Charlie Chaplin's visits and Vi's negligence. A similar collection of individuals would gather for a social drink in the evening to exchange their stories. Mercifully times have changed little at The Land.

The Heronsgate Residents Association has become increasingly important during the years of this chapter. It dates back to 14th February 1947. The association came into being with the buying of the Wesleyan Chapel (which had been largely unused since before the war), by Hubert Birdwood, Frank Heyworth Talbot and Hugh Leonard and its subsequent selling to the Heronsgate Association. Mr Talbot guaranteed the mortgage, and land for a car park was donated by the owners of The Orchard. The principal figures in the early days of the association were Heyworth Talbot, barrister (The Grange), Hugh Leonard, petroleum refiner (Ladywalk), S.R. Van Duzer, company director (The Firs), R.J. Parsons, director (Herons Court), Hubert Birdwood, civil servant (Sherwood), Tom Jones FCA (Whitegates), Stephen Richards, engineer (Stanmore Lodge), John Venn, notary public (Wiverton), R.K. Ross, launderer (The Pines), Peter Vezey, schoolmaster (Beaumont House), F.C. Blyth, gentleman (Midgham Cottage).

The objects of The Heronsgate Association as it was initially named were most honourable and aimed: 'To foster social intercourse among persons resident in Heronsgate and its vicinity and to provide facilities for social, political, cultural, recreational and other meetings and assemblies'. It would be fair to say many people since have devoted much time to the association and it has played an important role in the life of the community. From the 70s onwards it has become increasingly active.

In the early 1980s the association became known as The Heronsgate Residents Association. This was because the original constitution was not specific enough and it did not meet requirements of acting for residents in regard to external matters. This was particularly the case in matters involving the council. More recently the association has been involved in many happy social occasions, including taking on the responsibility from the church for organising and running the annual safari supper. The church ran the safari suppers for many years where residents would gather at Sherwood for an opening drink and then move round the Estate to eat a three-course meal with each course served at different houses. The evenings ended with dessert and a valedictory drink at The Grange.

The prettiest spring garden in May is another popular event. Almost every garden is open for viewing and then inspected by the residents before a secret vote in the Hall is taken and the winner receives a salver donated by Mr and Mrs Knight formerly of Pinhaye. Much hard work by all concerned goes into the gardens in spring and Heronsgate looks a picture in May.

John Jackson in his years of residency at Beaumont House delighted in carrying on the tradition of golf and each year there is a competition on John's immaculately prepared nine hole course. The Birdwood field, although still owned by the family, has been in the care of the community since 1983. The cost of maintenance is met from Heronsgate funds and many residents have been busy keeping it in good order. Working parties can often be seen trimming the trees, clearing, tidying and cutting the grass. It provides a most attractive asset for Heronsgate and has been used for many social events and car parking.

The lanes committee is always active and deals with many problems. The flash flood of 31st May 1992 caused considerable damage; on returning home that night Kali, my labrador had to swim from the car almost to the house. This flood led to an improved run-off system from the lanes. The introduction of a staggered speed ramp in Stockport Road highlighted the difficulties caused by the narrowness of the lanes, the many obscured accesses and junctions and the fact that some people do speed. Further improvements have been made including a system of clear signs warning people of speed limits, the imminence of humps, the fact that children are playing, concealed entrances and the narrowness of the lanes making them unsuitable for large vehicles.

The social committee has been active in other areas. In September 1990 a grand ball was held at the Memorial Hall in Chorleywood with a buffet supper provided by outside caterers and music by the Roy Galler jazz band. The main purpose of the ball was to provide funds for the building of a new kitchen and cloakroom for Heronsgate Hall. Following the success of the ball it was decided to bolster the funds for the improvement of the Hall further by holding a street fair. This event took place in September 1991: numerous stalls, side shows and games were organised. It was another triumph and attracted many people not only from Heronsgate, but also from the neighbouring villages and towns. Unfortunately, as in the garden open days of the 1970s, a spate of burglaries followed and the concept of street fairs also had to be abandoned.

An enjoyable but time-consuming activity of the committee was the organisation for the celebrations of the 150th anniversary of the founding of the Estate. This involved the setting up of an exhibition of Heronsgate life since its foundation, and the invitation to lecturers to speak. It is very pleasing to write that Dorothy Thompson and James Epstein, who contributed chapters two and four in this book, accepted our invitation to speak. Both gave most informative and interesting lectures in the Hall to full houses and their talks were very well-received by their audiences.

The celebrations went on for a fortnight: they started with a black tie dinner at Ladywalk, on Saturday the 24th of May 1997, where there was music, dancing and entertainment, and continued with an exhibition in the Hall. Festivities ended with a grand family anniversary day, on Sunday the 8th of June. The anniversary day began with a thanksgiving service in St John's Church. The church was full: Christine Ross played the organ, Michael Hatfield read the lesson from Genesis chapter 28, and the Reverend Canon Dr Alan Horsley, after welcoming the congregation and praising the hymn singing, gave the sermon. His main theme was to remember and thank God for the lives of Feargus O'Connor and the Reverend W. J. Neild, the first vicar of the combined parishes of Mill End, West Hyde and Heronsgate, who was born by a happy coincidence 150 years ago and, like O'Connor, was concerned with the underprivileged. Canon Horsley ended his sermon with the comment that out of the failure of the original settlement had come a loving and caring community with which both O'Connor and the Reverend Neild would have been pleased.

From the church, the congregation paraded in Victorian dress to the Hall where Richard Warman, the chairman of the association, spoke about the first settlers. Katie Warman and Katie Ralph read extracts from works of the Chartist poet Ernest Jones; then a plaque was unveiled in recognition by the residents of Heronsgate to its founder Feargus O'Connor.

The idea of the plaque came from the Chorleywood and Rickmansworth Labour Party who, not unreasonably, wanted the residents to share the cost of the plaque and for the plaque to include a reference that it was erected by the Chorleywood and Rickmansworth Labour Party. The members of the Heronsgate Residents Association at their Annual General Meeting held in 1996 rejected this idea on the grounds that the Land Company was non-political, the Labour Party did not exist at that time and O'Connor was an Independent Member of Parliament and inclined to support the reforms of the Liberal or Whig party of the mid-19th century. They decided to erect their own plaque to be placed at the entrance to the Hall. It reads:

In
Proud Memory of
O'CONNORVILLE
founded here in
1847
by FEARGUS O'CONNOR MP
Chartist, Idealist &
Social Reformer

Then with banners waving, trumpets blaring and chanting of the Heronsgate song written by an Australian friend of Donna and Mick Flinn, the 1997 residents of Heronsgate with their friends and ex-residents marched to the Birdwood field where the afternoon was spent in the atmosphere of the mid-19th century. Roast pig cooked by Higgins, the Chorleywood butcher and picnics prepared by the ladies were eaten; beer and wine was consumed. Entertainment included morris dancing by a visiting troupe, craft demonstrations, tug-of-war competitions and Victorian games. Music was played by John Jackson and singing of varying quality was heard. The last people went home in mid-evening and in good order – just like the early settlers after O'Connor's meetings – including the four residents who had been celebrating their birthdays on that day.

Not all, over the years, have seen Heronsgate in the most favourable light. Arthur Horner, the Australian cartoonist, who lived at Homeland in the 1970s and died in March 1997, dreamt up Colonel Pewter and used him to depict the essentially English bowler-hatted city gent, or the crazy collector of golf putters or the accumulator of status symbol cars. After the death of Arthur Horner, Christopher Bell (resident of Shire Lane, Chorleywood) wrote to The Guardian on the 11th of March 1997

'Whimshire, drawn by Arthur Horner with such affection, was actually leafy Heronsgate in Hertfordshire. The artist's gentle sense of irony delighted in the fact that opulent, swimming-pooled mansions now stood on the site of O'Connorville, one of the original Chartist settlements built for working men by Feargus

O'Connor in the 1840s. But the Horner family and their left-leaning donkeys were on good neighbourly terms with the Colonel Pewters and mine cannot be the only house with a Horner original proudly on its walls'

To continue this theme, Paul Foot, the son of Michael Foot, the former Labour Party leader and old boy from Leighton Park (my school) wrote in 'The Guardian' on Monday the 2nd of June 1997:

'Christopher Bell, a Labour party member in Hertfordshire, tells me a story which shows how labour history is acceptable, even admirable, until it interferes with what is happening today. His constituency includes Heronsgate, one of the settlements built by the Chartist Land Company to provide homes and votes for factory workers. Heronsgate was inaugurated as O'Connorville by huge jubilant crowds on May Day 1847. The Labour Party resolved to commemorate the 150th anniversary of that joyful May Day with a slate plaque on Heronsgate Hall "in proud memory of O'Connorville founded here in 1847 by Fergus O'Connor, Chartist, Idealist and Social Reformer". Underneath the plaque in very small letters they proposed to add: "Erected by the Chorleywood and Rickmansworth Labour Party on May 1, 1997". This was too much for the Hall's owners, the wealthy burghers of Heronsgate Residents' Association, most of whom live in newly built mansions complete with swimming pools. They voted to ban the plaque if it contained the slightest reference to the Labour Party. So the memorial was never installed. Last week, the Residents' Association sponsored an exhibition of documents about O'Connorville – all old "historical" and safely irrelevant.'

And Paul Barker writing in 'The New Statesman' of the 25th July 1997 comments:

'Nowadays, the Chartist model town of O'Connorville is a leafy, arcadian village, much sought after by the Mercedes-owning classes.

O'Connorville was launched with a march from London to the fields of Hertfordshire: "Labour's Procession to Labour's own Land, purchased with Labour's own Money". Special songs were written, including "Beautiful Villas" and "No Longer to be a Slave". Fergus O'Connor had founded his Chartist Land Company to set up new settlements as a form of workers' self-help. (His fiercest rival, Bronterre O'Brien, derided it for undermining the great aim of land nationalisation). Here were the first fruits.

At Heronsgate, near Rickmansworth, 103 acres were bought. In Manchester, O'Connor presided over a ballot for 35 smallholdings. He spoke of clear skies and rich soil; of children at school, not in the mill; of vice withering and virtue abounding. On 1 May 1847 the first tenants moved in. Ten years later the bankrupt Estate was auctioned off. An experiment was over. The way forward, it turned out, was the building society movement, also sustained by northern working men, and now being destroyed. (When they asked the chief executive of the Halifax about the change, he said he would spend much more time in the City of London. QED.)

On a reprint of a Chartist poster, I am touched to see that plot 31 (four acres) was taken by a man, James Greenwood, from my native village in the Yorkshire Pennines, Hebden Bridge. He was also the first to sell – to a London tradesman, who wanted a retirement house. O'Connor's Northern Star carried angry correspondence. I like to think it was sheer local shrewdness. I am kindly shown the poster by the people who live in the old brick schoolhouse O'Connor built. The new-fangled name, "O'Connorville" was ditched and long forgotten; but earlier this year the Heronsgate Association marked the 150th anniversary with a dance ("best frock and dinner jacket," one celebrant reports, "unlike our Chancellor") and a barbecue (roast pig, stove-pipe hats.) An old Wesleyan chapel acquired a fine blue plaque, "In proud memory of O'Connorville" and "Feargus O'Connor MP, Chartist, Idealist and Social Reformer.

You turn off the M25 at exit 17, into gentle countryside. In half a mile you are among some gritty-sounding addresses: Nottingham, Stockport, Bradford and Halifax Roads, named after towns that early supporters came from. But O'Connor made the roads only nine feet wide; lanes, really. Today hawthorn and laurel overhang them. Houses in Heronsgate are much sought after. It is a private, arcadian world. The smallholdings, never less than two acres, have become huge gardens with luxuriant trees, swimming pools, double or triple garages (some as big as O'Connor's original cottages).

A Mercedes for him, for example, and a Hyundai hatchback for her. You look out over fields of meadowsweet, or into paddocks. A man goes by on a bike, exercising two liver-coloured Weimaraners. Houses have been rebuilt and enlarged. But, enwrapped within many of them, you see evidence of how it began; a modest but elegant two-storey semi in classical style. On each gable-end is O'Connor's little device: a logogram of the People's Charter, partly unscrolled like a sacred text. As a businessman he failed; but he planned better than he is given credit for. A semi in the country, with garden, has become the enduring English ideal — working-class or middle-class — in spite of eco-campaigners' arguments that people should prefer a close-packed terrace house in town. His villas, with fitted book-shelves, surprised contemporaries: "tradesmen", rather than "working man", standard:

> Has Freedom whispered in his wistful ear,
> "Courage, poor slave! Deliverance is near"?
> Oh, she has breathed a summons sweeter still.
> "Come, take your garden at O'Connorville."

There are 60 houses in these green lanes. "It is the sort of place you only leave in a box," a man says, as he sweeps up in the front of the church. Even then you may come back. Your ashes can be scattered in the little garden behind. In the chancel I find a brass to Frederick Felkin, born in Nottingham 1834, died 1903. He must have been one of the handful of settlers who stayed on.' (In fact, Felkin was not an original settler-author.)

'The Watford Labour Party, I'm told, tried to use the church porch as a nomination platform at the last election, wheeling Tony Benn on as further proof of Labour continuity. (But O'Connor wrote: "My plan has no more to do with socialism than it has to do with a comet." Halley's comet had reappeared in the 1830s.) The present citizens of O'Connorville were not amused.

Like many reformers O'Connor was better at giving instructions than at following them. He lived at Hope Cottage (now Hope Lodge) with resident poodle, where he fathered two sons by a local woman, but didn't marry her. He was to die of drink, but he insisted that O'Connorville should be dry. Just outside the settlement limits, however, there is a pub called The Land of Liberty, Peace and Plenty. The front of the sign shows O'Connor speaking in favour of voting by ballot; the reverse shows King John signing the Magna Carta. The bar is full of men wielding samples of the ten guest beers and watching rugby via satellite. Liberty comes in many packages.'

Whilst I respect all these critical articles they do not depict the Heronsgate I know. Heronsgate is a caring community, the only qualification to live here is that you can afford to buy a house, and property prices are often lower than in neighbouring areas. Its inhabitants offer a complete cross section of support for the political parties; they come from differing social backgrounds; and they have a wide variety of talents and abilities. Most have been attracted to the settlement by its unique atmosphere, its historic connections, the leafy lanes, the sense of isolation and – although it is now within shouting distance of the M25 – the sense of peace and tranquillity and safety. They are attracted by the amenities offered to old and young from gardens to foxes, from birds to tennis, from badgers to horse riding, from deer to the space for their dogs, from fields to trampoline. But, perhaps above all, they are attracted by the freedom to chat and wave, stop and talk or ignore it all as the mood takes. As one couple described it 'When you turn into Stockport Road, it is like driving into your own driveway and a sense of well-being creeps over you'. But Heronsgate does not suit everyone; some find it both claustrophobic and lonely and they quickly move on. However, the majority stay and think of Heronsgate as their Shangri-la: some have been born here and are still here, some have lived here for close to 50 years, many have been here for more than 20 years. Some are newcomers, but above all there is a happy mix of talents between the older and younger elements; if there is a common factor today, it can be seen in the enterprising, artistic, musical and creative interests of its inhabitants.

As we move away from the 150th year since its foundation and towards the millennium, a new cycle in the development of Heronsgate begins to emerge. Residents with long-standing associations with the Estate have moved, new owners have taken their place and a younger element is now clearly discernible with different ambitions and ideals. The pace of life has increased but hopefully the old traditions of a care for the community and the peace and tranquillity will remain. Thus the big houses, Ladywalk and the Grange, sometimes known as the 'bookends of Heronsgate' have new owners and Herons Court, in the middle, also has new occupants. Many of the larger houses along Long Lane are witnessing extensive renovations and houses in the inner regions are seeing their improvements too. As in the days of the original O'Connorville, there have been movements within Heronsgate; for instance, the McMurtries have moved from The Grange to The Birches and the Shaws, formerly of Amberwood, now live in School House (Beaumont House).

Two new houses have appeared in Nottingham Road South; firstly the old Beaumont House School science cottage and at one time the masters' accommodation has been knocked down and a two-storey building has been constructed. Secondly, at Homeland, a new house has been built on the former tennis court and orchard to the south of the house to replace the cottage at the back of Homeland. Although it is quite possible for old houses to be knocked down and new houses constructed to specifications in keeping with the character of the Estate, it is unlikely that any new houses will be permitted in this conservation area. The increased traffic in the lanes and the demand on services is already a major cause of concern.

As the year 2000 comes closer, so the preservation of the character of the Estate becomes a more important issue. Many are concerned about the increasing air traffic above their houses and the possibility of the construction of a service station on the M25 close to Heronsgate and the consequent increase in noise is another problem; but in the main, residents look forward to the year 2000 and beyond with confidence. Heronsgate will remain a desirable area in which to live;

the facilities of the Estate will be protected. Much work has been done recently to keep the Hall in a good state of repair and the people continue to be concerned about the church, the lanes and the expectations of the inhabitants. A quarter-acre section once part of High Holly land and used for bee-keeping, has recently been purchased by the Hatfields and will be used by the church as a quiet garden and one is reassured about the future by the continued presence of dogs, horses and the abundance of wild life.

A millennium celebration is planned for New Year's Eve; the Birdwood's field will, as in the 150th celebration, be the venue and once more it is expected the field will reverberate with the sound of music, singing and dancing and the next period in Heronsgate's history begins with high hopes. This is the story of Heronsgate and its patterns of change and development, of success and failure. The overriding picture is of residents working together to achieve a community where the individual is important but the welfare of all is paramount.

CHAPTER NINETEEN

Heronsgate Remembered

THE FOLLOWING CHAPTERS invoke the memories of current residents, former residents and friends of Heronsgate. Some memories go back to the earliest years of the century and some are very recent. They are presented to the reader as a concluding insight into a cross-section of people who are interested in Heronsgate and have contributed to its character.

Terry Wearing who has been farming in the area for many years and plays dominoes on a Sunday at The Land of Liberty, remembers the 1950s when he was pig farming. After the sows had had their litters, they let the piglets out to grub in the woodlands; one day he received a frantic call from Mrs Ross at Breve House saying: 'I have over a hundred piglets asleep on my lawn, they are causing no harm but I don't know what to do with them.'

Moyra Nockolds came with her husband to Chartist Cottage after Harold was demobbed at the end of the Second World War. Harold Nockolds, writer and author, was the motor racing correspondent for The Times and then a director of IPC. Moyra's loves were pottery and horse riding. She had ample opportunity for both in Heronsgate. Heronsgate's association with hunting goes back to the earliest days of the Estate and in Moyra's time The Old Berkeley met regularly. The Old Berkeley used the kennels (Dog Kennel Lane) on The Common and later amalgamated with the Whaddon Chase (Vale of Aylesbury). In those times the Master was Dorien Williams who was to become the BBC commentator on show jumping. Dorothy Haigh, who lived at Wood Weye, hated the hunting season as horses and hounds meeting at Ladywalk ran all over the Estate. Windsor Park was not too far away and here Moyra indulged herself in carriage driving. The grounds of Chartist Cottage were, under the Nockolds, a delight and Moyra enjoyed her pottery in the garden shed. Moyra now lives in the shadow of Windsor Castle. She moved there in 1975, when her husband developed cancer and the horses and children had gone, but she remembers Heronsgate as an old-fashioned village with its croquet and tennis parties and a church. The church was enlivened when the very knowledgeable, dry, but popular QC, Frank Heyworth Talbot, gave the sermon and the boys of Beaumont House produced the carol service. Mr Vezey used to roar at the boys, but they were very well behaved.

The Clark family bought the original Walnut Tree Chartist cottage from J.F. Marchant in 1929, having previously lived at Wood Croft. Roy, one of Victor Clark's sons, was to marry Di Topley, who lived almost next door at Pixie House. In the 1970s they moved out of the original Chartist cottage to the new Walnut Tree Cottage where they live in happy retirement. They have many tales of Heronsgate. They remember others talking about Mr Bird and Dorothy Haigh going to the Miss Richardson School in Halifax Road and Mr Bird speaking of Whitegates being rebuilt in 1925. They remember the Second Heronsgate Girl Guides, who used to march the lanes of Heronsgate and take in the church parade in the prewar years with Jane Aston, Sylvia and Ruth Clarkson, Betty Bird, Pamela Simeon, Ann Venn with, of course, Di and her sister Pat, being amongst its members. Dorothy Harman who at that time lived at Newell's Cottage was persuaded to be the first Guides' captain and a little brick shed on the grounds of Rosecot was the Girl Guides HQ.

The triangle of cottages Crowthorne, Wood Croft and Bramble Close are remembered as the homes of the gardeners White, Clarkson and Bunce. Mr White was the gardener for the Astons and Birdwoods, while Mrs White sorted for Heronsgate residents. Clarkson was the Bowlers' gardener, while Bunce worked for the Morris's at The Grey Cottage. Bowood next to Wood Croft was the home of the Bradbury brothers who collected newspapers and kept very much to themselves.

Miss King and her charges had by now stopped using the Wesleyan chapel and it was empty until 1947 when the residents bought it. The Hall, as it was now called, became the focal centre of the Estate and the Clarks remember the Friday Club with fond memories for its progressive table tennis, dancing, whist drives and other events. Money from these evenings was used to pay the mortgage. Perhaps their most exciting memory goes back to the early 1950s, when the police in their attempt to find Kim Philby, blocked the exits of Heronsgate. Nowadays the Clarks are devoted to their badgers and monkjacks and garden.

Ann Venn recounts that her parents bought The Nook in 1930 when she was six months old and the name of the house was changed to Wiverton after a happy family holiday at Wiverton in Norfolk. The coal sheds in the yard were originally greyhound kennels. Main drainage was introduced in 1936 and before that 'the drainers' as Ann called them dealt with this matter. The Venns paid an annual tithe to the Parsons at Herons Court, somewhat strangely as the Hagyards also thought, since Wiverton had been the original Chartist cottage (see explanation about fee rents in Chapter 8). Sammy Clark was a lovely character. He was a member of St Peter's Church, Mill End and played a shepherd in the nativity play of 1948, in which Ann also had a part. But Sammy is remembered for driving the horse drawn milk float and allowing Ann to take the reins. Ann was a member of the 2nd Heronsgate Girl Guides and earned her stripes and guide badge working 96 hours 'really hard' at Miss Elsie Kidner's rabbitory at The Orchard during the war. Miss Kidner bred rabbits for fur and meat having formerly had boarding kennels and a cattery. The camps for the Girl Guides were fun. They were in the grounds of Chorleywood House and Dick Harman and Mr Topley used to escort the girls and help establish camp. Mr Clempson, the organist at St John's, was remembered for giving excellent music lessons at St Cecilia.

Sandy and Gill Gibbins remember Arthur Horner as a handsome, bearded, slightly piratical, eccentric man who lived next door with his wife, two daughters, rabbits, a donkey, a goat, a peacock, a peahen, hens and a worshipping golden retriever bitch. All of these strayed from time to time; to their surprise and slight alarm, late one evening there was a stomping outside. On investigating, they saw a procession of Arthur's animals proceeding slowly past their lower windows out through the back gate to return home. Where had they been? Why was it that the animals were in such perfect formation? Visions of Noah and the animals escaping from the flood came to mind. Arthur Horner was the man who dreamed up Colonel Pewter when 'The News Chronicle' wanted a cartoon strip and the Colonel was soon winning popularity medals. Horner also did straight political cartoons.

In March 1997, I visited Fred Babcock's widow. Mrs Peta Babcock walked enthusiastically towards the western end of her 14-acre property now known as Long Lane House – 'rather a pretentious name' she said, and 'I am going to show you where I think Herringsgate Farm is sited'. I was excited too as Terry Wearing, farmer and fountain of local knowledge, had spoken of Herringsgate Farm, the original Putnam farmhouse of the O'Connorville Estate being on the Babcock property. Peta showed me evidence of an old pond, wine cellar and well. Later I hurried down to Chorleywood library and looked at the 1805 Ordnance Survey map which shows Herringsgate Farm in the grounds of The Grange or Laburnums / The Hop Garden but it does confirm High Ash Farm to be on the boundary of Long Lane House acres and Bullsland farmland now owned by Robin Taylor. More recently it has been established that the ruins Peta Babcock had shown me on her property were those of High Ash Farm. It was a farm until the 1870s.

Mrs Babcock's property is interesting in that originally it was the farrier's cottage, named Mumfistells; so called because it was built on a mound, where the spring waters emerged from the ground. It was built in the 1790s in a two-up and two-down style. The forge where the farrier worked is to be found just by the Stag Pub. Part of the Babcock acreage may have been acquired from the original Chartist Estate, but Peta continues the Chartist ideology of living off the land by keeping hens and goats, sheep and horses and growing vegetables.

Mick Hatfield speaking at a farewell party in 1982 about the departure of Brenda and Nigel Birdwood for Wales remembers that this was the end of 52 years of association of the Birdwood family with Heronsgate. Hubert and Brenda, Nigel's parents, had bought Sherwood in 1930 and sold it to the Hatfields in 1957; the Birdwoods moved to Charters. As Mick Hatfield explained, the Birdwoods were great supporters of The Heronsgate Association and, with Sylvia Evans, who lived at Field Cottage were meticulous in welcoming new arrivals. In the Hatfield family it extended to knitting bootees for each of their newly-born children and thus Penelope, Adam, Sam and Emma became the proud owners of 'the best bootees in England'. 'Brenda and Hubert's love and friendship extended throughout, and no more so than in all they did for the church, whether it was Hubert tending the church garden or Brenda making and looking after the vestments'. Although they have gone, the Birdwood's field is a constant reminder of their former presence. Isobel and Francis O'Loughlin amongst others speak of their helping hand when they arrived in 1963.

Jane Garnet, grandaughter of Harold Aston, whose mother had been secretary to Mr Vezey, and who lived at Craven Cottage, was another member of the 2nd Heronsgate Girl Guides. She remembers the giggling and subsequent dressing-downs at the church parades. During the war she recalls how Mrs Evans kept rabbits and that when a German plane came down in Bottom Wood there was great excitement inspecting the wreckage. The post office-cum-sweet shop at Laurel Cottage was a constant source of pleasure.

When Dorothy Haigh died on Christmas Eve 1988 an era in the history of Heronsgate ended. Dorothy Haigh was born in 1905 at The Hut, now called Sunnyside. Her father, an architect remembered for his building of the First World War memorial and many houses and extensions in Heronsgate, had moved his family to Nottingham Road South because he wished to be closer to the land. In 1910 the Haighs moved to Wood Weye, where Dorothy was to live for the rest of her life. Dorothy grew into a beauty with a delicate, fair skin and auburn hair. She could have had many suitors, but in the twenties and thirties dutiful daughters stayed at home to care for their parents. She lived at Wood Weye working in the house and garden and living quietly. In these years she studied painting and the difficult art of wood engraving, buying blocks and tools from Mr Laurence of Bleeding Heart Yard in Clerkenwell; this was the start of a lifetime's association with a man well-known for his impatience with any lack of talent.

When the war came in 1939, Dorothy was in her mid-thirties. She volunteered for the Land Army and worked on the land locally until her talents were discovered by the Foreign Office and she became a cartographer. Mystery shrouds her work as a wartime map maker, but she did well enough to be asked to stay on and she became head of the Foreign Office's map making department, a position in which she was closely associated with the Scott Polar Research Institute. In recognition of her work, Haigh Island in Antarctica was named after her and she was elected a Fellow of the Royal Geographical Society.

By this time, Dorothy's mother had died and her father was ailing, but she continued to work in London despite the arduous journey by steam train from Chorleywood which included a forty minute walk each way. Her invalid father was becoming increasingly demanding. However, she continued with her wood engraving, specialising in rural scenes and subjects from nature. She became a member of the Society of Wood Engravers and one of her engravings 'Combing the Hives' was chosen for inclusion in 'Forty-five Wood Engravers', a volume illustrating the best work done in engraving in this century. In her lunch hours at the Foreign Office, Dorothy used to research among back copies of The Times into the rise and fall of the Chartist Land Company. Alice Hadfield used her research and some wood engravings in her book 'The Chartist Land Company'.

By the time Dorothy retired, Heronsgate had changed into an estate of gracious homes but Wood Weye remained much the same, and so did Dorothy. Watched over by her brother's family and by Dennis Heckford, her gardener and longtime friend, she filled her retirement with painting and engraving, tending her garden, collecting for the RSPCA, watching the deer and foxes in her orchard, making honey, feeding the wild birds and worshipping on Sundays in the church where she was christened.

The residents of Heronsgate gathered en masse for her funeral on January 10th 1989, and found they were saying goodbye not just to dear Dorothy, the occasionally vague, rather unworldly maiden lady who did the beautiful lettering in the memorial book in the church produced in 1979/80, but to Miss Dorothy Haigh, FRGS, member of the Society of Wood Engravers, artist and cartographer. We shall not see her like again.

Pat Hausseur gave me a letter from Dr J. Stuart Richardson, who, writing from Taunton in 1982, aged 70, to Pat said he could remember acting as sidesman at St John's Church in 1920 (aged 8) and taking round the plate. He was then at school at The Firs, the swot school for boys and girls run by his aunts Evelyn (who died in 1956) and Ethel. A chestnut tree which he planted grew into quite a big tree and was transplanted by his devoted aunts to Heronsfield where it grew even bigger but 'Alas, it must have got out of hand, for when Heronsfield School closed down and the building was sold, the new owners had it sawn down'.

An obituary for Frank Heyworth Talbot QC appeared in the Parish Chronicle of April 1990, written by Roddy Pickis:

'I vividly remember one evening when, as an impressionable teenager attending evensong at St Peter's, I heard a sermon by a most impressionable lay reader, in flowing surplice and blue scarf. He conjured up the feelings of the shepherds in the fields (it must have been at the Christmas season) as they heard the angelic message and of one shepherd of whom in tones of great judicial hesitation he said "I venture to call him Reuben".

On enquiry, I gathered that I had been listening to one of our most distinguished lawyers, Frank Heyworth Talbot QC who died on 6th March 1990, aged 94. For many years he lived at The Grange, Heronsgate, and was an active member of St John's Church. In addition to a most faithful execution of his duties as a lay reader, as a member of the parochial church council (1946-1959) he added legal gravitas to the discussions. Although perhaps slightly Olympian in his legal manner he provided unstinting advice to the council: one recalls a cause celebre with St Mary's over some plate belonging to the ancient parish. He was always generous and kindly in advising friends, particularly the Heronsgate community. Above all he was faithful in his service to St John's Church.

After the death of his first wife he lived in Lincoln's Inn (his second wife was also a lawyer who came from Rickmansworth) and to a very advanced age, though living out of London, continued to drive on the motorway in pursuance of his London practice in Regent Street.

He was a remarkable man whose many doings included on one occasion winning a case on the toss of a coin, and escaping a poisoning threat, as recorded in The Times obituary. His like will not be seen again. Our sympathy goes to his widow and family - may he rest in peace. Incidentally he will now know beyond peradventure the name of that shepherd ..!

Michael Bowler, born in Heronsgate in 1939, was educated at the local schools until his early teens: he started at the nursery school then run by Mrs Henson (sister-in-law of Lesley Henson, the actor) in the stables at Oakhill, before going on to Heronsfield, run by Miss Neville and Miss Curtis and finishing his preparatory years at Beaumont House. He remembers Heronsgate in the forties in terms of people and buildings described below.

Mrs Gilbey lived in one of the now demolished bungalows, she was the long suffering cook at Beaumont House, who cut wartime ham wafer thin, and you only got extra if you said you liked ham. Mr Clempson, the St John's organist lived at St Cecilia, while Bircham Cottage was the rather dingy Beaumont House masters' accommodation, which occasionally doubled up as a spare fifth form room, if their own form room was too cold. Moyra Nockolds used to pass motoring magazines through the fence and Dorothy Haigh was there but seldom seen. Sailor the tramp lived in the pigsty nearest the road at Ladywalk Cottage. Beaumont House boys used to use the Whitegates/Ladywalk path to get to Long Lane. Field Cottage was occupied by the Evans family – Austen, Sylvia and son Philip. It had been built by the Birdwoods in the 1930s on what was possibly the site of the Sherwood Cottage mentioned in the fee farm rent sale. The field was regarded as a 'No thoroughfare' and was guarded by impossible and impassable geese for some twenty years.

Elsewhere some of Michael's memories include the Van Duzer's Armstrong Siddeley returning from Pixie House after a tennis tournament covered in plum stains; Walnut Tree Cottage (now a garage) being a house; Willy Webb's, The Swillett butcher, (Briar Wood) being a little bungalow; Mrs Darby still ran the Misses Kidner's kennels at The Orchard; Heyworth Talbot, who helped Michael with his Beaumont House general knowledge test, was a regular winner with Mr Bird at the flower shows (although Marty Kristian was to complain that when he bought Rosecot in the 1970s there were no roses in the garden). Pinecroft was known as The Bevinry and Breve House was called The Pines.

The author remembers that Dorothy Haigh among her many achievements designed and painted the sign which hung outside the Land of Liberty for many years. It bore the intriguing illustration of a downcast Chartist pointing to a TT (teetotal) badge on his lapel, side-by-side with a jovial character holding a mug of beer aloft and smiling broadly. The original beer shop had been subsequently named The Land of Liberty, Peace and Plenty in about 1870 because of its position beyond the borders of the former strictly teetotal stronghold of O'Connorville. One day in the 1970s the sign was damaged by a passing lorry and for many days lay in the hedgerows of Long Lane; however, after an evening of revelry involving the author, the sign found its way back to Rosemary Cottage where the following morning it was cleaned, straightened and returned to Wood Weye – Dorothy never knew how it got there, but she was, indeed, pleased. The sign was never to be rehung, but the pub does have a splendid new sign depicting the signing of the Magna Carta and the presentation of the Charter to Parliament.

One October lunch time in 1996, the occupants of Rosemary Cottage had unexpected visitors. Ray and Joyce Williams from Woodbridge in Suffolk called and asked if they might look around. It transpired that Ray's aunt, Mrs Clare Neal (over 90 years old) wished them to visit the area to see if it had changed. Her mother, Mrs Agnes Williams, a widow from Pinner, had bought Rose Marie (as it was then called), in July 1930 from Dr J. Wilkins. She lived there until April 1938 when the freehold property was sold back to Frank Warman. Ray Williams had visited Heronsgate many times as a child. He remembered well the post office at Laurel Cottage (Ray and Joyce now run the post office at Grundisburgh in Woodbridge, Suffolk!). He said his aunt used to hire horses from the stables at Ladywalk Cottage from a Mrs Goodman. Mrs Goodman ran the Heronsgate Riding School for Hacks and Hunters. Thus was born and a tradition for horse riding for pleasure created; firstly with the former Ladywalk stables and which has been continued with the now well established stables opposite Farfield and with the ownership of horses by some Heronsgate residents. Ray enjoyed his afternoon reminiscing and felt that Heronsgate had not changed too much.

Many will remember the Gilham brothers, the shoemakers of the High Street, Rickmansworth. The following information in immaculate copper plate writing was found in a ledger for the years

ClaireWilliams at Rose Marie (plot 29) in 1931

1908 to 1913. Gilhams used to deliver by foot to some residents of Heronsgate. For instance, Mr Giffard of Beaumont House School spent £29 6s 6d on various items during these years, including 71 pairs of black canvas shoes costing £9 3s 6d and 72 laces costing four shillings and three pence. Mr Giffard was obviously a man of foresight as he purchased one spare pair of laces. Cricket balls cost 4s 9d and wicket keeping gloves cost 17s 6d, and batting gloves were 9s. Other residents to have accounts with Gilhams at this time were listed as Mr Haigh of Bowood, Mr Felkin of Sherwood, Mr Foster, Mr King and Mr Taylor. In later years in the late 40s, I remember going to Gilhams and seeing all these shoes packed in boxes. Mr Gilham knew exactly what was in each box but, one day, he did bring down a box full of money, and in some boxes were kept hens' eggs which he used to deliver to Heronsgate residents.

Mick and Donna Flinn, from Australia and the north of England respectively, remember driving into Heronsgate in 1975 through the overgrown hedged lanes to see Bircham Cottage, the then unoccupied and rather derelict former home of many Beaumont House masters. It was full of old newspapers and forgotten cricket gear. They were not married at the time and were noticeable for their long hair and large transit van full of strange and loud looking recording gear, being well known in the pop music business of the 1970s. Bircham Cottage was just what they were looking for and Heronsgate was the perfect place, offering the rural tranquillity which they were seeking. Linda Fernandez and her husband were renovating Crowthorne and it looked good, and Mick and Donna were determined to buy Bircham Cottage, despite the estate agent's warning that Heronsgate was not a very desirable area. Mr Vezey at first did not want to sell to them and he was difficult to deal with. One day, however, Mick appeared in a Harvard University sweatshirt, and Mr Vezey suddenly decided they were an ideal couple.

Just as the time came to complete the negotiations, Mr Vezey fell into a life-threatening coma, but the initiative of the solicitor, Mr Vezey's son-in-law, enabled the deal to be completed. Later the Flinns were able to purchase St Cecilia the other side of Bircham Cottage (Little Whaddon as it was then called) from the Department of Transport and they transformed the two cottages into a fine house. Dorothy Haigh was somewhat sceptical of the new arrivals but soon warmed to them. During their years at Bircham Cottage they purchased the cashier's desk, which once belonged to Snook, The Swillett butcher. It was designed by Bertram Haigh and dated 28/6/1910. It now, as at Bircham Cottage, acts as the Flinns' bar in their home at Glenthorne.

Following closely in the Flinns' footsteps came their friends in the pop music business, Marty and Carol Kristian. Their musical and entertaining talents were quickly at home in Heronsgate where their gregariousness was welcomed. They too moved into a derelict Chartist cottage, Woodene. Marty continued with his musical career, while Carol was making her mark in her own way. Being a professional dancer, she started with adult keep-fit classes for the likes of Jane Broadbent, Moreli McDougall, Diana Pollard, Rene Gillott, Colin Green and Pat and John Jackson. Some children joined these classes. Soon Carol branched out with a dancing school for the sons and daughters of Heronsgate families. In no time she had spread her wings by establishing dancing schools in Wembley and the Chorleywood Memorial Hall. The classes in Wembley were run in a small hall also used for a nursery school. Coincidentally, the nursery school was run by a lady who had been a governess at Myrtle House and had run a nursery school at the Heronsgate Hall before the days of Mr Wright. The Flinns and the Kristians have played an important role in ensuring a happy and mixing community in Heronsgate.

In the 1950s The Post Office put its first pole into Heronsgate and suddenly the world was at our feet. But there was a snag – the new telephones were on party lines, the operator worked from The Swillett and was often not there; the main exchange was at what is now the General Accident Property Services in Chorleywood (Weller Hill & Hubble). Often it was not clear to whom one was speaking and one would find oneself speaking to three people at the same time, only one of whom you really wanted to talk to.

Mrs Grimshaw at the Hall nursery school found Alistair Gibbins and Anthony Ross rather a handful and they were asked to attend school on alternate days. Elizabeth Ross quickly placed Anthony at another school and Alistair continued his education peacefully at Mrs Grimshaw's.

When Gill (my sister) produced her kneeler for the church, it did not entirely satisfy the powers that be: although the kneeler was very well done, it had been done in tent stitch and not cross stitch as required and hence was not thick enough – having taken only half the required amount of wool! Hopefully it will survive long enough.

Two former residents, Ron Clarkson and Betty Bird, have memories of Heronsgate going back to before the Second World War. Ron Clarkson was born in 1935; firstly the Clarksons lived at Cherry Cottage, but soon moved the family home to Woodene. Within six months Wood Croft had been bought and there the Clarksons lived until it was sold in 1973 to the Lamberts. Ron's father was the gardener, while his mother looked after the Bowler and other households. Mrs Clarkson is remembered as a woman who did not mince her words, as a woman to be trusted whose role it was to wash and lay out the deceased of Heronsgate. Her characteristics were to earn her the major part in the 'Hidden Gem', a book written by Josephine O'Reilly of Myrtle House and first published in 1946. The book describes Myrtle Cottage (at one time during the Second World War it had been used as a Sun Alliance office) as a house of medium size, with five bedrooms, three sitting rooms with cobwebbed walls, thick furry carpets of dust and a lovely jungle of a garden. The house itself was coated with ivy and provided excellent accommodation for rats, bats and other small animals. All in all it was a first class buy for the family from Ireland. The book mentions Mr Ross at The Pines who kept bees and ran the Watford Steam Laundry and Mrs Ross who welcomed the O'Reillys with 'We are like one big happy family here'. It portrays Mrs Robinson (Mrs Clarkson) as the sort of person who solved problems, did an excellent job in the house, could be trusted with innermost secrets, was attractive and a real lady. The Land of Liberty pub is mentioned as being run by Jessie Box (Jesse Cox); also mentioned are the Hills of Hope Cottage.

Ron remembers his childhood as a happy one: playing in Bottom Wood and his father summoning him home for meals with a few loud blasts on a trumpet. The bus only went twice a day and if you wanted to get anywhere you walked. Ron believes Heronsgate changed in the 1950s – previously there were the wealthy with the maid and gardener, the professional class and the working class, but everyone respected each other. The new arrivals in the 1950s were not the same. At about this time he began to work for the Wearing brothers and then became a gardener for Sir Norman Kendall at Roughwood Park; he later set up a smallholding enterprise with five and a half acres at the back of the present Flinn and Redhead homes. The O'Connor ideal had reared its head again. Ron milked his cows and sold the milk, which was collected each day, to the Marketing Board in Wing; he reared pigs and kept chickens until Ron Skilton wanted to build on part of Ron's small-holding and he was forced to move out. In a short while Wood Croft was sold. Ron remembers one Sunday having a routine mow at his smallholding when Heyworth Talbot from The Grange came to tell him it was the sabbath and he should not mow on the sabbath. The present incumbent of Wood Croft might think the same, but Ron was not pleased.

Amongst Ron's other memories were the Esperanto International Language School which had its offices at Lindens between the late 1930s and 1950s – a source of intrigue to a young boy. 'I can remember the signs just by the St John's crossroads advertising this mysterious Esperanto'. Ron's middle sister worked for the Philbys and his younger sister used to baby-sit for the neighbours at a very young age.

Iris Fitzsimmons who lived at Amberwood (The Beehive) and whose husband worked at Beesons in Rickmansworth as a carpenter, emigrated to Australia. She was almost certainly a descendant of Fitzsimmons, the original Chartist settler, who stayed on in Heronsgate; but the seed of adventure and hope for better things had once again re-emerged in the Fitzsimmons blood. Descendants of the original Chartist settler, the Ford family, lived at The Limes.

Fanny King was another with Chartist blood who ran the epileptic home at Laburnums; she is reputed to have said to Mrs Clarkson, 'If you come to chapel every week the larder will never be empty'. Mrs Clarkson never went to chapel. When the road was being improved or, some might say, being ruined, from a grass track full of pot holes, to a tarmac lane, Ron picked up the cement slabs and placed them in the correct place (normally it was four men to a slab!). Simon Farr, a Beaumont House old boy and a resident with his family at Hope Lodge in the 50s and 60s, remembers his father, then a wing commander and later an air vice-marshall helping Ron with these slabs and speaking of his strength with awe.

Betty Bird talks about Rosecot in the following terms: She was two and a half years old when her parents moved into Heronsgate in 1928. She recalls that her grandparents had used it as a holiday cottage at the turn of the century, coming from London by train and then pony and trap to Heronsgate. It was in 1910 that the main architectural changes were made to Rosecot under the supervision of Bertram Haigh. She remembers her parents talking about the planting of the original fir tree and that it was her aunt, Mrs Davidson, who built Penny Firs in 1937 on a half-acre site on the Rosecot two-acre plot. When Francis O'Loughlin moved into Penny Firs he found an original map and plan of the O'Connorville Estate in the loft. It must have come from Rosecot. There is no date on this map and comparing the names of the homeowners for the known occupiers for 1846, 1851, 1857 and 1858 it dates the map for the years between 1851 and 1857. Probably it originated in 1854 soon after William Goodchap, the Government Receiver, took over the running of the Estate. The Wheelers – father and son – are shown as occupying plots 17 and 25. Thomas Wheeler was the secretary to the Land Company, and although shown as having paid money for a lot, was not an original lottery winner, nor was he an occupier of a plot, although his son was by 1851. On this plan, Joseph Barnett is shown as owning plot 6 (Rosecot) and is pencilled in as owning four plots of land (33, 1, 2 and 3) and he was associated with other plots at a later date. This would establish the date of the map to be 1854.

Betty recalls that their two-acre plot was cut with scythes by the menfolk of the family; she bought coronation stamps from the Dyers post office in 1937 and saw Endlands burnt to the ground at around the same time. This reminded her of her parents saying that Whitegates suffered a similar fate in 1925 or 1926. Betty's father ran a bookshop in Bedford Square, London, importing books from America and establishing publishing distribution rights, but the business was hit by the war and a shortage of dollars. Life was pleasant in Heronsgate; people called themselves Mr or Mrs and leisure time was filled with tennis and bridge. Then in 1957 she moved away to marry, leaving her parents in occupation until the 1980s when they sold to the Kristians who found the house was full of fine furniture formerly belonging to Betty's parents.

I remember rumours of there being a ghost in Heronsgate. One day Christine Ross phoned me and told me that often she would be sitting in her sitting room at Whitegates and there would be a feeling of stillness and yet someone was there. Christine remembers one particular evening, when she was sure she was not alone. Jimmy her husband, was in Africa and on his return she said 'I think we have a ghost.' Jimmy replied, 'I know we have a ghost; it stands in the garden by the apple tree watching me practising putting. It is very benign.' On another occasion, Christine had friends to a dinner party. As they entered Whitegates, one of the guests said, 'there is a presence here, but do not worry it will do you no harm.' This guest was a spiritualist and knew about ghosts. After a while,

Christine, some guests and the spiritualist went upstairs to see Alexander who at that time was 18 months old. He was asleep and so they tiptoed back downstairs. Later, Christine felt a touch on her shoulder, a sort of warning, and went upstairs to find Alexander sleep walking and tottering at the top of the stairs. 'Don't worry,' said the spiritualist, 'he is protected.' Frequently Christine and Jimmy would see 'their presence' walk through the french doors in their sitting room and out onto the lawn. She was a tall, stately figure dressed in grey with a white v-necked collar and grey hair drawn back.

Alfred Mansfield, who lived at Croft House in the early 1930s and 1940s recalls:

'My sister-in-law, at that time editor of the ladies page in a national newspaper, the Daily Mirror, was more often than not in London where she maintained a flat. She was the proud possessor of a Sealyham terrier named Bonzo. This hound was usually resident with us, as she had to spend most of her time in London. A regular hell-hound he was, always up to mischief. One could be quite sure he would be at the centre of any dog fight. I shall always maintain that he organised such affairs and having started them sneaked out leaving his canine 'friends' hard at it tearing bits off one another.

How well I remember hearing a commotion in the lane, an angry voice using ungentlemanly language and then observing Bonzo sneaking into the garden - unfortunately someone had left the front gate ajar. Minutes later a tall dignified but ruffled man banged loudly on the front door. From the window I recognised the irate knocker as the butler from 'The Grange', a residence some hundred yards up the lane from us. The Grange had at one time been occupied by Madam Melba, the world-famous singer. At the time of which I write it was owned and occupied by a well-known King's Councillor (K.C.), Talbot by name, with whom I had a nodding acquaintance.

I gathered from the butler that he had been peacefully strolling down the lane to the postbox, when the 'mad' dog rushed out from my garden and savagely attacked him (the rushing out part I could readily accept). He had, he said, raised his foot to ward off the dog and the wretched animal had then taken a firm grip on his trouser leg and savaged the material obviously preparatory to biting him. He pointed to his trousers where one leg was split from ankle to well above the knee, evidence of a considerable tug of war. Bonzo, one imagined, thought he was about to receive a hefty kick. He may have been right, and considering attack the best means of defence, grabbed hold of the trouser leg and held on regardless. The butler pulling would have done the rest. Rapid visions beset me of my being hailed before a judge and being prosecuted by a K.C. on the grounds that my (it wasn't mine actually) man-eating, savage dog, had been allowed by me to rush out and attack his faithful man-servant without warning, care and attention etc., etc., causing grievous bodily harm while the said man-servant was proceeding on his lawful occasions on the King's Highway, to wit, our lane.

Obviously something had to be done and done quickly. I invited the victim in and offered a drink which he accepted. I then humbly apologized adding that the damaged trousers would be replaced and that Bonzo had never, to my knowledge, attacked anyone previously. Privately I thought that all Bonzo's attacks were reserved for his friends and enemies in the canine world. My abject apology and remarks mollified the complainant who returned to his usual dignified manner, in spite of the damaged nether garment. We parted on reasonably friendly terms. An account for a new pair of trousers arrived in due course and nothing further was heard of the incident. I could not help but think what a charming and reasonable chap has was, all considered.

To set the stage for the next Heronsgate incident it would be helpful to have some idea of the position of the houses at our end of the road. Across the lane from my property stood 'Myrtle House' facing east and overlooking my meadow. Proceeding up the lane for about 100 yards 'The Grange' faced south, a small gate giving access to the lane, the main entrance and drive being from Long Lane. The lane, actually called Stockport Road, took a sharp turn to the left near 'The Grange' gate and after passing one more house standing well back amidst trees terminated abruptly at some large gates a hundred yards further on. The gates bore the legend 'Endland' and were always locked. As the lane was a cul-de-sac any unfortunate motorist reaching this point was in trouble. The lane was so narrow that it was impossible to turn a car around and it was necessary to reverse over two hundred yards and back into my drive. This happened quite often. I recall one lady having reached Endland and trying this reversing business unsuccessfully was on the verge of hysterics when I went to her aid. I had never passed the Endland gates, but vaguely understood that two elderly ladies lived in the large house and were rarely seen by anyone other than tradesmen calling by appointment.

My wife and I had spent a day in London at the Ideal Home Exhibition, a 'must' with us every year. On our return we had a meal and retired to bed about 10.00 p.m. Tired with all the standing about at the exhibition, we were soon asleep, a sleep that was soon to be disturbed.

About midnight my wife nudged me into semi-wakefulness asking 'What was that?'. 'Nothing', I replied 'go to sleep'. I dozed off again, only to be prodded once more and to be told to 'listen'. Having no alternative, I did, but still could hear nothing. On being further pressed I left the bed and went over to the window. Looking out and down, I could see nothing, the night being very dark, but a faint cry of 'Help! Help!' seemed to come from somewhere below. Calling out, I enquired who was there and what was the trouble. The only reply was a further thin cry for help. There seemed nothing for it but to don dressing gown and slippers and wend my way downstairs. Along a passage down the stairs and through three rooms and the hall to the front door I went, grumbling to myself at being so rudely disturbed.

Opening the door I saw, with the aid of a torch, an elderly lady clad in a dressing gown. She was unknown to me, and was standing under the covered porch, still feebly emitting a cry for help. Enquiry revealed that she was from 'Endland', the large house at the end of the lane, and she needed help for her sister. I recall thinking, 'Here's a pretty kettle of fish at one o'clock in the morning'. She seemed unable to give any further information and no solution other than going along to Endland presented itself. The elderly lady was clearly very upset. So together we wandered up the lane, my torch throwing shadows as the light reflected from the hedges lining both sides of the narrow lane.

It was so dark that the lane seemed endless; actually, it was less than 300 yards. We arrived at the gates I had never seen open, one was now slightly ajar and we entered the grounds. The house, I knew, was a large one standing well back and, so far as the limited range of my torch allowed, it seemed there were lots of tall trees. The entrance door of massive proportions also stood open and as we entered, I could see in the light of the torch a wide staircase. Suggesting to the lady it would be useful if the lights were switched on, I was informed they did not have electric light in the house. We then proceeded up the stairs, she by this time having a lighted candle in her hand, which, together with my torch, added to the eerie feeling by throwing dancing shadows all around.

Reaching the top of the stairs she went straight forward to a heavy door containing a spy hole through which she peered. I was still wondering, with some misgivings, as to what had happened or was about to happen when she opened the door and beckoned me in. At the far end of the room I could discern a bed that appeared to have no occupant and what looked, in the feeble light, to be a heap of bedclothes lying on the floor. On a bedside table, a lighted candle had almost run its course. Bracing myself for the unexpected, I went up to the bed to investigate. The bed revealed nothing save that it had no occupant or bedclothes. Gingerly, I moved some of the heap on the floor and there found a very old lady covered completely by clothes. Apparently she had fallen out of bed dragging all the bedclothes with her. She was unconscious but appeared to be still alive. How the lighted candle had not fallen from the table and set fire to the bedclothes and to the old lady seemed to be a miracle. Disentangling her from the bedclothes gently, I lifted her up on to the bed. She weighed so little, it was as though she were a child four or five years old. Having made her as comfortable as possible, I suggested that we telephone a doctor immediately, only to be told there was no telephone in the house. There was nothing for me to do but return home and telephone for the doctor. Going down the lane I remember thinking "What a night and what a way to spend it wandering up and down a scarey lane in a dressing gown and bedroom slippers".

My call raised Dr. Cardew from his bed, it was now about 1.30 a.m. He said he would be along shortly and suggested I keep Miss Beatson company until he arrived. I set off again up the hill and gained entry into the house where I found my former companion sitting on the top stair awaiting the doctor and my return. I joined her there. We sat still on the stairs chatting. It was, I recall, decidedly chilly. I learned that the old lady I had recently returned to her bed was the dominant partner and that she would not permit any new-fangled appliances or conveniences in the house - no electricity, radio, gramophone, telephone, etc. It was almost as though 'you name it and she was against it'. It was not a case of money shortage. Miss Beatson said she and her sister had ample cash. In due course the doctor arrived on foot and carrying a torch. After examining the old lady and making her comfortable, he had a few words with her sister. He and I then started down the lane. Knowing the snag of the cul-de-sac he had parked his car in the land near to my entrance gate. This, he said, was his usual practice when he visited 'Endland'.

The engine would not start and I felt I could do nothing less than get my car out and drive him home. On arrival there he suggested we have a nightcap. I accepted gratefully and during a chat gathered he made a daily visit to see Miss Beatson, the elder, and that he was afraid she would not be around much longer. This proved to be the case. She died a few weeks later. The surviving sister, May, was approaching seventy years of age, but after the passing of her sister she really 'went to town'. Engaging a youngish companion and ample help, she was out daily in a hired car - visits to London theatres and concerts became frequent. She also called quite often on my wife, with whom she became firm friends. May Beatson presented her with several valuable trinkets.

I saw her only rarely, but one occasion soon after the declaration of war with Germany in 1939, she unburdened herself to me explaining that a certain gentleman had pestered them for years trying to buy 'Endland' from them with its four acres of rate and beautiful fir trees. The two ladies was so annoyed by the constant approaches that they vowed, some what may, they would ensure he never got the property. May went on that she was now even more determined over the question and, no matter how much he was prepared to pay, he should not have the property. Miss Beatson went on to say that if I would buy the property, she would be delighted. She named a purchase price far below its value and added that, if I would do this, it would 'settle Mr...'s hash for good and all'. I reluctantly had to decline, explaining that, as much as I would love to have the property, the war just started might well last a long time and as everything was so uncertain, it would be unwise for me to commit myself to such a project. It was only a matter of months before May died leaving the estate to a distant relative whom we never met.'

On July 14th 1991, The Mail on Sunday under the heading 'Scandal in Toytown' wrote the following article about Jeffrey Levitt a resident of Home Close at that time:

'Leading antique toys trader Jeffrey Levitt carried out a £12 million fraud on the Department of Trade and Industry, which then gave him a Queen's Award for Exports. The Mail on Sunday has discovered that Levitt's company "Mint & Boxed" used fake sales invoices and shipping documents purporting to show the export of toys. They were enough to win him the award in April – and to raise £12.5 million in loans from the DTI's Export Credits Guarantee Department in conjunction with the Midland and NatWest banks. Last month Levitt's 60% personally owned company collapsed and he declared himself bankrupt. 'Mint & Boxed enjoyed a dramatic rise in the specialist world of antique toys which was matched only by the lifestyle of 34 year old Jeffrey Levitt. He paid himself a salary of £700,000, owned two Mercedes, a Rolls Royce Camargue, a Bentley, a second vintage Bentley which he claimed was worth £300,000 and cars for his domestic staff and chauffeurs.

Living in a seven-bedroomed house with a swimming pool in Heronsgate Hertfordshire, he regularly crossed the Atlantic with his wife, three children and nanny on Concorde. Two years ago he paid around £30,000 for the personalised car registration number LEV IT. He complained he had had to fork out so much because he was bidding against his namesake Roger Levitt, the top insurance salesman whose business, once worth £150 million collapsed last December. Levitt (Jeffrey) says he is not related to Levitt (Roger) now facing fraud charges. But they shared an extravagant lifestyle, self-aggrandizing corporate videos portraying them as jet setting businessmen, and an ability to attract blue chip investors.

The world's toy dealers looked on in amazement as Levitt J., known as"Toytown's Top Trader", paid high prices for antique models at auctions then claimed to sell them on to customers for 20 times more. Levitt's accounts show sales rising from £350,000 in 1984 to £14 million in 1990 and he was forecasting £27 million for the year to June 1991. Profits supposedly rose to more than £2.5 million. He splashed out on lavish advertising, beautiful colour brochures and the opening of a gallery on New York's Madison Avenue attended by a host of celebrities. Clients, he claimed, included film director, Steven Spielberg and Frank Sinatra. One for certain, was Sir Anthony Joliffe, a former Lord Mayor of London, who is now a creditor. Levitt's 30 employees in New York and London were intimidated by his highly-strung, driving personality, confused by his secretiveness and made suspicious by his claims to have sold the same toy to different people. The antique toy trade was equally sceptical. "It seemed incredible to me that people would pay Levitt maybe ten times above the market value", said John Badeley, a toy expert at Sotheby's.

The scepticism proved well-founded when the banks, backed by ECGD loan guarantees, called in accountants Arthur Anderson as administrative receivers. They had tried to collect debts, sending repeat invoices to dealers who had apparently bought models but not paid. But about 90% of the deals were fake. "The vast majority of sales simply never existed", said one insider. The DTI said on Friday that it gives Queen's Awards on the basis of three year's accounts submitted by the companies. It does not carry out checks of its own.'

CHAPTER TWENTY

And More Memories

GEOFFREY LEAKE was born in Heronsgate in 1936 and lived at Rowandene until 1967. He went to the nursery school at Oakhill, then to Beaumont House, but he did not survive the strict regime long. He moved on to York House in Rickmansworth, Leighton Park (the Quaker school) and Christ Church, Oxford, and finally made his career in teaching mathematics which at one time involved missionary work in Kenya. About Rowandene, Geoffrey says, 'The house was built in 1860 and may be the first to have been built after the original Chartist settlement.' (Ordnance Survey maps show it was built in the 1890s. When I pointed this out to Geoffrey he agreed the OS maps must be regarded as definitive but he still maintained that he and his father had come across some evidence that made them decide that it dates from 1860). He continues:

> 'Rowandene was known until 1930 as May Cottage when my father bought it from Gerald Boyle who then moved to The Bungalow on the other side of Heronsgate.' When the Leakes bought May Cottage in 1930, they bought it in two lots. Lot 1 was described as a prewar substantially built detached house with a secluded old established garden consisting of lawns, fruit trees and herbaceous borders; Lot 2 was a plot of land to the southeast consisting of a garden well stocked with with fruit trees. According to the conditions of sale the abstract of title to Lot 1 commenced with conveyances in 1890 and 1895, and to Lot 2 with a conveyance dated 1899.
>
> My interpretation is the conveyance of 1890 refers to the partition of the original Chartist plot with a piece of land 75 feet along Nottingham Road and a depth of 137 feet to Halifax Road on which May Cottage was to be built. By the conveyance of 1895, Philip Ford sold the remaining, but majority, part of Laurel Cottage to George Antill. Philip Ford now moved to The Limes. George Antill thus owned the larger part of the original plot and in 1899 he sold the property to Sydney Walker. Therefore Rowandene was built between 1895 and 1898.
> At some date after this and before 1930, the owners of Rowandene purchased land, i.e. Lot 2 (47ft 8ins x 137ft) from Sydney Walker, owner of Laurel Cottage. Most likely it was Gerald Boyle, who purchased the land. The conditions for sale for 1930 say, in regard to Lot 2, 'A mistake appears to have been made as to the number and area of the piece of land but that the purchaster shall not make any objections ...'.

Geoffrey carries on:

> 'My father chose the name Rowandene to identify it with two rowan trees in the front garden and the

191

dip (or dene) in the road outside. The may tree by the gate survived until 1961 when it was felled to make way for a garage. Father was a keen gardener and lived in the house until he died in 1967. The features that stand out in my memory are the many cypress trees which he planted, two old pear trees, the cherry tree, the russet apples; the chickens we kept for some ten years from 1942; the well; the laurel hedges, one near the house, one at the bottom of the garden; the air raid shelter; the centre path; the puddles.

When he bought the house, it was in a poor state of repair, but one of my father's relaxations after a long day in the City, was carpentry. This was long before DIY became popular. He rebuilt the staircase and landing himself and had proper plumbing and sanitation fitted. He designed and built a new front porch. I remember helping fill in the old cess pit at the bottom of the garden in later years. He also had electricity installed. The well, just behind the house, was a real one, some twenty feet deep and there was water at the bottom. My father made a decorative cover for it, and it became a feature of the garden.

What we knew as "the centre path" had a history which we never finally resolved. This path ran the length of the garden from the side gate. It was probably the boundary of one of the original Chartist plots. The previous owner had bought the ground between this path and the next boundary hedge and integrated it into the garden as a whole. The path had a much more solid foundation than any normal garden path of the time. My father understood that it had once been a right of way used by cattle to reach a watering-hole in the garden beyond. Being at the lowest spot in Heronsgate, this is a very reasonable explanation.' (The footpath, no doubt, was used by cattle but it remained as part of Laurel Cottage until Sydney Walker sold a parcel of land to Rowandene [May Cottage] and the boundary line of the original Chartist plot ran to the left of the present garage. The land to the left of the garage was bought from Rosecot by the Greens, the present owners.)

'And the puddles … Rowandene (together with the houses on the opposite side of the road) was at the lowest point. When the rains came, the road became a river. I guess it still does! The road outside became a lake. The cars made it worse! Stones from the gardens on either side filled the worst of the holes. Ash from the fires was added! Nothing we could do made any lasting difference – except to raise the level of the road! The road could be almost impassable. One of the first acts of the Heronsgate Association was to make storm drains, to ask the neighbours to allow them to be run into their gardens and to organise a work party to install them. With these came reinforced concrete slabs as car tracks. Ugly as they were, they did help.'

Geoffrey's father wrote the following verse:

> At long, long last the day has come
> Through willing work so ably done
> Dry shod, we now enjoy the lane
> And fear no longer mud or rain.
> Our thanks to one and all we give
> There's no lane, now, like ours

In 1982 the Heronsgate Residents Association decided according to responsibilities laid down in the original constitution of 1947 'to disseminate information about matters of common concern to residents of Heronsgate' by printing and distributing a newsletter which was to be called 'The Heronsgate Gazette'. The Gazette as such was to last until the early 1990s. It was then discontinued and a diary of the year's happenings was published instead. There follow some extracts from these Gazettes. Needless to say the first Gazette was dominated by the Lanes Committee and the problems of raising finances, resurfacing the lanes, the question of easy access for the emergency services (in particular fire and ambulance); in this context residents were reminded of the importance of keeping their hedges well trimmed!

The Gazette of 1982 also included the following:

'Mr and Mrs Knight, who lived at Pinhaye for many years, have very kindly given a salver for competition for the prettiest Spring garden. Judging during the first two weeks in April will be by a personal vote of the Heronsgate residents and papers will be delivered nearer the date. Jonathon and Angela Ingrams have just managed to move into Stanmore Lodge (you know, the Vicary's house) after having extensive internal refurbishment. Jonathon prepares films and journals designed to keep doctors up to date with the latest developments in the fast changing world of medicine. So if your doctor still cauterizes your wounds with boiling pitch, refer him to Stanmore Lodge. Angela is a teacher of speech and drama.

Meanwhile, down at Four Acres, recently vacated by the Wageners, Johnny and Connie Speight have moved in. They form a valuable addition to the Heronsgate entertainments industry, as Johnny has been known to write a script or two for the Beeb. Normally reliable sources tell us that they have three children, Francis, David and Samantha and a Rolls called Clara. We wish them all a long and enjoyable stay in Heronsgate. Our new vicar, the Rev Malcolm Cherry, and his wife Peggy, have settled in at St Peter's Vicarage, Mill End, and have met quite a number of Heronsgate parishioners at coffee after the Family Service in January. We shall continue to have one service each Sunday, to which all are welcome.'

The Gazette of 1983 included the following extracts:

'After Morning Service on June 12th a presentation will be made at The Lindens (by kind permission of Mr and Mrs Aitken) to Mr G. Kidman. Now aged 88, Mr Kidman has been a lay preacher for over 60 years and has been helping with services at St John's since Mr Heyworth Talbot moved to London nearly 20 years ago.

The funeral took place at St John's on May 25th of Mr Arthur Bird and many of us were there to pay our respects to the man who had been our oldest inhabitant. He was born 92 years ago at Rosecot, the house once owned by his grandfather, and those of us who had the opportunity of hearing his stories of characters and happenings in Heronsgate over that time span much appreciated his wit and memory. He and his wife Gladys, who died in December, spent over 60 years of married life at Rosecot and took an active part in local affairs. They were both demon whist players and often held whist drives at their home. Mr Bird also grew a mean tomato and his name was usually amongst the prizewinners at the horticultural shows of the past. When failing health made it no longer possible for them to look after themselves, it was with real pleasure that many of us responded to Mrs O'Loughlin's suggestion that we formed a rota to take them coffee, lunch and tea each day. This worked well for a few months, and Mr and Mrs Bird were always cheerful and pleased to chat. It was with regret that they eventually had to move into a residential home in Bushey and it is sad to think that they are no longer with us. However, we all have many memories of a hardworking couple who provided a real link with the past.

The Lanes Fund is still £400 short of what is required to enable a contract to be placed for this year's work. And this is in spite of £700 carried forward from the £930 raised by the auction held in October 1982. The majority of this year's non-subscribers, and those only partially subscribing various amounts, are residents living in Nottingham Road, where far and away the bulk of lanes funds have been applied for many, many years. As notified in the last issue of the Gazette, a further £1000 is proposed to be spent on Nottingham Road and £2000 is to be allocated to Halifax Road South which, after about twenty years during which nothing has been spent on it, is now in a worse condition than any of our lanes. Halifax Road South residents have a long record of a high and consistent subscription rate, all of which has been spent to the advantage of residents in other lanes. They have indeed been very loyal to our community effort, and patient in waiting for what is now their turn this year.

Grateful acknowledgement is also due to the group of regular subscribers who have homes fronting on Long Lane and whose use of our lanes is minimal. These residents and those living in Stockport Road are consistently the most fully paid up subscribers. May we make another plea to the community spirit of residents who have still to subscribe, or who have not subscribed the full £40. Time is very short now if we are to have any work done this summer.

In regard to the M25 motorway. Following the circular to Heronsgate Residents dated 29 June 1983 the consulting engineer to the Department of the Environment has passed on the following information. "The adverse weather conditions have hampered progress with the cutting at the end of Nottingham Road. However, if the weather improves earthmoving in the section at the end of Nottingham Road could be completed in 10-12 weeks. Construction of the bridge connecting the Heronsgate side of the motorway with Ladywalk Wood will be started after earth moving is completed and could be finished in mid-1984".'

The Gazette of February 1991 included the following:

'Kay Bowler died in October 1990. She had lived in Heronsgate for 54 years and was well known and respected in the community. She served on the Residents Association Committee for many years and had chaired the Lanes Committee until she retired three years ago. Her immensely valuable voluntary work in Rickmansworth and the surrounding area during the dark days of the Second World War is still talked about. In 1981, she was awarded the OBE in recognition of her work for the Conservative Party. Her warm personality and dominant spirit will be missed by all who knew her.

A working party of willing helpers assembled at the Birdwood field on Sunday 21 October. The purpose was to clear as much as possible of the fallen timber following the storms earlier last year, to cut the grass and generally clear up. A lot of hard work was put in and it proved possible to make a start on clearing the large tree at the bottom corner of the field near Halifax Road. The field was put in a fit state for the winter.

The 1990 AGM of the Association was held on 12th July at the Hall and was attended by 45 residents. Reports were received from three sub-committees. Roger Talbot explained the work of the Lanes Committee which was followed by a wide ranging discussion on subjects such as the flooding in Nottingham Road South, the bollards at the corner of Stockport Road and the status of the lanes. Christine Ralph reported on the very successful social events held during the year. The Valentine Supper and the Safari Supper were of particular note; the residents of Heronsgate are clearly fond of their food! Francis

194

O'Loughlin detailed the matters considered by the External Affairs Committee, including the proposed restriction of heavy goods vehicles in Long Lane and planning applications in respect of properties in Heronsgate. The Chairman also reported on a number of matters not covered in the sub-committees' reports, and Terry Redhead presented the accounts for the year to 31st March 1990. Councillor Ann Shaw has initiated a programme of tree planting in the District to replace the trees lost over the past few years.'

The gardener for many years at Herons Court was Wilfred Atkinson, who died in 1996. Pam Hatfield wrote his obituary in the Parish Chronicle of October 1996:

'Wilfred Atkinson 1906-1996

The funeral of Wilfred Atkinson of The Swillett took place on 30th July at Chiltern Crematorium. John Warren officiated, and spoke of Mr Atkinson's pride in his two sons, Raymond and Wilfred, and of his legendary helpfulness to others throughout his long life. He came from Yorkshire to work at The Old Rectory in Chenies, before moving to Heronsgate, where Herons Court garden became "his" garden. Mr Atkinson did not advertise his presence in Heronsgate, but his quiet content spread beyond the garden he worked in for over 60 years, first for Mr and Mrs Parsons, and then for Mr and Mrs McDougall. He went to ground among the dahlias and the raspberries; only the scritch-scratch of a hoe betrayed him. He was a man of few words, but great kindliness: a true Yorkshireman. He did not change his ways. Though the traffic in Long Lane increased over the years, he still rode his bicycle up and down from The Swillett with the slow dignity of a countryman.

His wife Bertha's death in 1982 was a great blow, but he continued to work and to help others. When he could no longer manage he was lovingly cared for at Cheriton in Chesham Bois, and was well enough to enjoy a game of scrabble the day before he died. His favourite hymn, "All things bright and beautiful" was sung at his funeral. He must often have thought of it in the beautiful garden he helped to create and maintain over so many years. May God rest his soul'.

Richard Warman and I went to see and talk to Ray Newell one autumn evening in October 1996. It was the first arranged interview with a Heronsgate resident and the only time we went armed with a tape recorder. Ray moved into Heronsgate in 1963 as a middle-aged man, married to Nan and with two daughters. By this time Ray had fought in the Second World War as a gunner, been captured by the Germans at El Alamein and eventually released from prison in Germany by the Russians. He spent his prisoner of war years painting his fellow prisoners and recently an exhibition of his portrait paintings was shown in Leeds. The following description appeared in The Times of January 28th, 1998:

'The work of a man who spent most of his war years in a German prison camp recording the faces and stories of hundreds of people captured during the Second World War has gone on show at the Royal Armouries, Leeds. "Portraits From a Prison Camp", is the work of former gunner Ray Newell, now 78, who was captured by the Germans in North Africa in 1942. "It started with me doing sketches of fellow prisoners in exchange for cigarettes. I did them on pay books, in bibles and on the inside of novels. Everybody had beards in the camps and wanted to show their friends and families after the war what they looked like. When we were moved to Stalag IVb just south of Berlin I began a sketching and painting class. It was a wonderful place to find subjects – there were 20,000 men in the camp with 40 different nationalities.

When I did proper paintings, I paid them with cigarettes to sit, But if they wanted the painting, they paid me; and a Russian, who was an architect, even designed a house for me in exchange for a portrait."

As a prisoner Mr Newell had to scavenge for materials. He created his drawings and paintings which took up to three hours to complete, under the most difficult conditions. Until now the pictures have been kept in a big case in his home in Heronsgate, near Rickmansworth, Hertfordshire. "They haven't been seen by the public eye since 1946 when I displayed them in a library in Islington." The subjects include Sugar, a member of the Canadian Air Force, who used to perform in the camp's plays dressed as a woman; Adamovitch, a Yugoslavian soldier, and the unnamed Russian who designed the cottage for him. Others show some of the German guards including one who posed for his portrait while British PoWs were excavating an escape tunnel under the hut.

Another picture shows a Russian, who was found scavenging for fat in empty tins in the garbage area. "He was scooping out the fat with his hands and licking it because he was so starving. British and American troops were fed the best, with the Dutch and French next. The Russians got the dross. I asked him if he would pose and he was very glad to make ten cigarettes which he could exchange for food." In Germany Mr Newell started an art class with the help of materials sent by the Red Cross. At best he would have twenty people in his class, but the number dwindled if it was cold "And it did get freezing in Germany."

He is "tickled pink" by the exhibition at the Royal Armouries. "I was recording these PoWs at a time when nobody was interested in them. Now other people can see them." He still draws, but these days needs two pairs of glasses to be able to see.'

On returning to England he went to art school, became a schoolmaster and then became a partner in a commercial art firm. In 1963 Ray says Heronsgate was a quiet backwater with little traffic using the unmade gravel roads and not a particularly popular area. Ray bought his two-acre plot from Dick Topley, Di Clark's brother, whose father had built Pixie House in 1934. The two-acre plot was part of Daphnes (four acres). The isolation of the area was mitigated by a good bus service; Dorothy Haigh, for instance, found not having a car no problem. The delivery of goods from the local shops, particularly P.C. Ball, the general stores in The Swillett and the friendliness of residents also helped to mitigate the sense of isolation. A clue perhaps to the lack of desirability of the area was that there were a number of houses for sale in 1963. Ray remembers well Dorothy Haigh working as a cartographer in the Home Office and her father, an architect; Bruce the former MP, lived opposite the Church and had been Bevan's permanent parliamentary secretary.

And there is a Heronsgate in New Zealand too. In the 1960s, Wing Commander Mac Morgan became New Zealand's Air Attaché in London. He and his wife, Juliette, rented Stanmore Lodge and lived there with their children, Guy, Peter, Kathy and Anna. They made many friends and came to have such happy memories of their friends and years in Heronsgate that they called their house in Waikenae, near Wellington, New Zealand, 'Heronsgate'. They have turned their Heronsgate into a typical English cottage garden; which has been written about in a number of New Zealand magazines. The Morgan's connection with Heronsgate lives on, for they both write to their friends and visit their favourite place in England. Only recently Kathy and Warwick (her husband) and their children Reuben and Wesley who live in Napier, New Zealand, came to stay with the Gibbins to remember their days in Heronsgate, England.

When O'Connor purchased Herringsgate Farm, the farm on its southern boundary was Woodwick. Its land was more fertile; being both acidic and alkaline. John and Sally Findlay, the current owners, are most interested in Woodwick's history. Its first mention was in The Domesday Book (1086) when it is shown as paying dues to the Abbot of St Albans. Most likely its history is even earlier. There has been found on its land, a Celtic dog weight and Roman coins. The name Woodwick is Saxon and means 'clearing in the wood'. It is possible the farm was established later; a 12th Century lozenge-shaped seal of the Abbot of St Albans was found in post Second World War times. 'The mixed hedgerow of hawthorn, blackthorn, oak, ash, silver scrub, elm, maple, blackberry, wild rose, honeysuckle found in some fields make it possible to ascertain that these hedgerows date back to 1100' says Sally Findlay. John adds: 'The footpath from the farmhouse through Ladywalk Wood, along the fields at the western side of Heronsgate and to Chorleywood dates from 1100'.

A 1760 map of the farm (see colour plate) shows Woodwick to be 409 acres, well hedged and fields with names like, 'Great Foggy Field', 'Great Stoney Field', 'Great Horn Field'. There was a coach lane from Maple Cross to the farmhouse and the footpath ran from the farmhouse through 'Wood Walk' to 'Charleywood', as they were both then called.

It was about 1850 that a new house was built on the original site; the cellars and woodshed remained from the old house. The central courtyard and other farm buildings were erected after 1760, but the vegetable garden and walls are shown on the 1760 map. At this time it was renamed Woodoaks; it was John Proctor, the owner of Woodoaks in the 1880s, who was responsible for the building of the Wesleyan chapel in Heronsgate.

The Findlay family connection with Woodoaks dates back to 1922. 'My father rented the land from the Ayres family (Lords of the Manor of Rickmansworth), before finally buying at the end of the war… It was a typical mixed farm in those days employing about 20 workers and using 12 carthorses to do the ploughing and other hard work.' Nowadays, I was told, two or three men do the work and contractors are hired at peak times. The last working horse was used in the mid-1960s; cart and horse, pony and trap were still used at the end of the war to deliver milk and do some farm work, but there has been a lorry and tractor since the 1930s.

One day in 1987, John Findlay was surprised to receive a letter from a Mr Nattkemper of Indiana, USA. informing him that the Lordship of the Manor of Woodoak had been purchased by Mr Nattkamper. Later a large American (over six feet tall) appeared in England to get married at St Albans Cathedral. He also took some soil from Woodoaks Farm back to America. It had to be sterilised before it could be exported.

When I asked about the possibility of there having been a convent on Woodoaks' land, I was given the response that there were ruins which could be the site of a former convent. However, the Findlays have never seen the 'Headless Lady'.

In 1972 Chris Quantrill of the Watford Observer wrote about The Swillett:

'Nearly 80 years ago, in the latter part of the reign of Queen Victoria, a daughter, Ella was born to Mr and Mrs Moor, who kept The Dove, in The Swillet, Chorleywood.' (Were they the Moors who co-owned Heronsgate House between 1884 and 1898?)

'It was a narrow country lane in those days. Pigs were kept in the sloping fields behind the public house and on the opposite side of the road there was a slaughterhouse. Close by stood a few farm labourers' cottages. As the little girl grew up she was to see many changes in her world. The Dove was quite small at first with a living room, a little private bar and a tap room. But later there were extensions.

She remembers the building of Manor Cottages and the coming of the shops. As she grew and took up employment, her mother, now widowed, felt the need for a man about the house. Mrs Moor let one of her rooms to a young man, William Webb. He was to fall in love with the daughter of the house and marry her. As Mrs Moor grew older she allowed the running of The Dove to pass to her daughter and son-in-law. They ran the business for more than 30 years until 1957. Until just before that time, the brewery had been Wellers, but they sold out to Benskin's. The Stag close by at the junction of Heronsgate Road and Stag Lane was also a Benskin's house. But there was one essential difference. It had a spirit licence whereas The Dove was only an ale house. The Webbs were unable to get a spirit licence and found they were losing trade. And so they decided to quit.

Mrs Ella Webb no longer lives in Heronsgate Road although she still lives in Heronsgate, at Briar Patch, Nottingham Road. When I spoke to her I said I had been told she knew some of the history of Heronsgate Road. She replied bluntly: "There is no such thing as Heronsgate Road. It's The Swillett and always has been. They started calling it Heronsgate Road because some people didn't like the sound of the name". The Swillett is merely a watercourse and there is a natural depression with many springs of fresh water. The largest of these now runs through a conduit which passes down Quickley Lane where the water disappears through a natural hole in the chalk.

After the Webbs left The Dove, the competition from The Stag proved too great and it is now a private house. It is the home of Malcolm and Margaret Henderson and is once again a business. In the past month Mrs Henderson has opened an antique shop in what was the old club room of the public house. She said: "I have been longing to do this for some time." The field where the pigs used to roam is now a pleasant garden of lawns, trees and shrubs and flowers.

One of the shops Ella Webb saw come to Heronsgate Road was that of P. C. Ball. Mr Ball started in the grocery trade in 1919 and had his first shop at Slough. He moved to Chorleywood in 1927 and took a lease on premises in Heronsgate Road near the junction with Bullsland Lane. In 1937 the lease ran out and Mr Ball thought the terms of the new one were too expensive and looked round for another shop. He found it less than 100 yards up the road at the present address. It had been used as a plumber's and also an under-taking business and was less than half the size it is today. The business prospered and on Mr Ball's death in 1957 it was carried on by his daughter and son-in-law, Mr and Mrs John Watson.

In the same year the shop was enlarged and also their son, Ian, began work there. Two years later Flora also started in the business. The shop took an advance in 1965 when it became an off-licence. This part of the business has become Ian's province and he has taken the opportunity to build up his wine knowledge as well as a varied list of wines ranging from inexpensive vins ordinaire to prewar vintage ports. It is a family grocery and wine business in the true sense of the word.

A newcomer to Heronsgate Road is Mr Brian Harmsworth, who with the increased interest in stamp collecting has opened a second shop in this a new area. He is offering examples for the serious stamp collector and also sells stationery, small antiques and reproduction pictures. He said, "Even in one's wildest dreams, Heronsgate Road would never be envisaged as another Oxford Street. But we have a selection of specialist shops in a pleasant country setting, offering personal service with courtesy and civility. And we have no traffic restrictions". This was echoed by Mrs Henderson who has lived in Heronsgate Road for three years. She said, "It is a nicely mixed community. I like it much better here than where we lived previously."

Despite the changes that the older inhabitants deplore, Heronsgate Road – or The Swillett – has an atmosphere of being a village High Street on its own, distinct from the rest of Chorleywood. The essential character would appear to be little different from what it was in Mrs Webb's childhood. By and large, the newer houses and the garage seem to have fitted into the scene fairly well.'

Tommy Killick remembers Miss Louise Calder. She had been a successful actress before the First World War in the USA. Her father was a doctor, who did not approve of her acting career; he once went to see a play in which she was acting, but he had not recognised her. In 1912 she was invited to take part in the Royal Command Performance at Covent Garden; the King and the Kaiser (Wilhelm II) attended the event.

When the First World War started Miss Calder returned to England, learnt to drive at Selfridges and became an ambulance driver. During the war she became ill and went to convalesce under Miss King's supervision at Laburnums. Thus began a long association with Heronsgate; at first she rented houses, including Stanmore Lodge. In the 1930s she purchased Long Meadow, sold it and bought Woodene. Her move to Woodene was most unconventional in that she simply knocked a hole in the wall which separated the two cottages and transferred her furniture through this hole in the wall. Kate Homburg became her wartime companion and lived with Miss Calder for many years.

Talent is no stranger to Heronsgate and throughout its history, the Estate has been blessed with people of ability, most of whom have chosen to live here because of its special atmosphere. Julie Felix, the country and western singer, has been here since the 1960s. Many remember the evening at the Hall in the early 1990s when the playwright, scriptwriter, socialist and Heronsgate resident, Johnny Speight spoke about his life and the world of show business. He died in July 1998; there follow extracts from his obituary in The Times, which remind us of his talk in the early 1990s:

'Johnny Speight was born on June 2nd, 1920 in Canning Town, East London, the son of a dock labourer. He attended a Roman Catholic school, leaving at 14 and working in local factories until called up for the Army at the start of the Second World War. He spent most of the war in England, but was posted to France after D-Day. After the war he was a drummer in a jazz band before he decided to try his hand as a writer. His inspiration was George Bernard Shaw. Without knowing anything of the author, Speight had read Shaw's witticisms in the newspapers and assumed he must be a stand-up comedian. A visit to Canning Town library revealed the truth, and Speight set about devouring Shaw's works.

Johnny Speight's most memorable creation was the monstrous Alf Garnett, anti-hero of the television comedy series "Till Death Us Do Part": A reactionary, loudmouthed bigot, brilliantly played by Warren Mitchell, Alf was a new phenomenon when he was unleashed on British television in the not-yet-swinging 1960s. Comedy programmes had traditionally kept clear of direct comment on political and social issues. Speight's intention was to use Alf to mock the right wing prejudices of many working class people. By getting the character to sound off outrageously on such subjects as coloured immigrants, religion or the monarchy, Speight hoped to expose such views to ridicule. To some extent the strategy backfired, for many viewers openly or secretly agreed with Alf and found themselves taking his side in his battles with his "Silly old moo" of a wife (another superb portrayal by Dandy Nichols) and his socialist son-in-law (played by Anthony Booth, himself now father-in-law to a Labour Prime Minister). Speight's uninhibited scripts often got him into trouble. The BBC was disturbed by the liberal use of swear words and there were complaints that the series was blasphemous and in bad taste. But it drew huge audiences, was turned into a successful cinema film, and made Speight one of the highest paid writers in the country. Not surprisingly, his later work tended to be seen as something of an anticlimax.'

It was Bank Holiday the 5th May 1999 that I met Charles and May Fitzgerald; the book was almost ready to be sent to the designer and then to be printed. I happened to overhear them saying that a relative of theirs had once lived in Heronsgate House (The Grange). I introduced myself and we began to talk. As mentioned earlier, they were the great-great grandson and great grand-daughter of William Prowting Roberts, the Chartist leader and radical lawyer who had lived at Heronsgate House between 1860 until his death in 1871. W.P. Roberts was married twice. His son by his first marriage died aged 40 before his own death. He had four children by his second marriage, two sons and two daughters. The eldest son Charles was educated at Harrow (W.P. Roberts had been friendly with the Headmaster). Charles became a missionary, first working in Ceylon and later became a parson at Chard in Somerset. He died in 1912 having had 11 children, one of whom, Molly, lived until she was 103. It appears that later some of the family emigrated to Canada.

William the second son was educated at Eton and after leaving school became a captain in the Hampshire Regiment. He carried the colours for the regiment at Mandalay in the Burma campaign of 1886. Later he too joined the church and in Heronsgate records regarding the fee farm rents is referred to as the Reverend William Prowting Roberts. Both daughters married civil engineers, one for a time living in Malaya and the other was associated with the East India Company. As Charles Fitzgerald told me, the family was well connected, but many of its earlier members were reluctant to acknowledge W.P. Roberts as an ancestor; he had been charged at the Wiltshire Assizes at Salisbury in 1840 for seditious libel and was subsequently jailed for two years. Some of the family regarded Chartism as an unworthy cause and family money had been inadvisably spent on the Heronsgate venture and money lent to O'Connor had not been returned. In the course of time a far more favourable picture of W.P. Roberts is presented and his ancestors accepted him. Firstly, his second wife Mary Hill Hopkins led a concerted attempt to improve his posthumous image, depicting him as a respectable Victorian lawyer. More recently, Raymond Challinor of Newcastle University in his biography about W.P. Roberts presents a balanced and supportive portrait. He and his second wife and eldest daughter are buried in the Christchuch churchyard at Chorleywood and their part in Heronsgate's history is respectfully remembered.

It has been a great joy researching and writing this book - a sort of living history filled with memorable moments and unforgettable personalities. What Feargus O'Connor might make of today's community is difficult to guess; but one thing is clear: he would recognise and warm to its friendly spirit.

APPENDIX ONE

References, Sources and Suggested Further Reading

Clive Birch	Chenies and Chorleywood in Camera
Jeremy Birkett and John Richardson	Lillie Langtry
Thomas Carlyle	Chartism. England in the Nineteenth Century
Raymond Challinor	A Radical Lawyer in Victorian England: W.P. Roberts and the struggle for workers' rights
Elizabeth Cull	An appreciation of the life and career of Dorothy Haigh
Geoffrey Dodds	A History of Chorleywood
James Epstein	Feargus O'Connor, the Lion of Freedom
James Epstein and Dorothy Thompson	The Chartist Experience (Editors)
A.H. Fordham	A visit to St. John's, Heronsgate
R.C. Gammage	History of the Chartist Movement 1837-1854
Alice Mary Hadfield	The Chartist Land Company
Keith Hodgkins	Chartist Settlements
Adrienne and Christopher Jacques	Rickmansworth. A Pictorial History
J.R. Lewis	The Village School
E. Grant Longman	Heronsgate Farm, Rickmansworth in 1689
Alfred Mansfield	I was in Kitchener's Army
Kenneth Norris	Chartists at Watford and Heronsgate (Aspects of 19th century Watford)
Edmund Parrott	Britain in Old Photographs: Rickmansworth, Chorleywood and Croxley Green
George E. Ray	History of Chorleywood
	The Book of Chorleywood and Chenies
Donald Read and Eric Glasgow	Feargus O'Connor. Irishman and Chartist
David Thomson	England in the Nineteenth Century
	England in the Twentieth Century
Dorothy Thompson	The Chartists: Popular Politics in the Industrial Revolution
Dorothy Thompson (Editor)	The Early Chartists
S.A.S. Treanor	A study of the settlement of Heronsgate
Mavis Waller (née Parrott)	The Journal of The Three Rivers Trust No. 22, Winter 1996
Transcript	The Trial of Feargus O'Connor and 58 other Chartists on a charge of seditious conspiracy

The Northern Star	1846-1853
Newspapers, National	The Times, The Guardian, The Daily Telegraph, The Mail on Sunday, The New Statesman
Newspapers, Local	The Watford Observer
Ordnance Survey Maps	1780, 1822, 1891, 1898, 1914, 1937,1962, 1976
Other Maps:	O'Connorville 1846
	The O'Connorville Estate 1853 (by Edward H. Burnell, Surveyor. February 1854) courtesy of Michael Bowler
	The 1854 map by courtesy of Francis O'Loughlin
	Air Raid Precautions Map 1940 courtesy of Ray Newell
Beaumont House Magazines	1907-1970 courtesy of John Jackson
Kelly's Directories	1882, 1890, 1895, 1899, 1902, 1906,1908, 1910, 1912, 1917, 1922, 1926,1929, 1933, 1937, 1942
Register of Electors	1950, 1960, 1970, 1980, 1990 (South West Hertfordshire)
Sumner - the chemist	1900-1950 registers (Rickmansworth)
Gilham - shoe shop registers	1900-1950
Hertfordshire Populations	1901-1991
Census Statistics	1841, 1851,1861, 1871, 1881
List of Occupiers of the O'Connorville Estate owners compiled by G. Cornwall	1846, 1851, 1857 and 1858

APPENDIX TWO

House Histories

In compiling the above information a number of difficulties and apparent discrepancies have emerged. Often Heronsgate houses were let and the information revealed in Kellys Directories, census and polling statistics (showing the occupants) is at variance with the facts which the deeds of houses (showing the owners) reveal. Thus, where possible, it is the occupants or residents who are shown. For instance, Charles Bond owned, between 1883 and his death in 1909, Breve House, Oaklands, Wiverton and Herons Court. Charles Bond lived in Breve House and his other properties were let. In his will, Charles Bond instructed that his son G.H. Bond and his daughter Ada Maria Davey, the wife of Charles Ward Davey and Alfred Frederick Prechtel would be the inheritors of the properties then known as The Pines, Hillmorton, The Nook and Herons Court. In 1912, Herons Court and Oaklands (Hillmorton) were sold; in 1913 The Nook (Wiverton) and in 1920 The Pines (Breve House) were sold. Owners and tenants where possible have been shown for these particular properties with the tenants in brackets.

A close look at the residents opens up the possibility of further research; for instance, was S Haigh, the first named occupier of Stanmore Lodge in 1908, a relative of Bertram Haigh the architect and, likewise, were Miss Goodman (1917) and Miss Fitzgerald also of Stanmore Lodge, the same Miss Goodman and Miss Fitzgerald who had been superintendents at the YWCA (Herons Lodge) and so on.

House names were not commonly used until he end of the 19th and early 20th Centuries; some house names have subsequently been altered and some earlier names have proved illusive to match to their current names. For instance, was Holly Villa the cottage at Homeland? Which cottage was 'Justacot'. People's names and initials and their places of residence have been inaccurately recorded; the facts in this section have been an attempt to rectify previous errors and to show changes.

The plots are shown starting at Bircham Cottage (plot 23) and working clockwise up the west side of Nottingham Road, along Bradford Road, down Nottingham Road South, up Halifax Road and finally along Long Lane north of the Grange. The Chartist plot number is shown in accordance with the plan on page 11 with the original Chartist cottage shown in italic lettering. Any houses built on the original plots are shown separately.

	PLOT NUMBER 23		PLOT NUMBER 23	PLOT NUMBER 24
CURRENT NAME	The Beeches	Woodside Cottage	*Bircham Cottage*	*Bircham Cottage*
YEAR BUILT	1935, demolished for M25	1937, demolished for M25	1846	1846
OTHER NAME			St Cecilia	Beaumont Cottage
OTHER NAME			Little Whaddon	
RESIDENT 1847			T Meyrick	A Barker
1851			T Meyrick	J Evans
1861			T Meyrick	J Birks
1871			T Meyrick	T Mead
1881			T Meyrick	
1895				
1910			H Clempson	
1922			H Clempson	J Luther
1933			H Clempson	
1942	J Tomlinson	D Gilbey	H Clempson	Rev A Robson
1950	Mrs S Tomlinson	D Gilbey	H Clempson	
1960	Mrs S Tomlinson	D Gilbey	H Clempson	
1970	C Jacobs	D Gilbey	J Bettle	
1980		D Gilbey	M Flinn	
1990			M Flinn	

	PLOT NUMBER 24	PLOT NUMBER 24		PLOT NUMBER 25
CURRENT NAME	Four Acres	School House	Beaumont House	*Chartist Cottage*
YEAR BUILT	C.1910	1907	1880	1846
OTHER NAME		Beaumont House School	Beaumont House School	Hollycroft
OTHER NAME				Holly Lodge
RESIDENT 1847				D Watson
1851				G Wheeler
1861				J Wooley
1871				J Wooley
1881			A Hawkins	W Chambers
1895			A Hawkins	W Chambers
1910	W Giffard	School	School	E Reid
1922	W Giffard	School	School	H Pierion
1933	W Keating	School	School	E Bagley
1942	P Vezey	School	School	W Williams
1950	P Vezey	School	School	H Nockolds
1960	P Vezey	School	School	H Nockolds
1970	P Vezey	School	School	H Nockolds
1980	M Seymour-Jackson	J Jackson	M Jackson	A Thomson
1990	J Speight	J Jackson	M Jackson	A Thomson

	PLOT NUMBER 26	PLOT NUMBER 27		PLOT NUMBER 28
CURRENT NAME	**Wood Weye**	Farfield	**Woodene**	**Long Meadow**
YEAR BUILT	1846	1942	1846	1846
OTHER NAME	Oak Cottage			Bush Cottage
OTHER NAME	Woodway			
RESIDENT 1847	M Griffiths		J Cole	B Vaughan
1851	M Griffiths			J Catell
1861	E Griffiths		J Evans	
1871	W Spooner			E Watson
1881	J Delone		T Meyrick	W King
1895				
1910	A Horwood			
1922	B Haigh			
1933	B Haigh			
1942	B Haigh	Miss L Calder	Miss L Calder	P Palmer
1950	B Haigh	Miss L Calder/Miss K Homburg	Miss L Calder	C Barker
1960	Miss D Haigh	Miss L Calder/Miss K Homburg	Miss L Calder	T Killick
1970	Miss D Haigh	K Grive	R Allen	T Killick
1980	Miss D Haigh	R Mawhood	M Kristian	T Killick
1990	G Thomas	R Mawhood	J Rice	T Killick

	PLOT NUMBER 28	PLOT NUMBER 29		
CURRENT NAME	Stanmore Lodge	Homeland	Homeland Cottage	Silver Birches
YEAR BUILT	1908	1906	C 1906	1950
OTHER NAME	Plain Cottage		Holly Villa	
OTHER NAME				
RESIDENT 1847				
1851				
1861				
1871				
1881				
1895				
1910	S Haigh	E Gyles	Mrs Gyles	
1922	Miss Fitzgerald	F Warman		
1933		F Warman		
1942	S Richards	Mrs L Warman	D Warman	
1950	S Richards	R MacPhail	J Page	D Warman
1960	Wing Com A Vicary	R MacPhail	J Page	D Warman
1970	Wing Com A Vicary	A Horner		D Warman
1980	Wing Com A Vicary	A Alexandrou	P Theodorou	D Warman
1990	J Ingrams	A Alexandrou		Mrs M Warman

	PLOT NUMBER 29	PLOT NUMBER 30		
CURRENT NAME	*Rosemary Cottage*	*Craven Cottage*	Charters	The End House
YEAR BUILT	1846	1846	C.1932	1928
OTHER NAME	Rosemary			Tighe-an-Rias
OTHER NAME	Rose Marie			
RESIDENT 1847	A Crowther	T Smith		
1851		J Purvis		
1861		F Bentley		
1871	J Burnet	C Barnett		
1881	J Purden	W Burchfield		
1895		W Burchfield		
1910	P Hill	Alice Ambrose		
1922	Dr J Wilkins	H Aston		
1933	Mrs A Williams	H Aston		Dr J Ross
1942	Lieut-Com A Preston	H Aston	G Alexander	
1950	Mrs L Warman	H Aston	R Milne	Brig. Hynes
1960	Mrs G Gibbins	R Marschall	M Hatfield	D Yiend
1970	Mrs G Gibbins	D Treanor	M Hatfield	D Yiend
1980	Mrs G Gibbins	D Treanor	H Birdwood	D Yiend
1990	Mrs G Gibbins	D Treanor	R Talbot	D Yiend

	PLOT NUMBER 30			
CURRENT NAME	Berry Cottage	Virginia	Newell Cottage	Westfield Lodge
YEAR BUILT	1928	1928	1928	1928
OTHER NAME				
OTHER NAME				
RESIDENT 1847				
1851				
1861				
1871				
1881				
1895				
1910				
1922				
1933		E Dilley		
1942	Mrs Willis	N Winwood	E Williams	G Sainsbury
1950	W Dale	H Greer	H Jones	G Sainsbury
1960	W Dale	H Greer	H Jones	G Sainsbury
1970	W Dale	F Brackett	H Jones	G Sainsbury
1980	J Wright	W Gillott	H Jones	G Johnson
1990	J Wright	W Gillott	H Jones	G Ralph

206

	PLOT NUMBER 31			
CURRENT NAME	Bowood	Wood Croft	Bramble Close	Pixie House
YEAR BUILT	1906	1906	1936	1934
OTHER NAME				
OTHER NAME				
RESIDENT 1847				
1851				
1861				
1871				
1881				
1895				
1910				
1922				
1933				
1942	P Bradbery	J Clarkson	G Bunce	A Topley
1950	P Bradbery	J Clarkson	G Bunce	A Topley
1960	P Bradbery	J Clarkson	A Webster	Mrs L Topley
1970	L Merrick	J Clarkson	R Carver	R Newell
1980	P Woodhead	L Lambert	R Carver	R Newell
1990	R Painter	Mrs P Lingwood	R Carver	R Newell

	PLOT NUMBER 31	PLOT NUMBER 32		PLOT NUMBER 18
CURRENT NAME	*The Daphnes*	*Walnut Tree Cottage*	Briar Wood	Rusper
YEAR BUILT	1846	1846; new house built 1970	1953	1954
OTHER NAME			Briar Patch	
OTHER NAME				
RESIDENT 1847	J Greenwood	T Smith		
1851	J Bailey	J Sevster		
1861	M Bailey	J Gibbon		
1871	F Armstrong	F Taylor		
1881	W Kingham	F Taylor		
1895	W Kingham	J Marchant		
1910	W Kingham	J Marchant		
1922	Mrs Kingham	J Marchant		
1933	J Gibson	V Clark		
1942	Miss E Anderson	V Clark		
1950	Miss E Anderson	V Clark		
1960	E Greaves	R Clark	W Webb	C McCulloch
1970	E Greaves	R Clark	Mrs E Webb	C McCulloch
1980	E Greaves	R Clark	E Wiseman	C McCulloch
1990	Mrs C Greaves	R Clark	E Wiseman	C McCulloch

	PLOT NUMBER 18	PLOT NUMBER 19		
CURRENT NAME	*Laburnums*	*The Hop Garden*	The Orchard	Heronsgate Hall
YEAR BUILT	1846	1846	c.1906	1884
OTHER NAME		Connorville (Post Office)		Wesleyan Chapel
OTHER NAME		Bieno		
RESIDENT 1847	J Short	W Oddy		
1851	G Pocock	E Bukhock		
1861	J Hardwick	W Howse		
1871	Mrs Chapman	W Howse		
1881	Mrs Chapman	P Chapman		
1895	Mrs Chapman/Miss F King	T Chambers		
1910	Miss F King		J Dinslage	
1922	Miss F King		F Thomace	
1933	Miss F King		Misses Kidner	
1942	W Oates		Misses Kidner	
1950	W Oates	S Halton	Mrs M Darby	
1960	E Morgan	S Halton	W Phillips	
1970	E Morgan	S Halton	W Phillips	
1980	E Lewis	S Halton	B Chilvers	
1990	E Lewis	R Sewell	B Chilvers	

	PLOT NUMBER 33		PLOT NUMBER 34	PLOT NUMBER 35
CURRENT NAME	La Casita	*Croft House*	*Glenthorne*	*Endlands*
YEAR BUILT	1928; rebuilt 1950s	1846; now includes original Glenthorne	1846; new house built 1965	1846; rebuilt 1950
OTHER NAME	Jennifer Cottage	The Nest		Endland
OTHER NAME		Mount Avon		
RESIDENT 1847		T Bond	J Taylor	J Openshaw
1851		J Gamble	J Sturgeon	F Hurlett
1861		J Barnett	J Sturgeon	S McKay
1871		J Barnett	J Sturgeon	T Mansfield
1881		T Baldry	C Light	A Mansfield
1895				L Beatson
1910		C Strong (J Reynvaan)	H Wallbank	Miss Beatson
1922		C Strong	F Ball	Miss Beatson
1933		A Mansfield		Miss Beatson
1942		A Mansfield	Miss E Scott	
1950	A Greasley	A Bird	P Hales	
1960	A Greasley	L Ellerd-Styles	D Beeston	W Tyrell
1970	J Greasley	L Ellerd-Styles	R Skilton	C Pollard
1980	J Jones	L Ellerd-Styles	R Skilton	C Pollard
1990	N Warner	T Redhead	R Skilton	C Pollard

	PLOT NUMBER 20	PLOT NUMBER 12	PLOT NUMBER 36	
CURRENT NAME	*Hope Lodge*	*The Limes*	*The Grange*	Grange Cottage
YEAR BUILT	1846	1846; rebuilt 1890	1846	c.1884
OTHER NAME	Hope Cottage	on new site	Heronsgate House	Grange Lodge
OTHER NAME			O'Connorville College	
RESIDENT 1847	G Richardson	W House	M Graves	
1851	W Betts	W House	J Lindon	
1861	J Cartwell	M Place	W Roberts	
1871	J Cartwell	G Place	W Roberts	
1881	J Cartwell	G Place	Mrs W Roberts	
1895	J Cartwell		W Hutchison	
1910	Mrs Lambert	D Ford	N McOstrich	
1922	Mrs Lambert	D Ford	G Richards	
1933	Mrs Lambert	D Ford	G Richards	
1942	A Seligman	D Ford	F Talbot	W Brodie
1950	Com G Hills	D Ford	F Talbot	
1960	Wing Com Farr	C Pope	F Talbot	P Fenton
1970	P Broadbent	C Pope	F Talbot	
1980	P Broadbent	C Pope	A McMurtrie	I Chapman
1990	D Matyus-Flynn	A Gower	A McMurtrie	D Miles

	PLOT NUMBER 11	PLOT NUMBER 10		PLOT NUMBER 9
CURRENT NAME	*(The Grange)*	Lindens	*Myrtle House*	*Heron Cottage*
YEAR BUILT	1846; demolished c.1890	1898	1846	1846
OTHER NAME		Esperanto House		Heronsgate Cottage
OTHER NAME				Herons Nest
RESIDENT 1847	J Neale		J Walwark	C Tawes
1851	A Hore		W Dimmock	T Heaton
1861	W Hore			T Heaton
1871	W Hore		H Gibbs	S Nife
1881	J Horwood		H Gibbs	R Gudgen
1895			J Dinslage	
1910		Mrs Reid	R Javal-Cremieu	Capt D Anderson
1922		G Reid		Mrs Anderson
1933		Capt. P Mangin		Miss Anderson
1942		C Goldsmith		G Gardiner
1950		C Goldsmith	J Measmore	G Gardiner
1960		K Aitken	T Barraud	G Gardiner
1970		K Aitken	W Sale	G Gardiner
1980		K Aitken	W Sale	G Gardiner
1990		Mrs C Aitken	W Sale	G Gardiner

	PLOT NUMBER 9		PLOT NUMBER 8		PLOT NUMBER 7	
CURRENT NAME	St John's Church		**Cherry Tree Corner**	Pinecroft	*Pinhaye*	
YEAR BUILT	1865		1846	1956	1846	
OTHER NAME			Cherry Tree			
OTHER NAME						
RESIDENT 1847			R Eveson		G Mansfield	
1851			R Eveson		R Smith	
1861	A Scrivenor	(1865)	J Woods		J Howard	
1871	J Aitken	(1867)	J Woods		J Howard	
1881	CW Neild	(1875)	J Woods		J Woods	
1895	CW Neild					
1910	FA Murray	(1897)				
1922	W Breffitt	(1912)				
1933	IF Smith	(1925)			C Arnell	
1942	WG Eeles	(1934)	A Haynes		C Arnell	
1950	GL Edwards	(1947)	A Haynes		J Jones	
1960	GL Edwards		Wing Com. E Panter	D Bruce	W Knight	
1970	GL Edwards		Ms J Felix	D Bruce	W Knight	
1980	RB Swift	(1972)	Ms J Felix	W Byrnes	W Knight	
1990	HJ Cherry	(1982)	Ms J Felix	D Allen	D Mead	

*Date of appointment
shown in brackets*

	PLOT NUMBER 7		PLOT NUMBER 6	
CURRENT NAME	St Joseph's	The Birches	**Rosecot**	Penny Firs
YEAR BUILT	1956	1956	1846	1937
OTHER NAME		Hunters Moon		
OTHER NAME				
RESIDENT 1847			C Smith	
1851			J Burnett	
1861			R Hammond	
1871			E Watson	
1881				
1895			AF Bird	
1910			AF Bird	
1922			AE Bird	
1933			AE Bird	
1942			AE Bird	Mrs Davidson
1950			AE Bird	I Davidson
1960	H Poxon	J Herring	AE Bird	I Davidson
1970	H Poxon	J Herring	AE Bird	F O'Loughlin
1980	Mrs C Poxon	D Barrett	AE Bird	F O'Loughlin
1990	Mrs C Poxon	L Wyllie	M Kristian	F O'Loughlin

	PLOT NUMBER 5			PLOT NUMBER 4
CURRENT NAME	Rowandene	*Laurel Cottage*	High Holly	*Crowthorne*
YEAR BUILT	1895	1846	1898	1846
OTHER NAME	May Cottage	(Post Office)	The Firs	
OTHER NAME				
RESIDENT 1847		P Ford		W Mann
1851		P Ford		E Whitmore
1861		P Ford		M Whitmore
1871		P Ford		A Crump
1881		P Ford		W Hewlett
1895		G Antill		
1910	E Bell	L Rickards	Miss Hocker	
1922	G Boyle	H Dyer	Misses E&E Richardson	
1933		H Dyer	S Van Duzer	
1942	R Leake	Mrs P Longhurst	S Van Duzer	F White
1950	R Leake	P Robertson	B Leech	F White
1960	R Leake	P Robertson	E Haussauer	F White
1970	C Green	P Robertson	E Haussauer	Mrs K White
1980	C Green	P Robertson	E Haussauer	Mrs L Fernandez
1990	C Green	P Robertson	E Haussauer	Mrs L Fernandez

	PLOT NUMBER 4	PLOT NUMBER 3	PLOT NUMBER 2	PLOT NUMBER 1
CURRENT NAME	Field Cottage	*Whitegates*	*Ladywalk Cottage*	*Sunnyside*
YEAR BUILT	1910; rebuilt 1930s	1846; rebuilt 1895 on new site	1846; rebuilt 1890 on new site	1846
OTHER NAME	Sherwood Cottage	Lawrence House (burnt 1925)	Nelson House (burnt 1919)	The Hut
OTHER NAME		Lawrence Villa	The Garden Cottage	
RESIDENT 1847		M Fitzsimmons	J Lambourne	J Westmoreland
1851		M Fitzsimmons	J Lambourne	
1861		M Fitzsimmons	L Beatson	R Port
1871		M Fitzsimmons	J Harrison	D Ford
1881		H Seaton	T Sharp	D Ford
1895			J Leeming	
1910		C Goodman		C Scott
1922		Mrs Goodman		D Ford
1933		Mrs Goodman		A Sparksman
1942	A Evans	T Jones		K Bristow
1950	A Evans	T Jones	A Willis	K Bristow
1960	A Evans	J Ross	J Melbourne	L Theodore
1970	A Evans	J Ross	S Campbell-Ritchie	J Pope
1980	A Evans	Mrs C Ross	S Campbell-Ritchie	J Pope
1990	A Ross	A McQueenie	S Campbell-Ritchie	J Pope

	PLOT NUMBER 1		PLOT NUMBER 13	
CURRENT NAME	Amberwood	Ladywalk	*Herons Lodge*	Cherry Cottage
YEAR BUILT	c.1898; rebuilt 1970	1890; rebuilt 1934	1846	1893
OTHER NAME	Beehive Cottage		Peace Cottage	
OTHER NAME	The Beehive			
RESIDENT 1847			H Smith	
1851			H Smith	
1861			T Bradford	
1871			T Bradford	
1881			M Fitzsimmons	
1895		T Wilks	Miss A Price – YWCA	
1910	W Fitzsimmons	Prof G Foster	Baron Kinnaird – YWCA	Miss Fitzgerald (Sup't)
1922	W Fitzsimmons	Miss Montague	Baron Kinnaird – YWCA	Miss Watson (Sup't)
1933	W Fitzsimmons	H Leonard	Mrs EM Bowler	J Clarkson
1942	W Fitzsimmons	H Leonard	H Bowler	
1950	G Longhurst	H Leonard	H Bowler	Miss A Nunn
1960	G Longhurst	H Leonard	H Bowler	Miss A Nunn
1970	G Longhurst	I Steers	H Bowler	P Rice
1980	J Abbott	I Steers	M Bowler	Mrs K Bowler
1990	T Shaw	I Steers	M Bowler	Mrs K Bowler

	PLOT NUMBER 14	PLOT NUMBER 15	PLOT NUMBER 16	
CURRENT NAME	*Sherwood*	*Chorheron*	*The Grey Cottage*	Home Close
YEAR BUILT	1846	1846	1846	c.1900
OTHER NAME	Herondale	The Bungalow	Laurel Mount	
OTHER NAME				
RESIDENT 1847	G Ramsbottom	W Mitchell	J Firth	
1851	J Bradford	E Newsome		
1861	M Deadson	J Gibbons	C Hayhs	
1871	M Halliday	J Gibbons	T Buckston	
1881	N Gibbs	H Saunders	S Abrook	
1895		E Jones		
1910	Mrs Felkin	E Jones	G Abbott	Col. H Rawson
1922	Mrs Felkin	T Summers	Capt. F Morris	Col. H Rawson
1933		G Boyle	Capt. F Morris	
1942	H Birdwood	G Boyle	Capt. F Morris	C Simeons
1950	H Birdwood	G Boyle	Capt. F Morris	C Simeons
1960	H Birdwood	P Wells	Capt. F Morris	I Steers
1970	H Birdwood	C Dinsdale	N Rice	J Shearman
1980	M Hatfield	C Dinsdale	N Rice	D Grainger
1990	M Hatfield	C Dinsdale	N Rice	J Levitt

PLOT NUMBER 17

	Wiverton	Herons Court
CURRENT NAME	*Wiverton*	Herons Court
YEAR BUILT	1846	c.1890
OTHER NAME	The Nook	
OTHER NAME	The Retreat	
RESIDENT 1847	R Kerfoot	
1851	H Ivory	
1861	W Cartmell (J Webb)	
1871	W Cartmell	
1881	W Cartmell (H Harvey)	
1895	C Bond	C Bond (W McKean)
1910	G Bond	G Bond (L Joseph)
1922	T Swales (J Copland)	R Parsons
1933	J Venn	R Parsons
1942	J Venn	R Parsons
1950	J Venn	R Parsons
1960	J Venn	R Parsons
1970	J Venn	I McDougall
1980	P Hagyard	I McDougall
1990	P Hagyard	I McDougall

PLOT NUMBER 21

	Little Aymers	Oaklands
CURRENT NAME	*Little Aymers*	Oaklands
YEAR BUILT	1846	c.1902
OTHER NAME	The Sun Box	Hillmorton
OTHER NAME	Layston	
RESIDENT 1847	B Knott	
1851	E Blackborough	
1861	S Blackborough	
1871	R Harding	
1881	A Thompson	
1895		
1910		A Davy (Lady Reed)
1922	Miss Hill	C Dellwik
1933	W Brunn	
1942	W Brunn	Lt-Col C Evans
1950	W Brunn	Ms C Dickinson
1960	A Ching	Ms C Dickinson
1970	A Ching	J Rew
1980	J Gordon	I Carter
1990	J Gordon	I Carter

PLOT NUMBER 22 / HOUSES OUTSIDE O'CONNORVILLE

	Breve House	Oakhill	White Lodge	Fernhill
CURRENT NAME	*Breve House*	Oakhill	White Lodge	Fernhill
YEAR BUILT	1846	c.1730	c.1890	1905–11
OTHER NAME	The Pines		The Red House	One Hundred
OTHER NAME			White House	
RESIDENT 1847	I Jowett	Grosvenor Estate		
1851	T Meads	Grosvenor Estate		
1861	R Tuck	Grosvenor Estate		
1871	S Carter	Grosvenor Estate		
1881	H Ward	Grosvenor Estate		
1895	C Bond	J Gill	Mrs Gill	
1910	G Bond		Mrs Gill	
1922	L Nicoll (Miss Smart)	C Cooper	Mrs Gill	
1933	G Royds	J Fullerton	Mrs Gill	
1942	R Ross		E Fay	Mrs Shiell
1950	R Ross	E Fay	Com B Taylor	A Escombe
1960	A Powys-Lybbe	J Gill	Com B Taylor	C Goldsmith
1970	A Powys-Lybbe	J Gill	M Jacobson	B Smith
1980	A Powys-Lybbe	D Formosa	J Williams	A Hadfield
1990	V Woczyk	D Formosa	J Williams	J Williams

HOUSES OUTSIDE O'CONNORVILLE

	Athelstan	Hillside	Long Lane House	Flint Cottage
CURRENT NAME				
YEAR BUILT	1905–11	1905–11	C.1790	C.1890
OTHER NAME			Midgham Cottage	
OTHER NAME				
RESIDENT 1847				
1851				
1861				
1871				
1881				
1895				
1910				
1922		E Collier	F Blyth	
1933	Mrs Braisher	Mrs Sharpe	F Blyth	C Baldwin
1942	Mrs Ranson	Mrs Thornton	F Blyth	Mrs Baldwin
1950	Mrs K Bolam	R Little	F Blyth	E Hare
1960	Mrs K Bolam	H Stacy	F Babcock	L Lambert
1970	R Whitehead	D Thornton	F Babcock	R Gay
1980	F Keeling	R Hills	F Babcock	R Gay
1990	M Halsey	T Williams	Mrs Babcock	G Winter

HOUSES OUTSIDE O'CONNORVILLE

	Land of Liberty public house	Waterfield House redeveloped 1983	The Dell
CURRENT NAME			
YEAR BUILT		C.1890	
OTHER NAME			
OTHER NAME			
RESIDENT 1847			
1851			
1861			
1871	J Swain		
1881	T Wheeler		
1895	J Thompson	A Camp	
1910	R Hunt	A Camp	
1922	R Hunt	J Camp	
1933	J Cox	Misses Richardson	
1942	J Cox	Misses Richardson	
1950	G Earnshaw	A Murray	K Ffitch
1960	G Earnshaw	G Brewer	
1970	V Cornhill	G Brewer	Z Bates
1980	V Cornhill	G Brewer	Z Bates
1990	S Parkin		Z Bates

INDEX